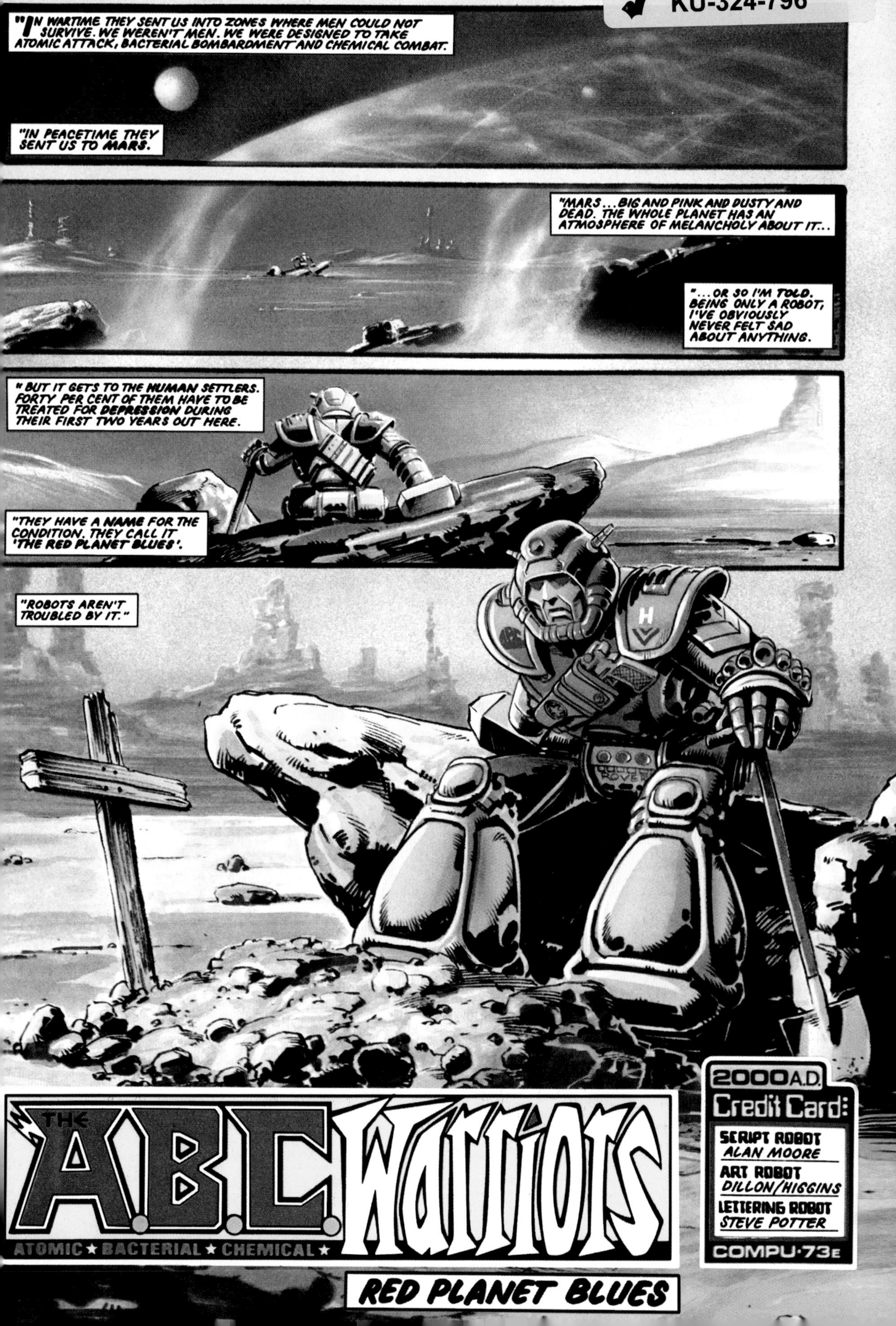
"IN WARTIME THEY SENT US INTO ZONES WHERE MEN COULD NOT SURVIVE. WE WEREN'T MEN. WE WERE DESIGNED TO TAKE ATOMIC ATTACK, BACTERIAL BOMBARDMENT AND CHEMICAL COMBAT.
"IN PEACETIME THEY SENT US TO MARS.
"MARS... BIG AND PINK AND DUSTY AND DEAD. THE WHOLE PLANET HAS AN ATMOSPHERE OF MELANCHOLY ABOUT IT...
"...OR SO I'M TOLD. BEING ONLY A ROBOT, I'VE OBVIOUSLY NEVER FELT SAD ABOUT ANYTHING.
" BUT IT GETS TO THE HUMAN SETTLERS. FORTY PER CENT OF THEM HAVE TO BE TREATED FOR DEPRESSION DURING THEIR FIRST TWO YEARS OUT HERE.
"THEY HAVE A NAME FOR THE CONDITION. THEY CALL IT 'THE RED PLANET BLUES'.
"ROBOTS AREN'T TROUBLED BY IT."
ROVER
THE A.B.C. WARRIORS
ATOMIC ★ BACTERIAL ★ CHEMICAL ★
2000 A.D. Credit Card:
SCRIPT ROBOT ALAN MOORE
ART ROBOT DILLON/HIGGINS
LETTERING ROBOT STEVE POTTER
COMPU·73E
RED PLANET BLUES

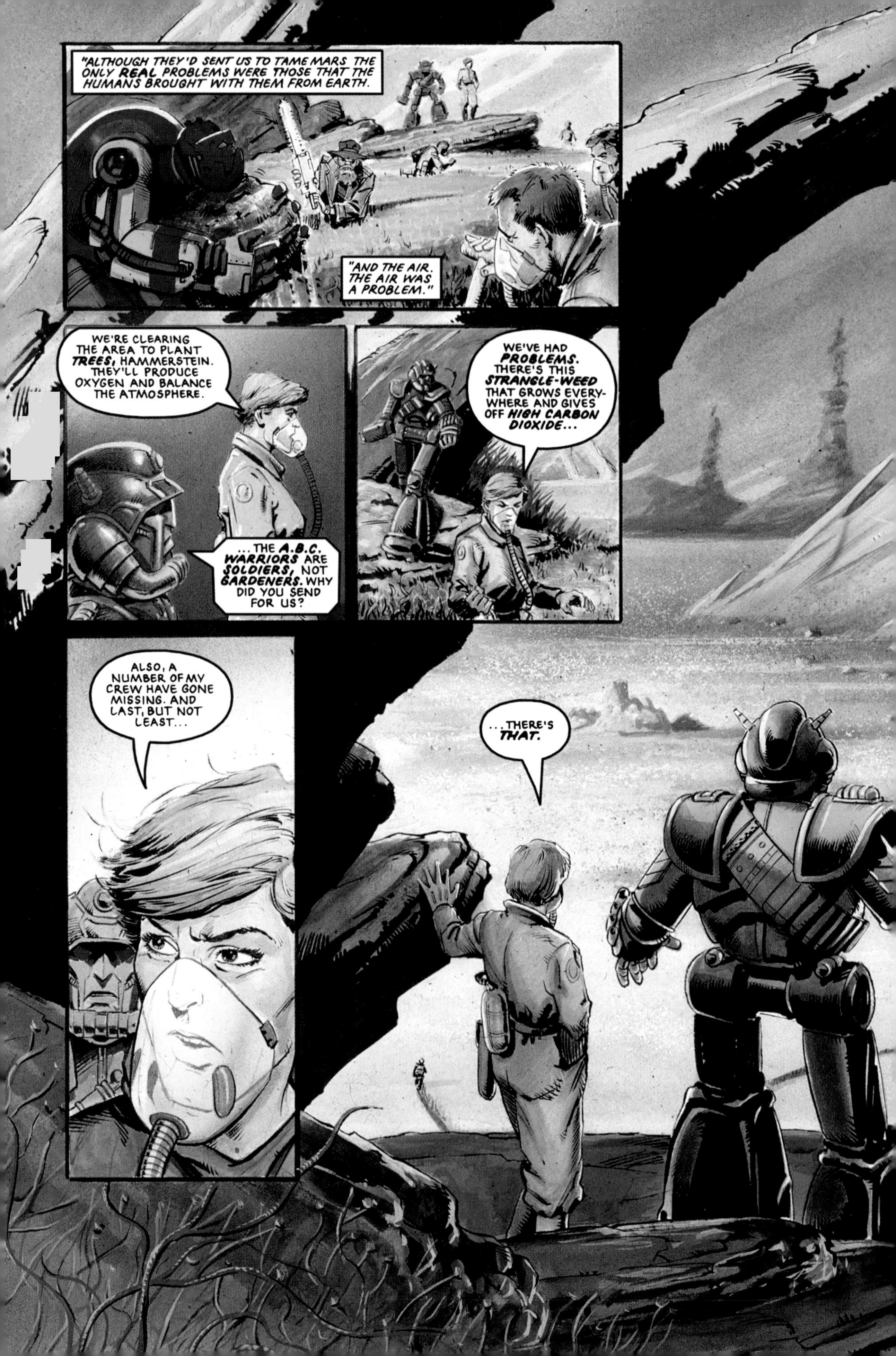
"ALTHOUGH THEY'D SENT US TO TAME MARS THE ONLY REAL PROBLEMS WERE THOSE THAT THE HUMANS BROUGHT WITH THEM FROM EARTH.
"AND THE AIR. THE AIR WAS A PROBLEM."
WE'RE CLEARING THE AREA TO PLANT TREES, HAMMERSTEIN. THEY'LL PRODUCE OXYGEN AND BALANCE THE ATMOSPHERE.
...THE A.B.C. WARRIORS ARE SOLDIERS, NOT GARDENERS. WHY DID YOU SEND FOR US?
WE'VE HAD PROBLEMS. THERE'S THIS STRANGLE-WEED THAT GROWS EVERYWHERE AND GIVES OFF HIGH CARBON DIOXIDE...
ALSO, A NUMBER OF MY CREW HAVE GONE MISSING. AND LAST, BUT NOT LEAST...
...THERE'S THAT.

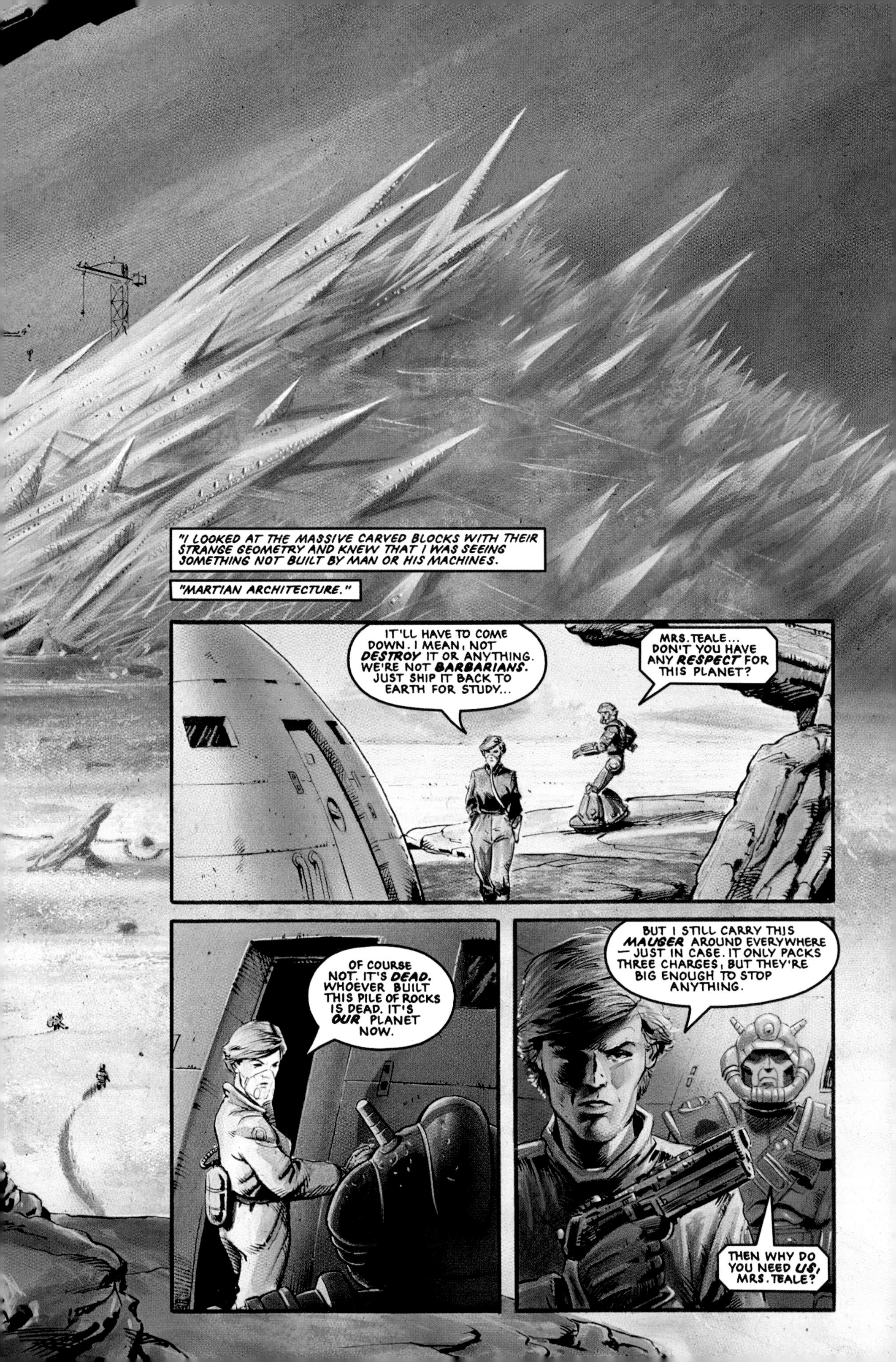
"I LOOKED AT THE MASSIVE CARVED BLOCKS WITH THEIR STRANGE GEOMETRY AND KNEW THAT I WAS SEEING SOMETHING NOT BUILT BY MAN OR HIS MACHINES.
"MARTIAN ARCHITECTURE."
IT'LL HAVE TO COME DOWN. I MEAN, NOT DESTROY IT OR ANYTHING. WE'RE NOT BARBARIANS. JUST SHIP IT BACK TO EARTH FOR STUDY...
MRS. TEALE... DON'T YOU HAVE ANY RESPECT FOR THIS PLANET?
OF COURSE NOT. IT'S DEAD. WHOEVER BUILT THIS PILE OF ROCKS IS DEAD. IT'S OUR PLANET NOW.
BUT I STILL CARRY THIS MAUGER AROUND EVERYWHERE — JUST IN CASE. IT ONLY PACKS THREE CHARGES, BUT THEY'RE BIG ENOUGH TO STOP ANYTHING.
THEN WHY DO YOU NEED US, MRS. TEALE?

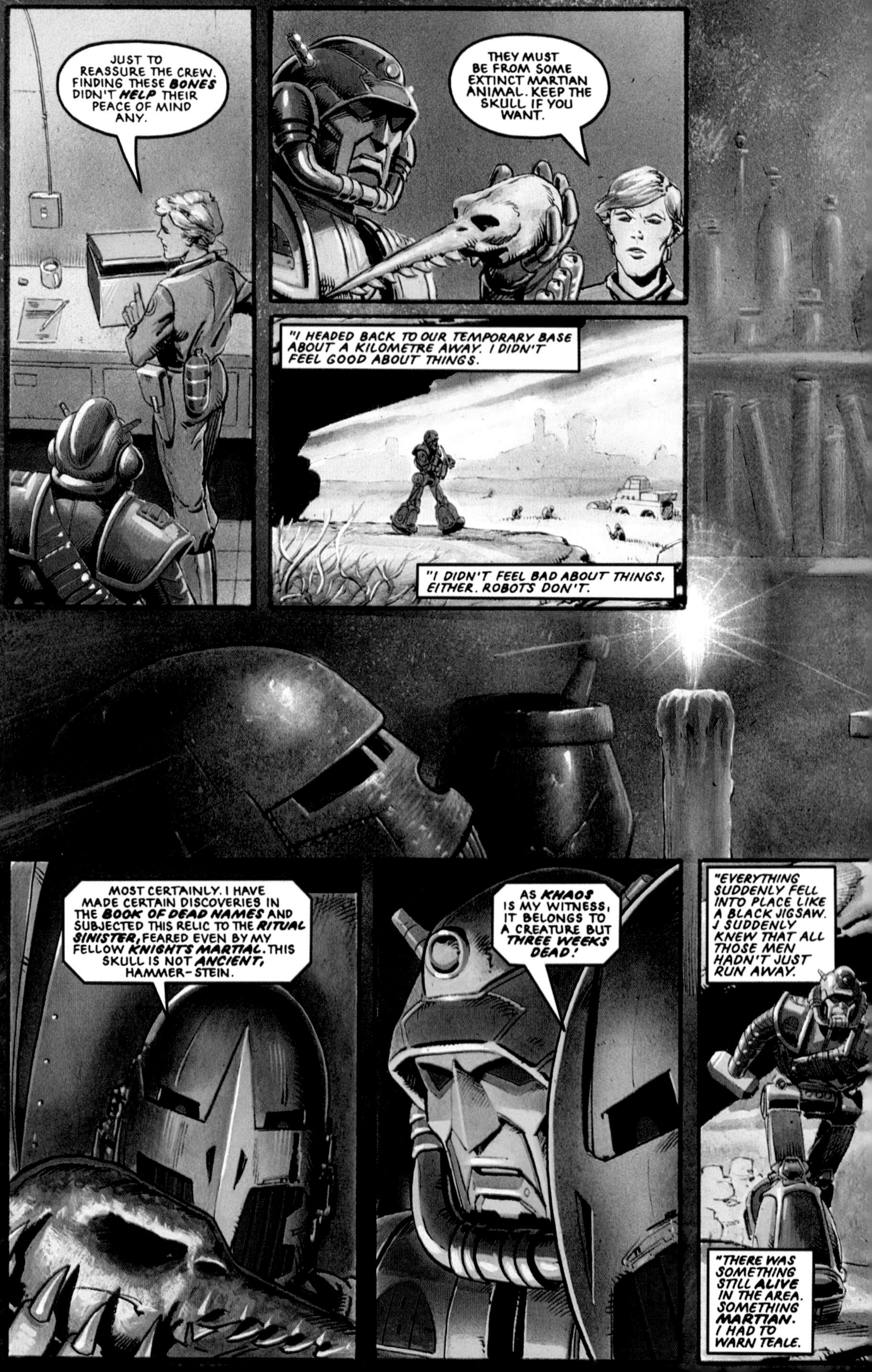
JUST TO REASSURE THE CREW. FINDING THESE BONES DIDN'T HELP THEIR PEACE OF MIND ANY.
THEY MUST BE FROM SOME EXTINCT MARTIAN ANIMAL. KEEP THE SKULL IF YOU WANT.
"I HEADED BACK TO OUR TEMPORARY BASE ABOUT A KILOMETRE AWAY. I DIDN'T FEEL GOOD ABOUT THINGS.
"I DIDN'T FEEL BAD ABOUT THINGS, EITHER. ROBOTS DON'T.
MOST CERTAINLY. I HAVE MADE CERTAIN DISCOVERIES IN THE BOOK OF DEAD NAMES AND SUBJECTED THIS RELIC TO THE RITUAL SINISTER, FEARED EVEN BY MY FELLOW KNIGHTS MARTIAL. THIS SKULL IS NOT ANCIENT, HAMMER-STEIN.
AS KHAOS IS MY WITNESS, IT BELONGS TO A CREATURE BUT THREE WEEKS DEAD!
"EVERYTHING SUDDENLY FELL INTO PLACE LIKE A BLACK JIGSAW. I SUDDENLY KNEW THAT ALL THOSE MEN HADN'T JUST RUN AWAY.
"THERE WAS SOMETHING STILL ALIVE IN THE AREA. SOMETHING MARTIAN. I HAD TO WARN TEALE.

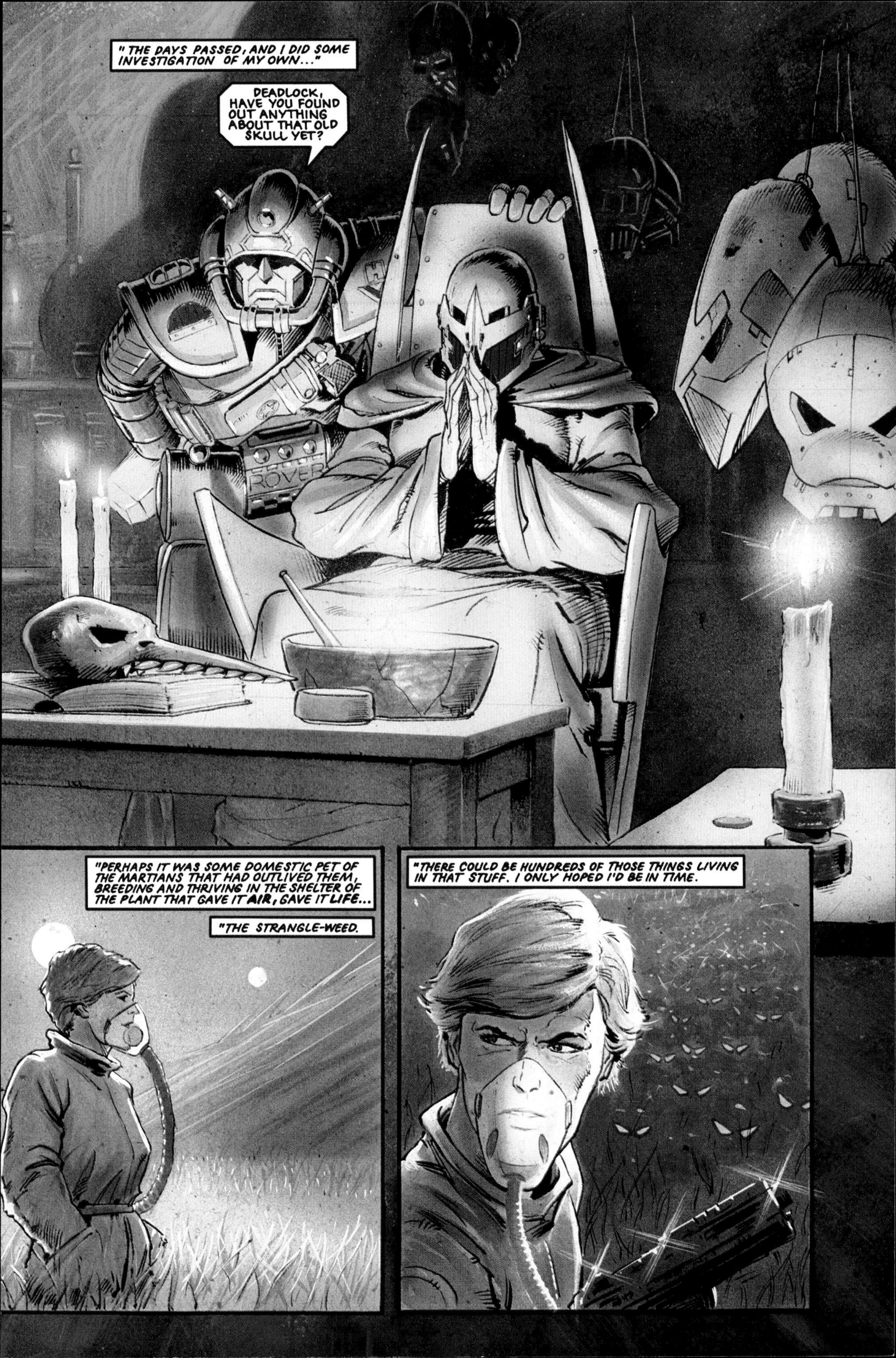
"THE DAYS PASSED, AND I DID SOME INVESTIGATION OF MY OWN..."
DEADLOCK, HAVE YOU FOUND OUT ANYTHING ABOUT THAT OLD SKULL YET?
ROVER
"PERHAPS IT WAS SOME DOMESTIC PET OF THE MARTIANS THAT HAD OUTLIVED THEM, BREEDING AND THRIVING IN THE SHELTER OF THE PLANT THAT GAVE IT AIR, GAVE IT LIFE...
"THE STRANGLE-WEED.
"THERE COULD BE HUNDREDS OF THOSE THINGS LIVING IN THAT STUFF. I ONLY HOPED I'D BE IN TIME.

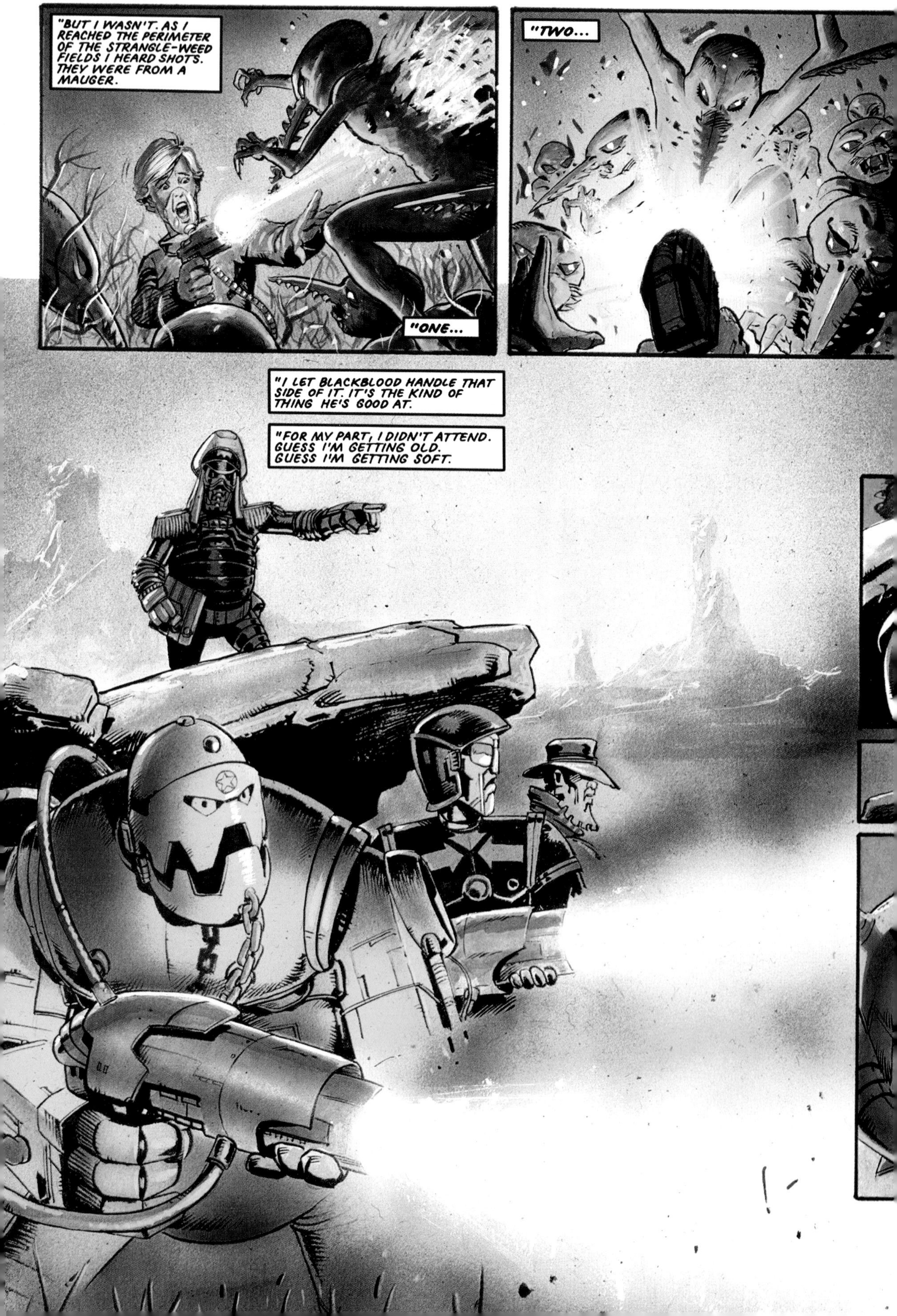
"BUT I WASN'T. AS I REACHED THE PERIMETER OF THE STRANGLE-WEED FIELDS I HEARD SHOTS. THEY WERE FROM A MAUGER.
"ONE...
"TWO...
"I LET BLACKBLOOD HANDLE THAT SIDE OF IT. IT'S THE KIND OF THING HE'S GOOD AT.
"FOR MY PART, I DIDN'T ATTEND. GUESS I'M GETTING OLD. GUESS I'M GETTING SOFT.

"THREE...

"I HOPED SHE SAVED THE LAST ONE FOR HERSELF.

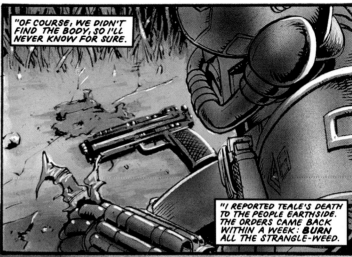

"OF COURSE, WE DIDN'T FIND THE BODY, SO I'LL NEVER KNOW FOR SURE.

"I REPORTED TEALE'S DEATH TO THE PEOPLE EARTHSIDE. THE ORDERS CAME BACK WITHIN A WEEK: *BURN* ALL THE STRANGLE-WEED.

"FUNNY THING... WE BURNED THE WHOLE UNDERGROWTH AND WE ONLY FOUND *ONE* DEAD MARTIAN ANIMAL. I FIGURE EVEN *THAT* WAS A FLUKE.

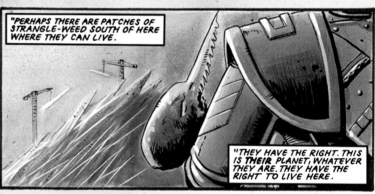

"PERHAPS THERE ARE PATCHES OF STRANGLE-WEED SOUTH OF HERE WHERE THEY CAN LIVE.

"THEY HAVE THE RIGHT. THIS IS *THEIR* PLANET, WHATEVER THEY ARE. THEY HAVE THE RIGHT TO LIVE HERE.

"...AT LEAST UNTIL MAN PUSHES HIS FRONTIERS FURTHER SOUTH AND THERE'S NO STRANGLE-WEED LEFT *ANYWHERE*.

"I BURIED THE ONE CREATURE THAT WE FOUND. LIKE I SAY...

"SOFT."

THE HUMANS ARE COMING, LITTLE ONE. THE HUMANS ARE COMING AND SOON ALL YOUR TRIBE WILL LIE AS STILL AS YOU.

THERE'S NOTHING YOU CAN DO ABOUT IT. IT'S *THEIR* PLANET NOW.

SPREAD THE WORD.

"TWO MOONS WERE CLIMBING IN THE SKY, CASTING A SICKLY LIGHT OVER THE WIDE CRIMSON EMPTINESS. THE HUMANS HAVE A NAME FOR IT. THEY CALL IT 'THE RED PLANET BLUES'.

"ROBOTS AREN'T TROUBLED BY IT."

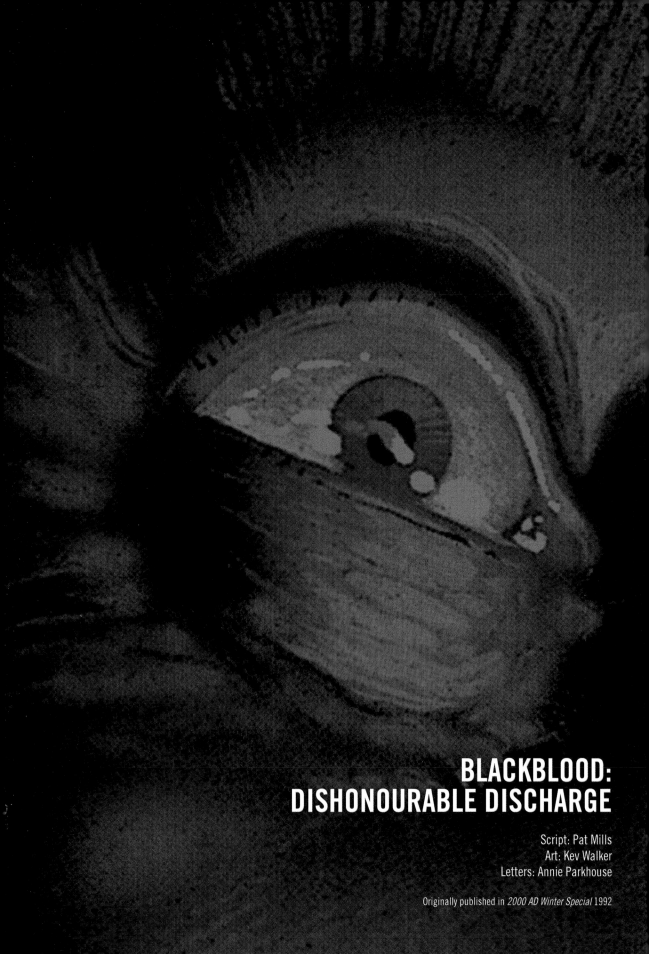

BLACKBLOOD: DISHONOURABLE DISCHARGE

Script: Pat Mills
Art: Kev Walker
Letters: Annie Parkhouse

Originally published in *2000 AD Winter Special* 1992

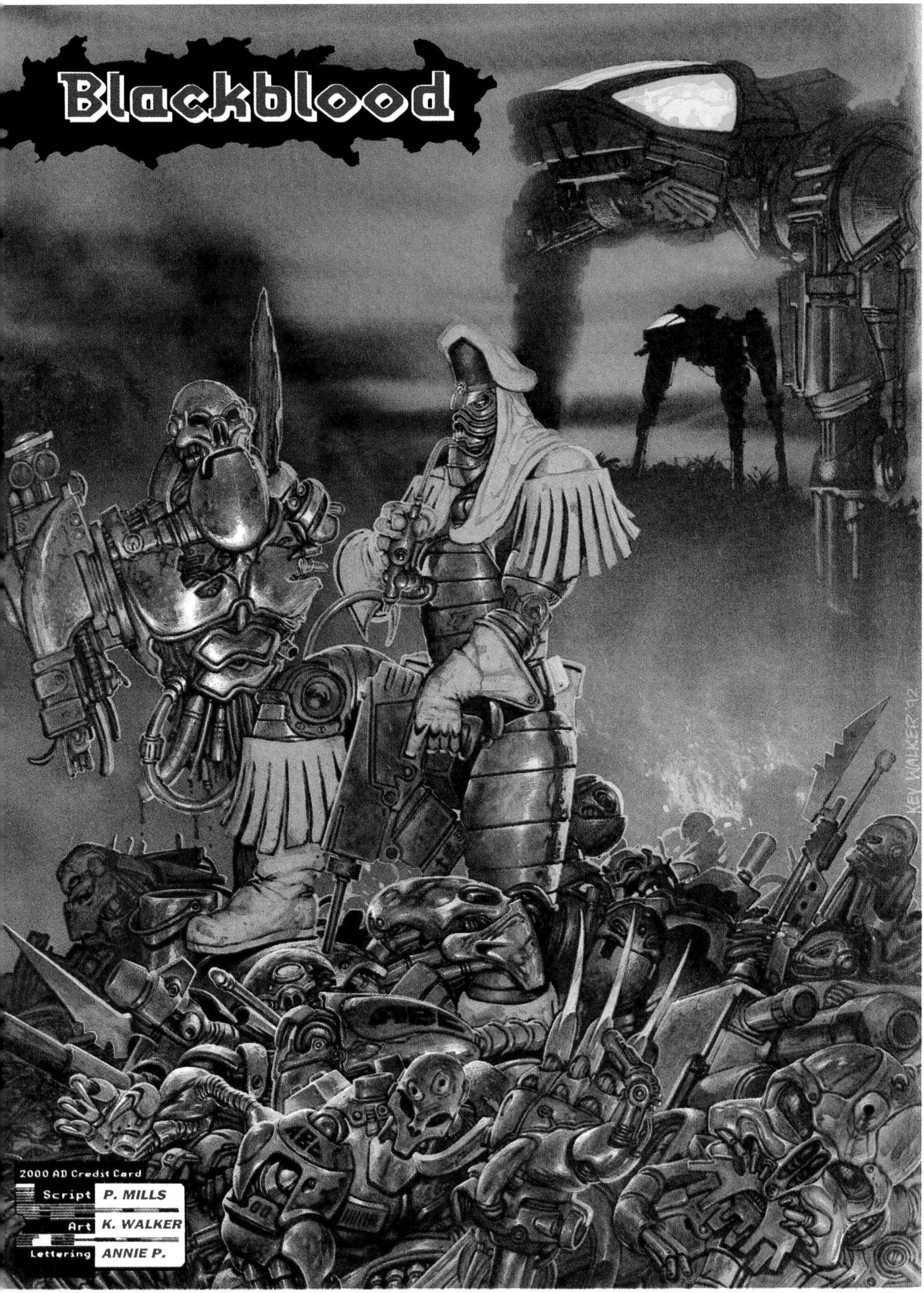
Blackblood
KEV WALKER '92
2000 AD Credit Card
Script P. MILLS
Art K. WALKER
Lettering ANNIE P.

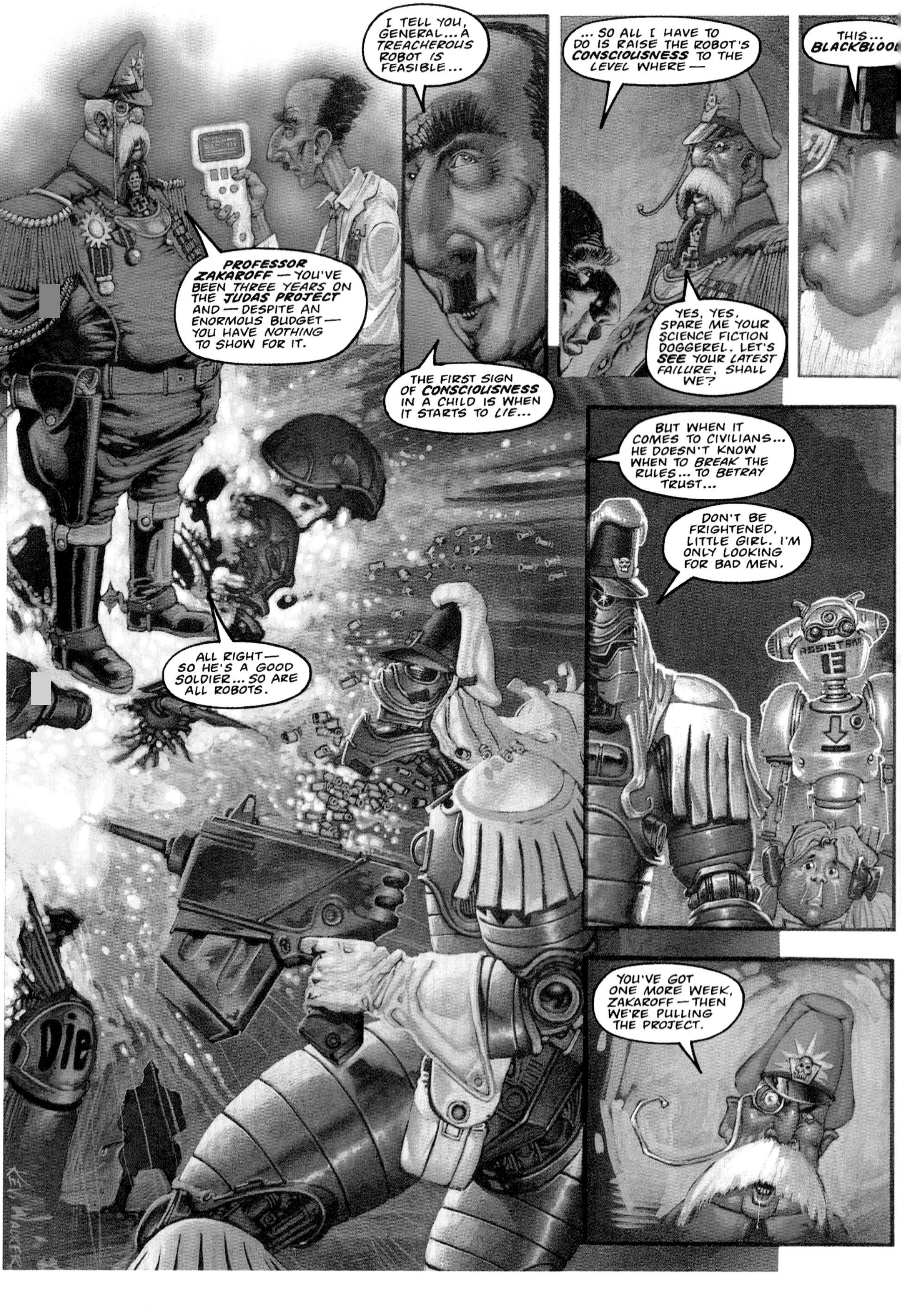
PROFESSOR ZAKAROFF — YOU'VE BEEN THREE YEARS ON THE JUDAS PROJECT AND — DESPITE AN ENORMOUS BUDGET — YOU HAVE NOTHING TO SHOW FOR IT.
I TELL YOU, GENERAL... A TREACHEROUS ROBOT IS FEASIBLE...
THE FIRST SIGN OF CONSCIOUSNESS IN A CHILD IS WHEN IT STARTS TO LIE...
... SO ALL I HAVE TO DO IS RAISE THE ROBOT'S CONSCIOUSNESS TO THE LEVEL WHERE —
YES, YES. SPARE ME YOUR SCIENCE FICTION DOGGEREL. LET'S SEE YOUR LATEST FAILURE, SHALL WE?
THIS... BLACKBLOO
ALL RIGHT — SO HE'S A GOOD SOLDIER... SO ARE ALL ROBOTS.
BUT WHEN IT COMES TO CIVILIANS... HE DOESN'T KNOW WHEN TO BREAK THE RULES... TO BETRAY TRUST...
DON'T BE FRIGHTENED, LITTLE GIRL. I'M ONLY LOOKING FOR BAD MEN.
13
YOU'VE GOT ONE MORE WEEK, ZAKAROFF — THEN WE'RE PULLING THE PROJECT.
DIE
KEV WALKER

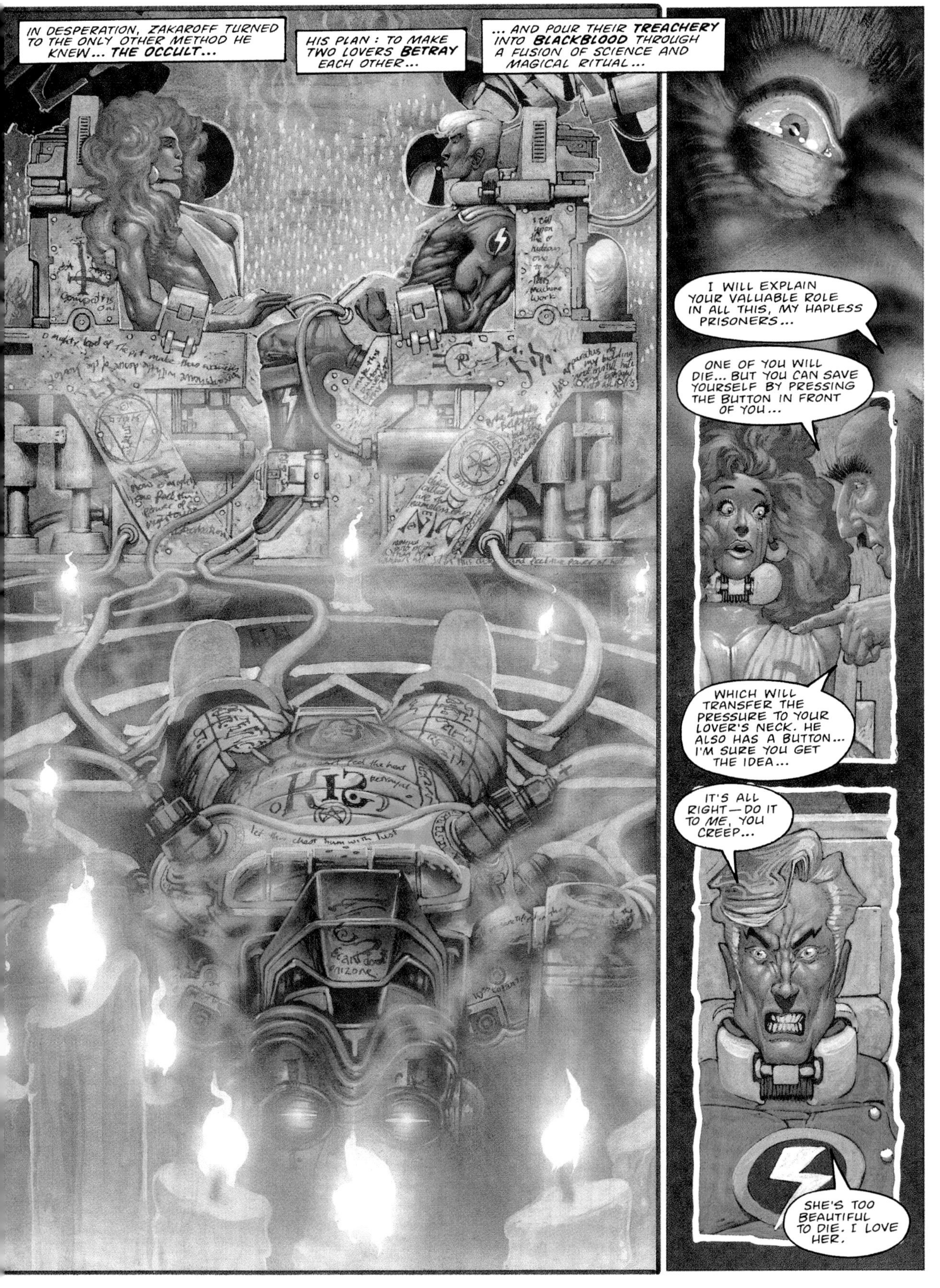
IN DESPERATION, ZAKAROFF TURNED TO THE ONLY OTHER METHOD HE KNEW... THE OCCULT...
HIS PLAN : TO MAKE TWO LOVERS BETRAY EACH OTHER...
... AND POUR THEIR TREACHERY INTO BLACKBLOOD THROUGH A FUSION OF SCIENCE AND MAGICAL RITUAL...
I WILL EXPLAIN YOUR VALUABLE ROLE IN ALL THIS, MY HAPLESS PRISONERS...
ONE OF YOU WILL DIE... BUT YOU CAN SAVE YOURSELF BY PRESSING THE BUTTON IN FRONT OF YOU...
WHICH WILL TRANSFER THE PRESSURE TO YOUR LOVER'S NECK. HE ALSO HAS A BUTTON... I'M SURE YOU GET THE IDEA...
IT'S ALL RIGHT—DO IT TO ME, YOU CREEP...
SHE'S TOO BEAUTIFUL TO DIE. I LOVE HER.

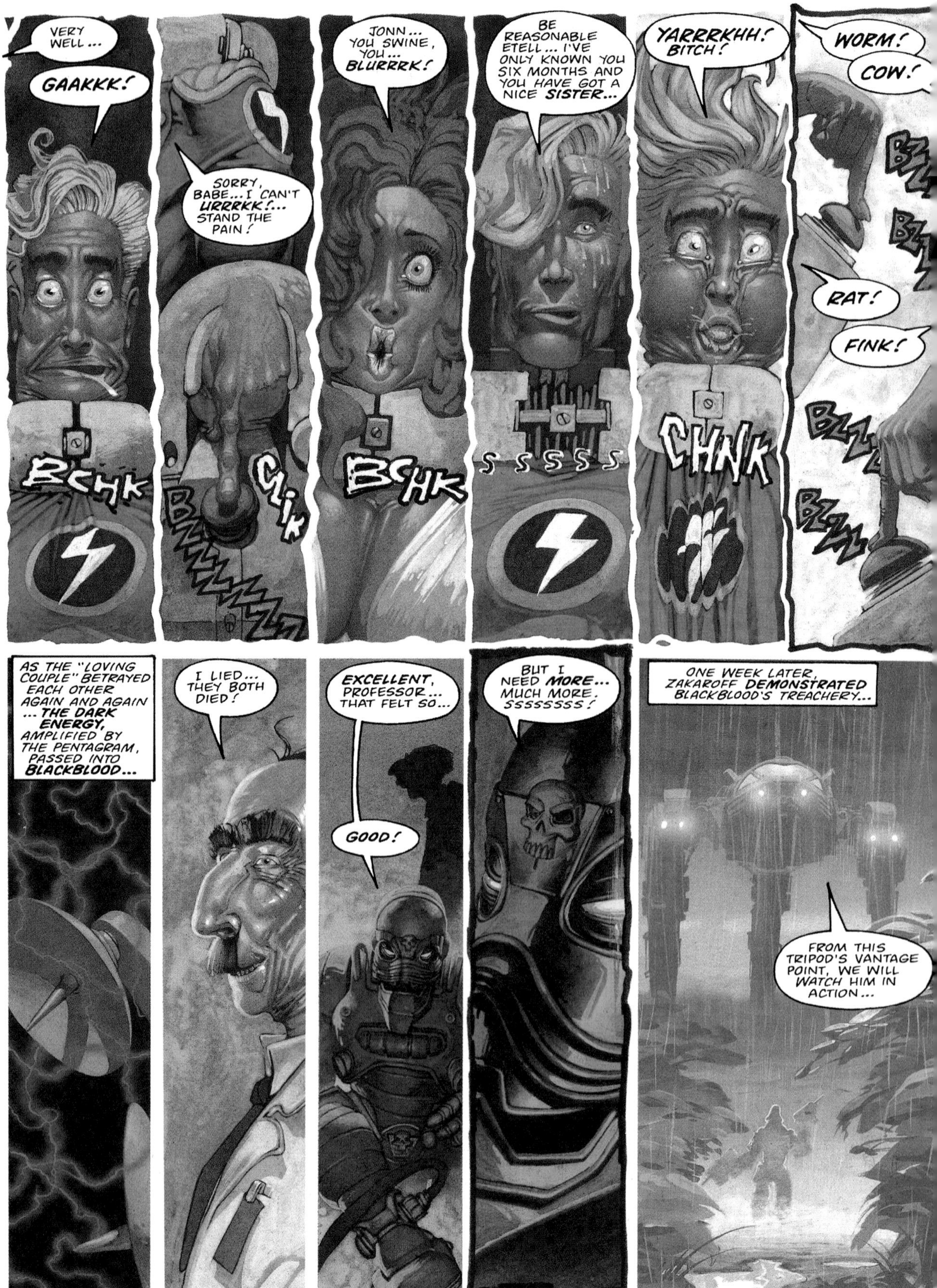

VERY WELL...
GAAKKK!
BCHK
SORRY, BABE... I CAN'T URRRKK!... STAND THE PAIN!
CLIK
JONN... YOU SWINE, YOU... BLURRRK!
BCHK
BE REASONABLE ETELL... I'VE ONLY KNOWN YOU SIX MONTHS AND YOU HAVE GOT A NICE SISTER...
SSSSS
YARRRKHH! BITCH!
CHNK
WORM!
COW!
RAT!
FINK!
AS THE "LOVING COUPLE" BETRAYED EACH OTHER AGAIN AND AGAIN ...THE DARK ENERGY, AMPLIFIED BY THE PENTAGRAM, PASSED INTO BLACKBLOOD...
I LIED... THEY BOTH DIED!
EXCELLENT, PROFESSOR... THAT FELT SO...
GOOD!
BUT I NEED MORE... MUCH MORE. SSSSSSSS!
ONE WEEK LATER, ZAKAROFF DEMONSTRATED BLACKBLOOD'S TREACHERY...
FROM THIS TRIPOD'S VANTAGE POINT, WE WILL WATCH HIM IN ACTION...

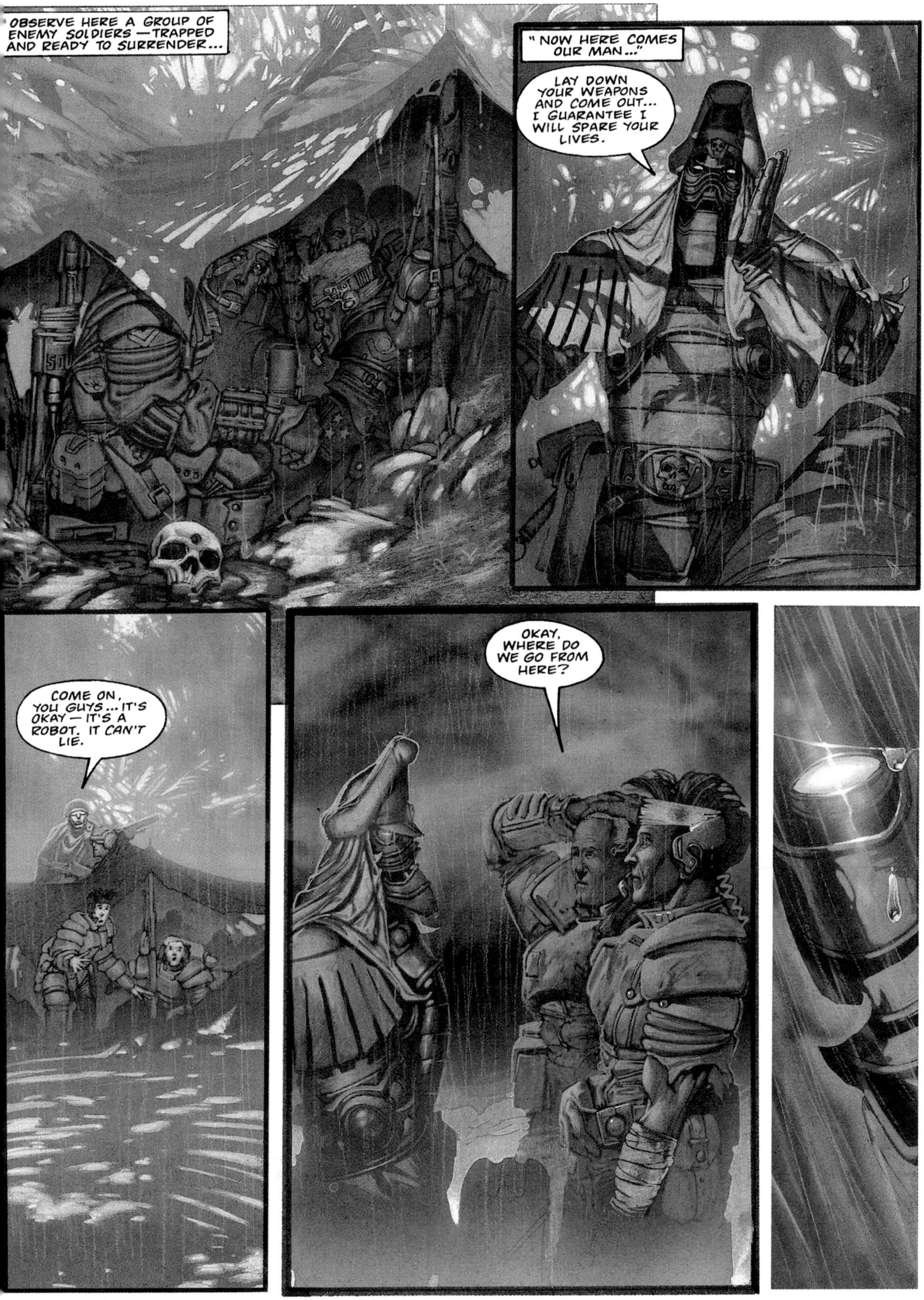
OBSERVE HERE A GROUP OF ENEMY SOLDIERS — TRAPPED AND READY TO SURRENDER...
"NOW HERE COMES OUR MAN..."
LAY DOWN YOUR WEAPONS AND COME OUT... I GUARANTEE I WILL SPARE YOUR LIVES.
COME ON, YOU GUYS... IT'S OKAY — IT'S A ROBOT. IT CAN'T LIE.
OKAY, WHERE DO WE GO FROM HERE?

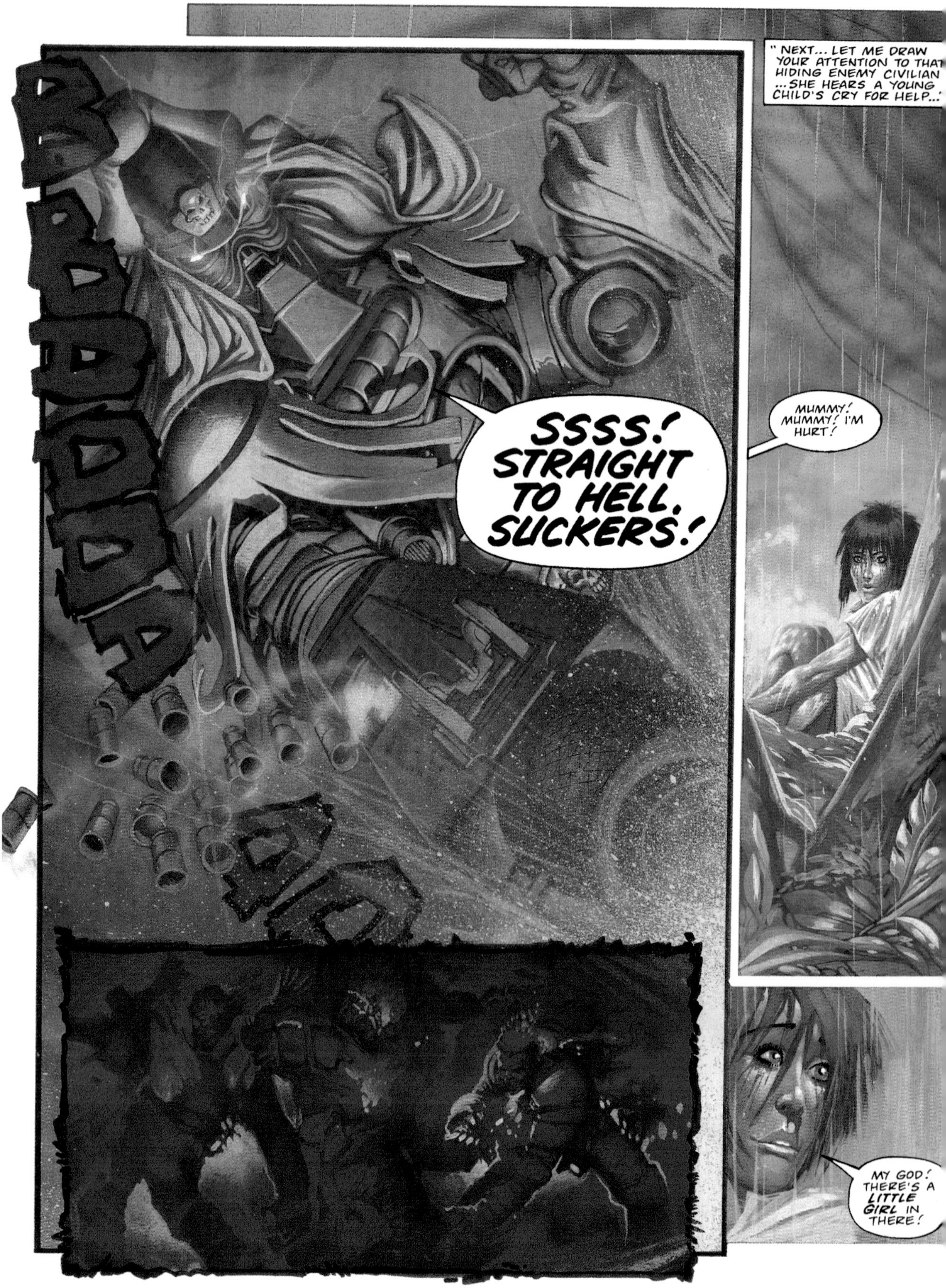

" NEXT... LET ME DRAW YOUR ATTENTION TO THAT HIDING ENEMY CIVILIAN ...SHE HEARS A YOUNG CHILD'S CRY FOR HELP..."
MUMMY! MUMMY! I'M HURT!
SSSS! STRAIGHT TO HELL, SUCKERS!
MY GOD! THERE'S A LITTLE GIRL IN THERE!

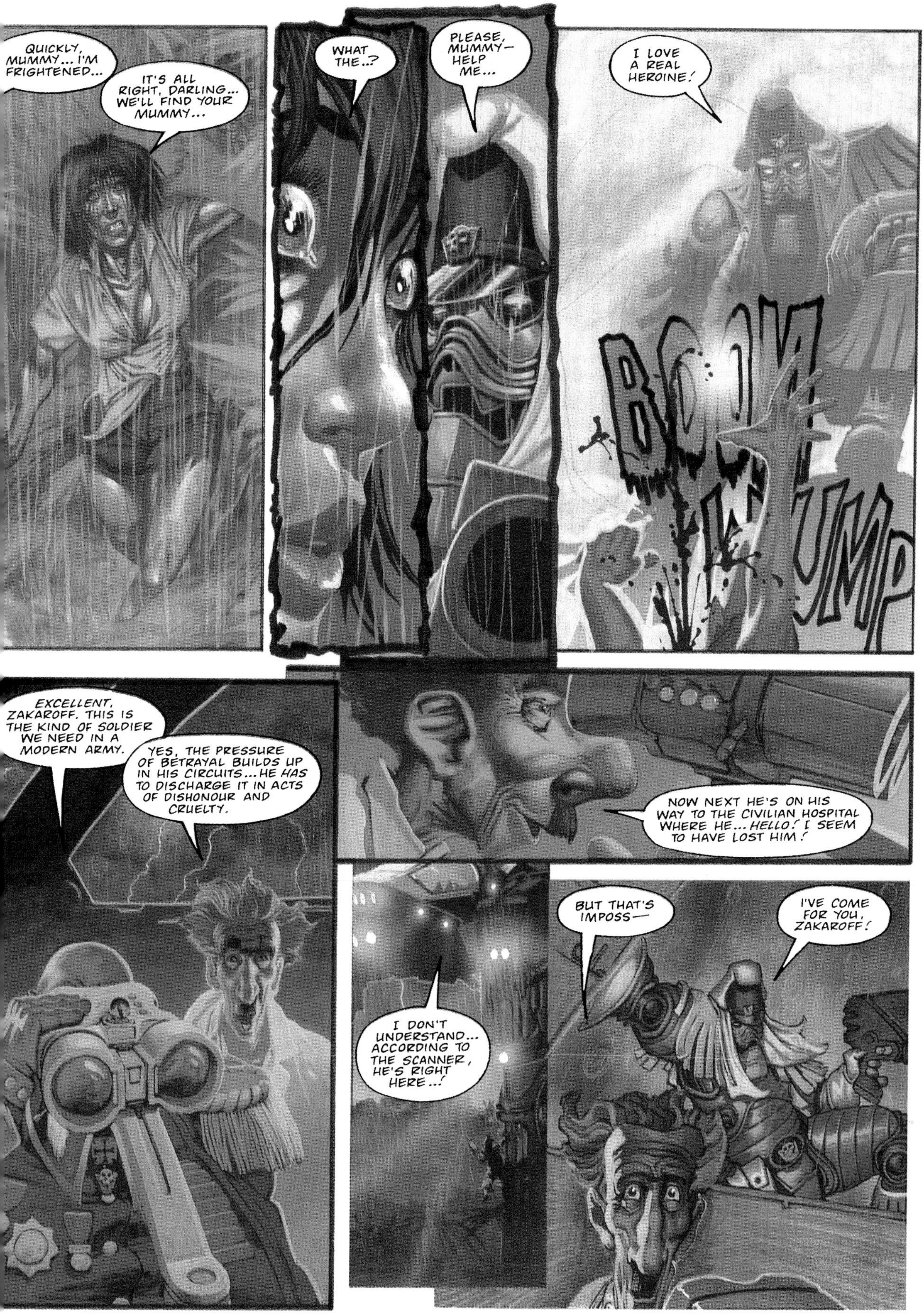
QUICKLY, MUMMY... I'M FRIGHTENED...
IT'S ALL RIGHT, DARLING... WE'LL FIND YOUR MUMMY...
WHAT THE..?
PLEASE, MUMMY— HELP ME...
I LOVE A REAL HEROINE!
BOOM
WUMP
EXCELLENT, ZAKAROFF. THIS IS THE KIND OF SOLDIER WE NEED IN A MODERN ARMY.
YES, THE PRESSURE OF BETRAYAL BUILDS UP IN HIS CIRCUITS... HE HAS TO DISCHARGE IT IN ACTS OF DISHONOUR AND CRUELTY.
NOW NEXT HE'S ON HIS WAY TO THE CIVILIAN HOSPITAL WHERE HE... HELLO! I SEEM TO HAVE LOST HIM!
I DON'T UNDERSTAND... ACCORDING TO THE SCANNER, HE'S RIGHT HERE..!
BUT THAT'S IMPOSS—
I'VE COME FOR YOU, ZAKAROFF!

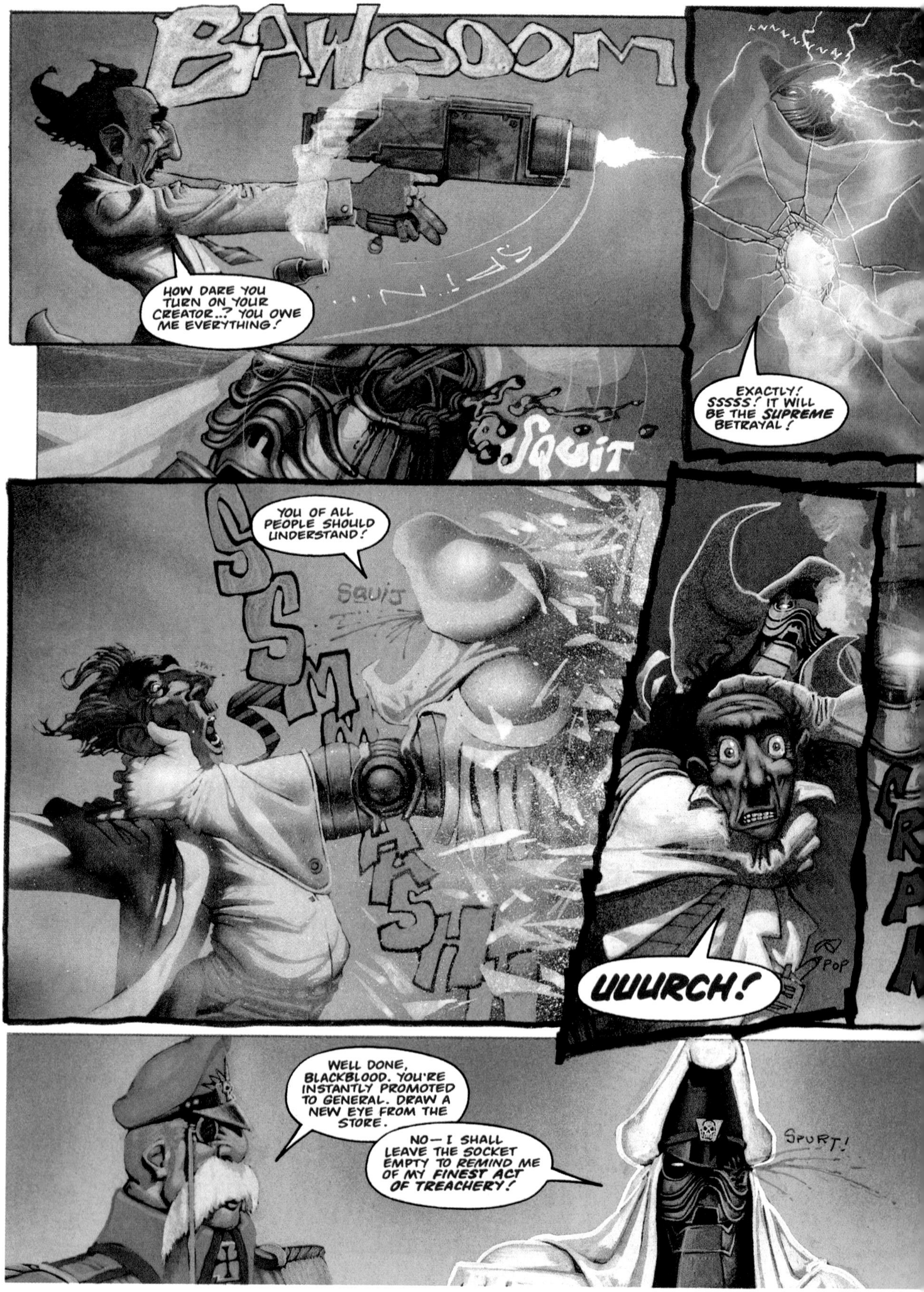
BAWOOOM
HOW DARE YOU TURN ON YOUR CREATOR..? YOU OWE ME EVERYTHING!
EXACTLY! SSSSS! IT WILL BE THE SUPREME BETRAYAL!
SQUIT
YOU OF ALL PEOPLE SHOULD UNDERSTAND!
SQUIJ
UUURCH!
POP
WELL DONE, BLACKBLOOD. YOU'RE INSTANTLY PROMOTED TO GENERAL. DRAW A NEW EYE FROM THE STORE.
NO— I SHALL LEAVE THE SOCKET EMPTY TO REMIND ME OF MY FINEST ACT OF TREACHERY!
SPURT!

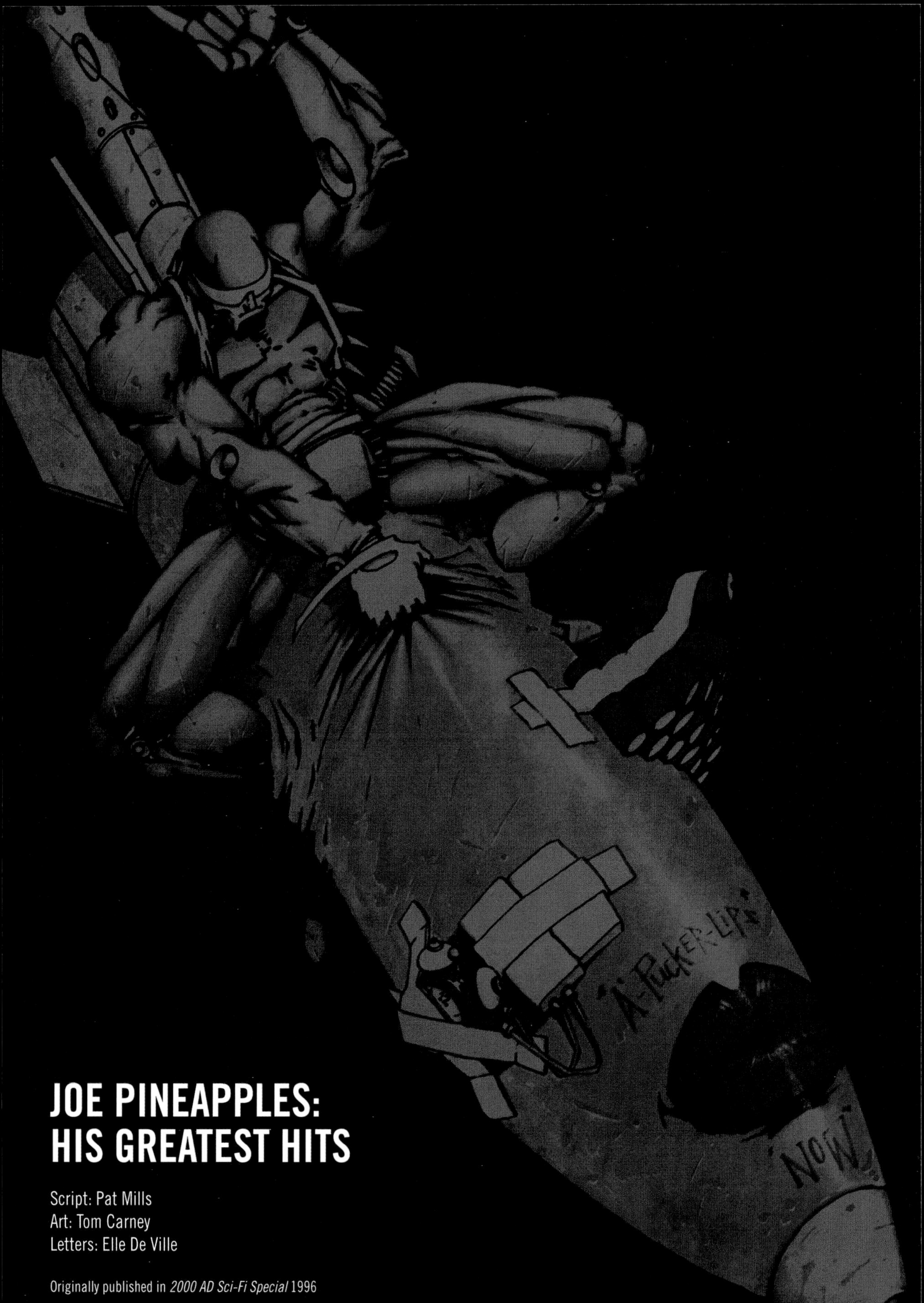
A-PUCKER-LIPS
NOW

JOE PINEAPPLES: HIS GREATEST HITS

Script: Pat Mills
Art: Tom Carney
Letters: Elle De Ville

Originally published in *2000 AD Sci-Fi Special* 1996

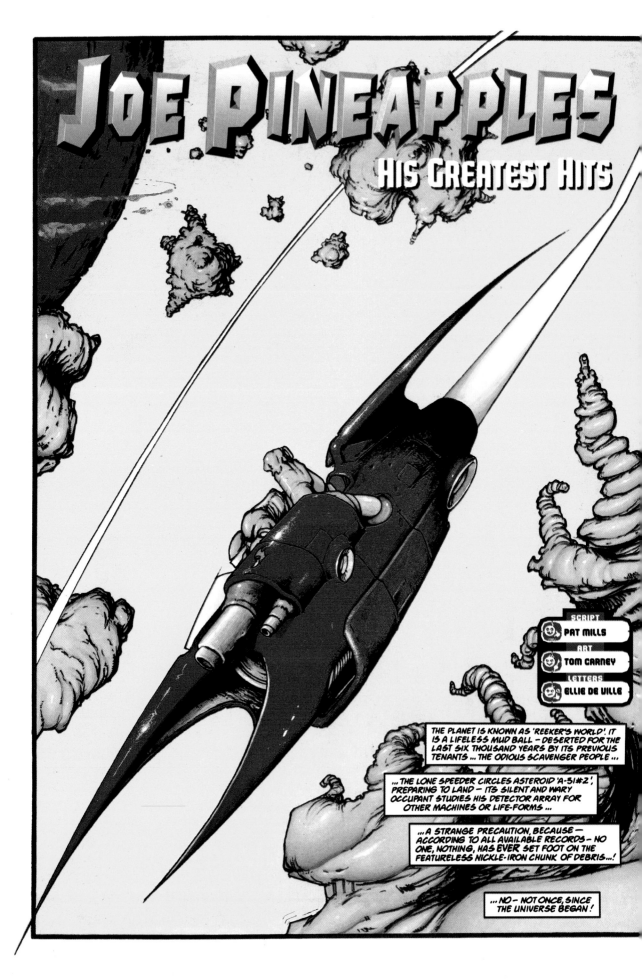

JOE PINEAPPLES

HIS GREATEST HITS

SCRIPT
PAT MILLS

ART
TOM CARNEY

LETTERS
ELLIE DE VILLE

THE PLANET IS KNOWN AS 'REEKER'S WORLD'. IT IS A LIFELESS MUD BALL — DESERTED FOR THE LAST SIX THOUSAND YEARS BY ITS PREVIOUS TENANTS ... THE ODIOUS SCAVENGER PEOPLE ...

...THE LONE SPEEDER CIRCLES ASTEROID 'A-51#2', PREPARING TO LAND — ITS SILENT AND WARY OCCUPANT STUDIES HIS DETECTOR ARRAY FOR OTHER MACHINES OR LIFE-FORMS ...

...A STRANGE PRECAUTION, BECAUSE — ACCORDING TO ALL AVAILABLE RECORDS — NO ONE, NOTHING, HAS EVER SET FOOT ON THE FEATURELESS NICKLE-IRON CHUNK OF DEBRIS...!

...NO — NOT ONCE, SINCE THE UNIVERSE BEGAN!

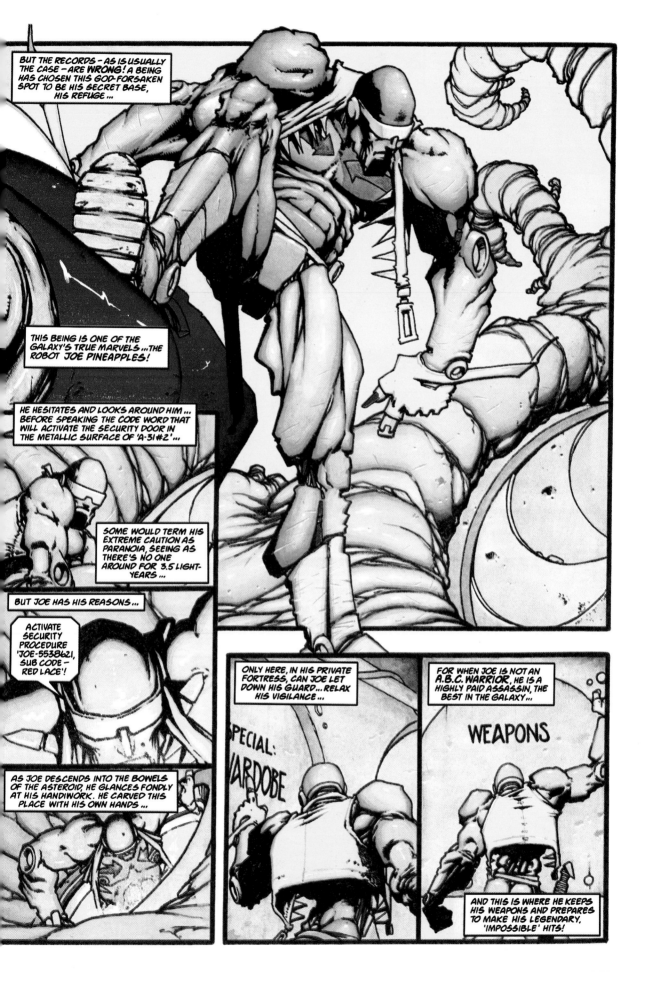

BUT THE RECORDS – AS IS USUALLY THE CASE – ARE *WRONG!* A BEING HAS CHOSEN THIS GOD-FORSAKEN SPOT TO BE HIS SECRET BASE, HIS REFUGE...

THIS BEING IS ONE OF THE GALAXY'S TRUE MARVELS ...THE ROBOT JOE PINEAPPLES!

HE HESITATES AND LOOKS AROUND HIM ... BEFORE SPEAKING THE CODE WORD THAT WILL ACTIVATE THE SECURITY DOOR IN THE METALLIC SURFACE OF 'A-31 #2'...

SOME WOULD TERM HIS EXTREME CAUTION AS PARANOIA, SEEING AS THERE'S NO ONE AROUND FOR 3.5 LIGHT-YEARS ...

BUT JOE HAS HIS REASONS ...

ACTIVATE SECURITY PROCEDURE 'JOE-5538621, SUB CODE – RED LACE'!

AS JOE DESCENDS INTO THE BOWELS OF THE ASTEROID, HE GLANCES FONDLY AT HIS HANDIWORK. HE CARVED THIS PLACE WITH HIS OWN HANDS ...

ONLY HERE, IN HIS PRIVATE FORTRESS, CAN JOE LET DOWN HIS GUARD... RELAX HIS VIGILANCE ...

FOR WHEN JOE IS NOT AN A.B.C. WARRIOR, HE IS A HIGHLY PAID ASSASSIN, THE BEST IN THE GALAXY...

SPECIAL: WARDOBE

WEAPONS

AND THIS IS WHERE HE KEEPS HIS WEAPONS AND PREPARES TO MAKE HIS LEGENDARY, 'IMPOSSIBLE' HITS!

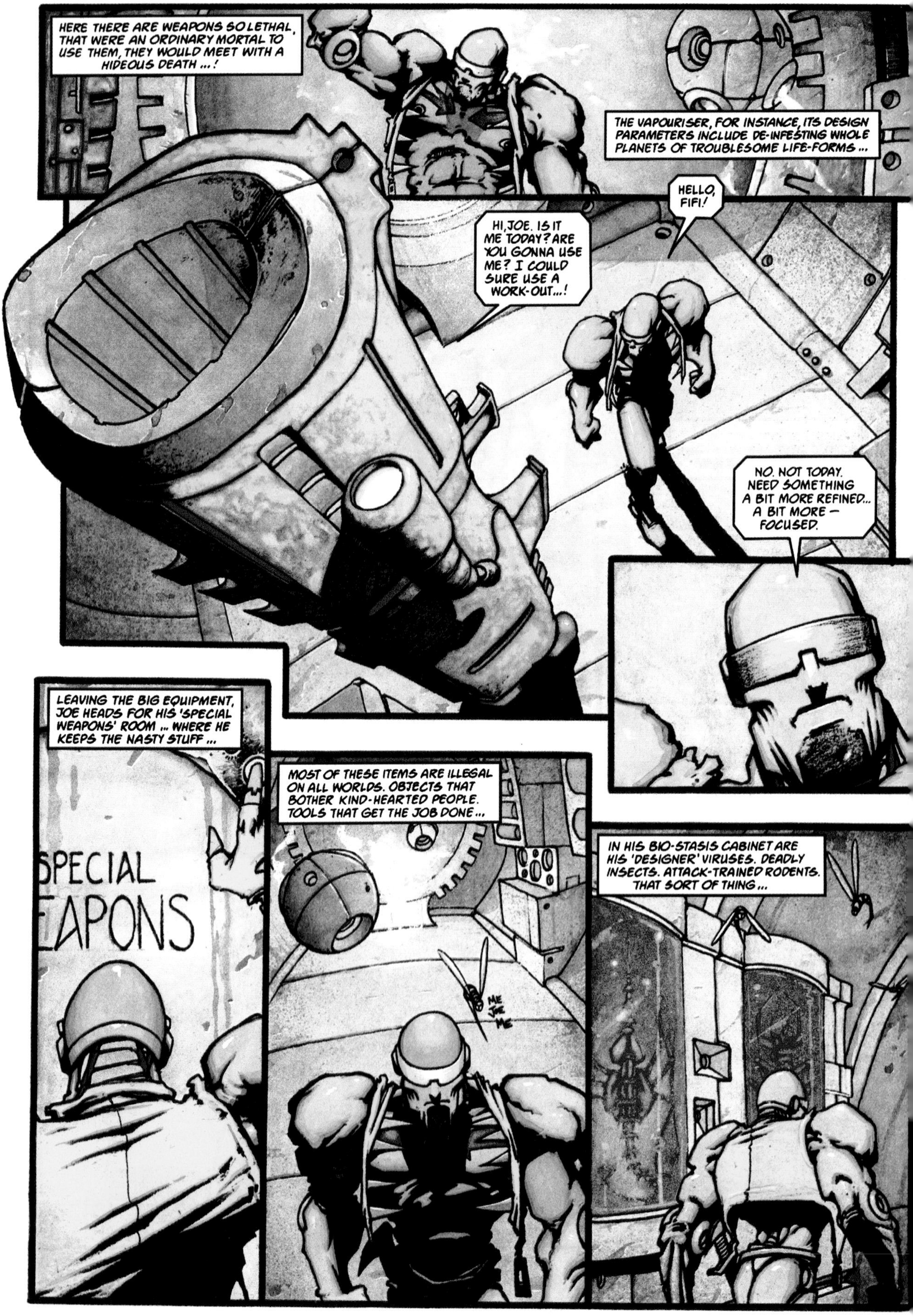
HERE THERE ARE WEAPONS SO LETHAL, THAT WERE AN ORDINARY MORTAL TO USE THEM, THEY WOULD MEET WITH A HIDEOUS DEATH ...!
THE VAPOURISER, FOR INSTANCE, ITS DESIGN PARAMETERS INCLUDE DE-INFESTING WHOLE PLANETS OF TROUBLESOME LIFE-FORMS ...
HELLO, FIFI!
HI, JOE. IS IT ME TODAY? ARE YOU GONNA USE ME? I COULD SURE USE A WORK-OUT...!
NO. NOT TODAY. NEED SOMETHING A BIT MORE REFINED... A BIT MORE — FOCUSED.
LEAVING THE BIG EQUIPMENT, JOE HEADS FOR HIS 'SPECIAL WEAPONS' ROOM ... WHERE HE KEEPS THE NASTY STUFF ...
SPECIAL
EAPONS
MOST OF THESE ITEMS ARE ILLEGAL ON ALL WORLDS. OBJECTS THAT BOTHER KIND-HEARTED PEOPLE. TOOLS THAT GET THE JOB DONE ...
ME JOE ME
IN HIS BIO-STASIS CABINET ARE HIS 'DESIGNER' VIRUSES. DEADLY INSECTS. ATTACK-TRAINED RODENTS. THAT SORT OF THING ...

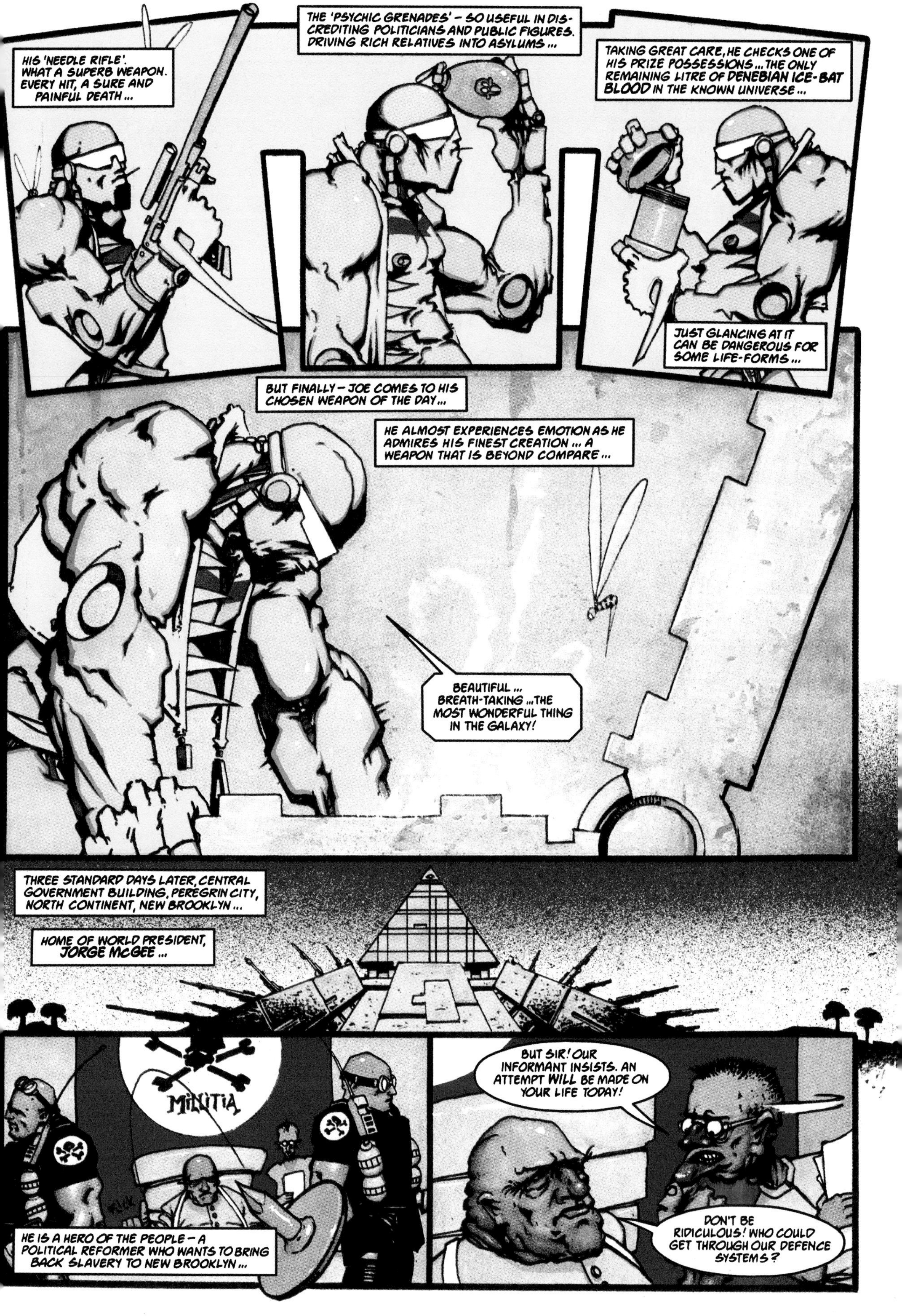
HIS 'NEEDLE RIFLE'. WHAT A SUPERB WEAPON. EVERY HIT, A SURE AND PAINFUL DEATH ...
THE 'PSYCHIC GRENADES' – SO USEFUL IN DISCREDITING POLITICIANS AND PUBLIC FIGURES. DRIVING RICH RELATIVES INTO ASYLUMS ...
TAKING GREAT CARE, HE CHECKS ONE OF HIS PRIZE POSSESSIONS ... THE ONLY REMAINING LITRE OF DENEBIAN ICE-BAT BLOOD IN THE KNOWN UNIVERSE ...
JUST GLANCING AT IT CAN BE DANGEROUS FOR SOME LIFE-FORMS ...
BUT FINALLY – JOE COMES TO HIS CHOSEN WEAPON OF THE DAY ...
HE ALMOST EXPERIENCES EMOTION AS HE ADMIRES HIS FINEST CREATION ... A WEAPON THAT IS BEYOND COMPARE ...
BEAUTIFUL ... BREATH-TAKING ... THE MOST WONDERFUL THING IN THE GALAXY!
THREE STANDARD DAYS LATER, CENTRAL GOVERNMENT BUILDING, PEREGRIN CITY, NORTH CONTINENT, NEW BROOKLYN ...
HOME OF WORLD PRESIDENT, JORGE McGEE ...
MILITIA
HE IS A HERO OF THE PEOPLE – A POLITICAL REFORMER WHO WANTS TO BRING BACK SLAVERY TO NEW BROOKLYN ...
BUT SIR! OUR INFORMANT INSISTS. AN ATTEMPT WILL BE MADE ON YOUR LIFE TODAY!
DON'T BE RIDICULOUS! WHO COULD GET THROUGH OUR DEFENCE SYSTEMS?

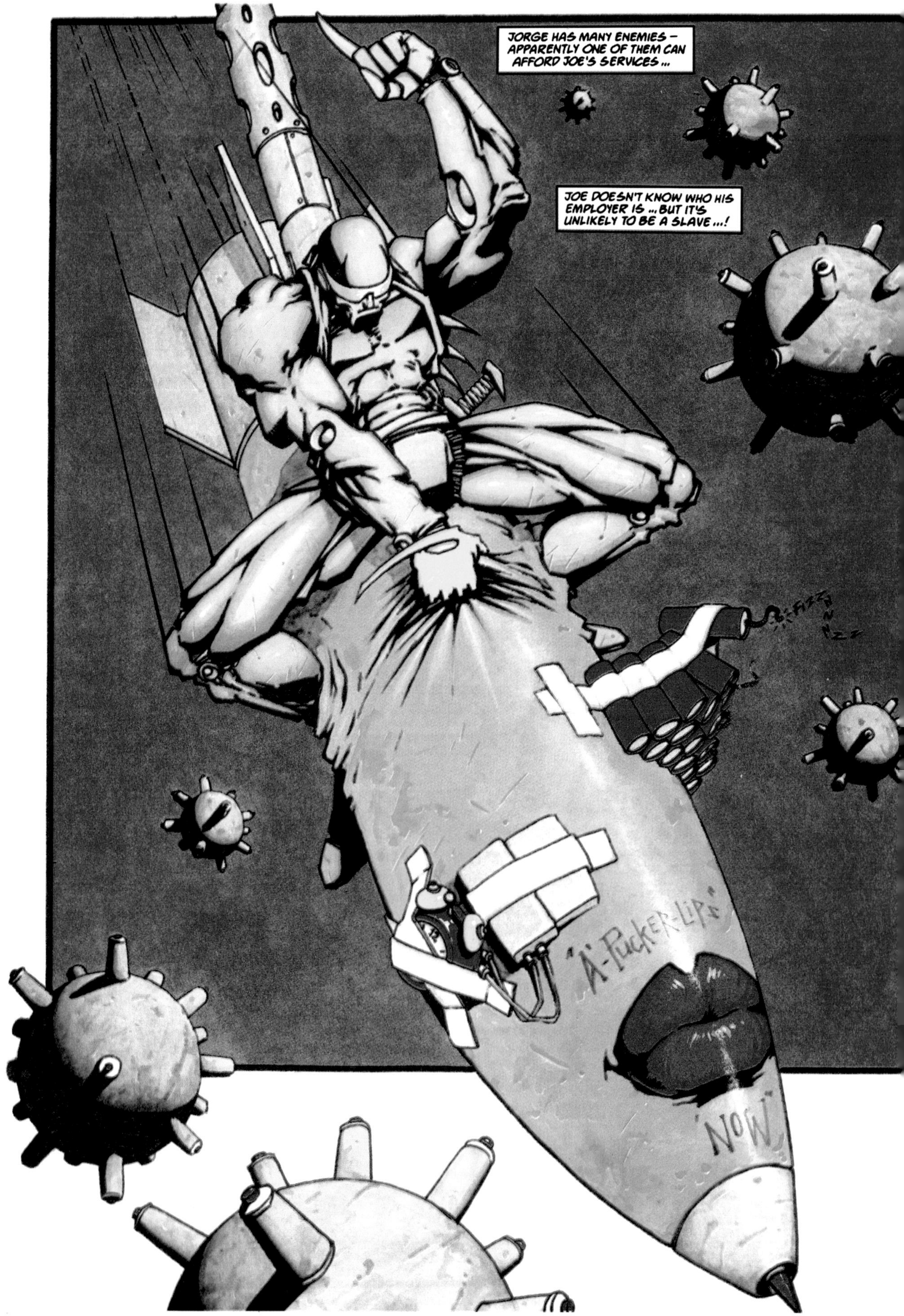
JORGE HAS MANY ENEMIES – APPARENTLY ONE OF THEM CAN AFFORD JOE'S SERVICES ...
JOE DOESN'T KNOW WHO HIS EMPLOYER IS ... BUT IT'S UNLIKELY TO BE A SLAVE ...!
FIZZ
"A-PUCKER-LIPS"
"NOW"

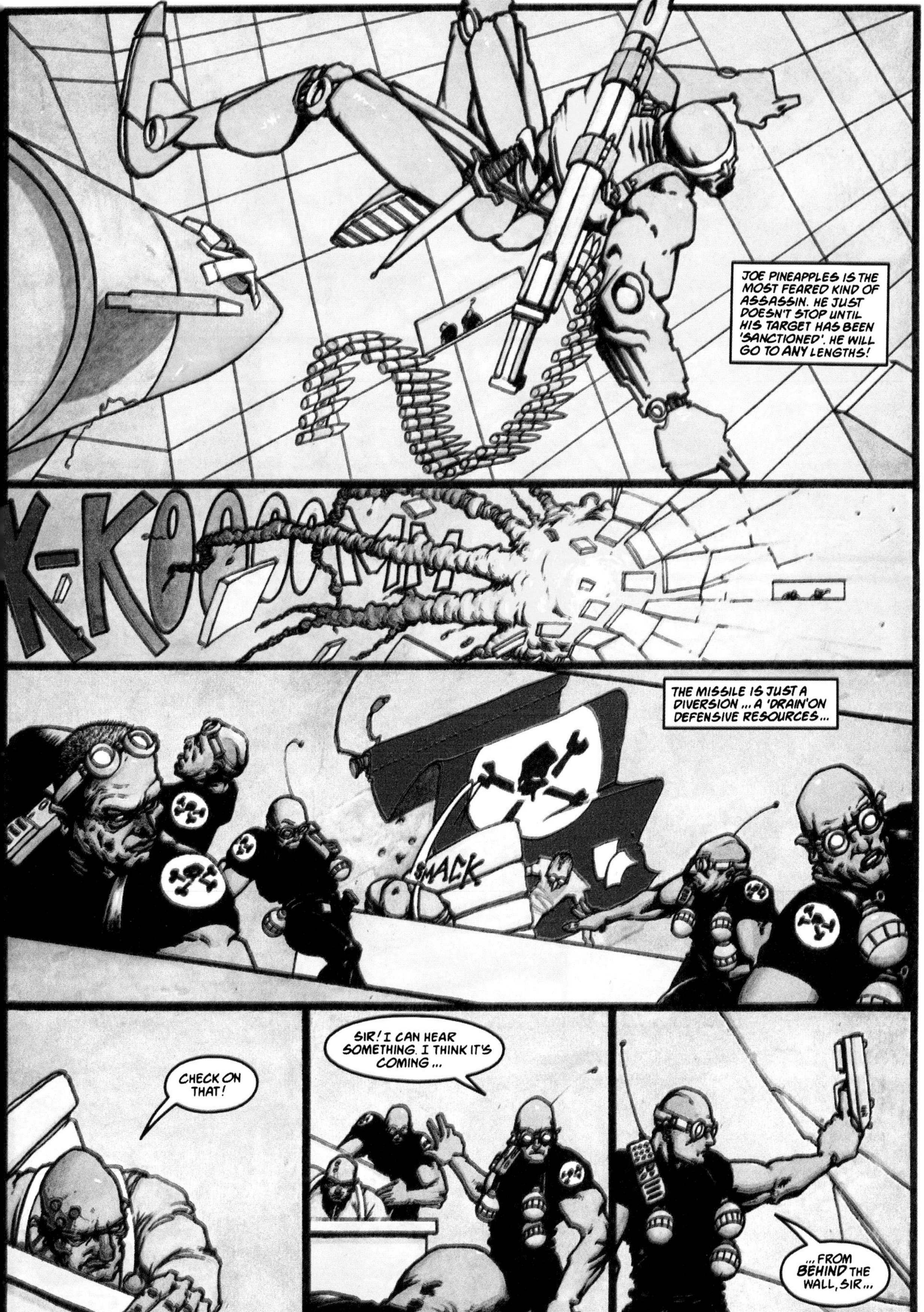

JOE PINEAPPLES IS THE MOST FEARED KIND OF ASSASSIN. HE JUST DOESN'T STOP UNTIL HIS TARGET HAS BEEN 'SANCTIONED'. HE WILL GO TO ANY LENGTHS!
K-KOOOOOMM
THE MISSILE IS JUST A DIVERSION ... A 'DRAIN' ON DEFENSIVE RESOURCES...
SMACK
CHECK ON THAT!
SIR! I CAN HEAR SOMETHING. I THINK IT'S COMING ...
... FROM BEHIND THE WALL, SIR ...

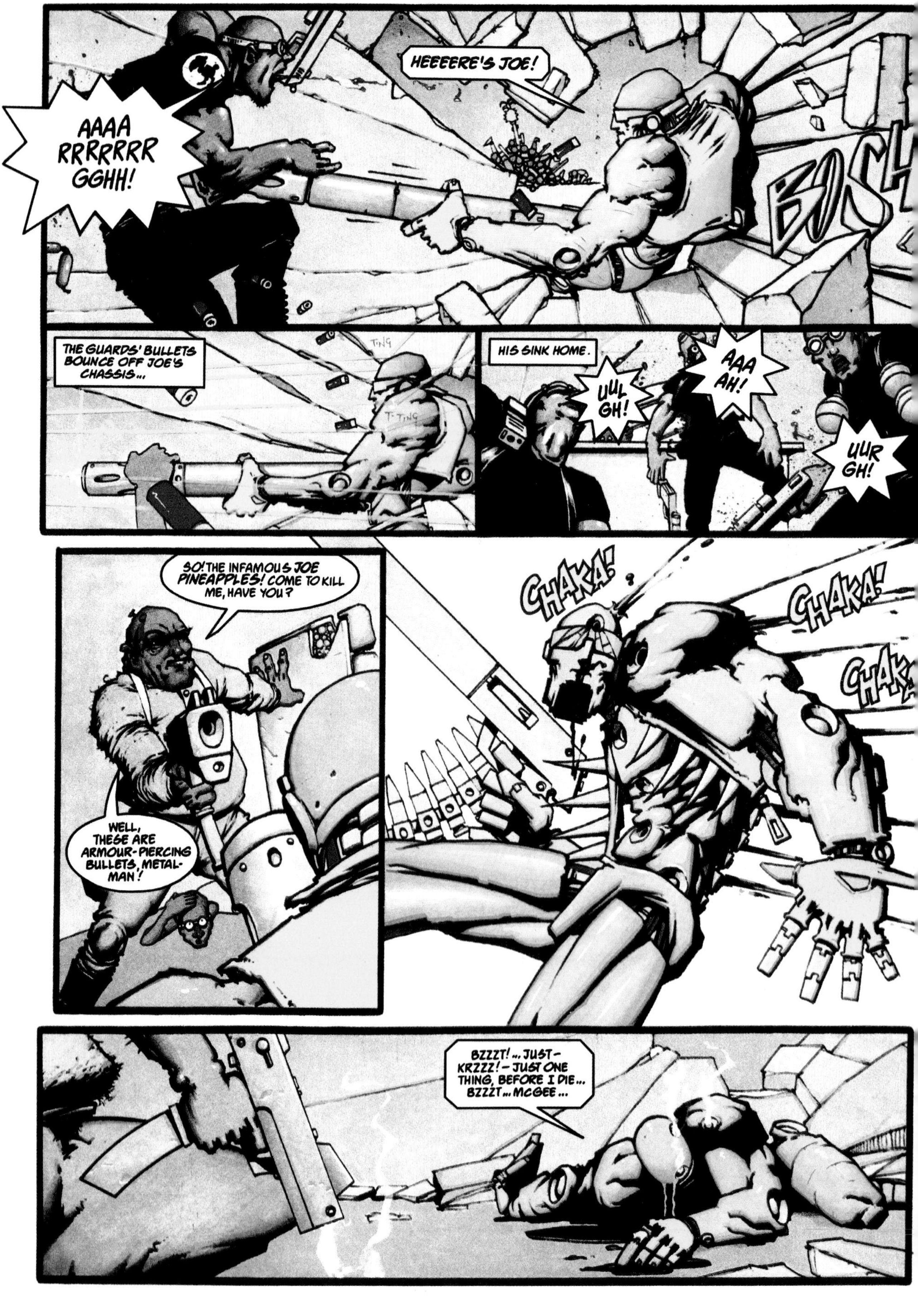
HEEEERE'S JOE!
AAAA RRRRRRR GGHH!
BOSH
THE GUARDS' BULLETS BOUNCE OFF JOE'S CHASSIS...
TING
T-TING
HIS SINK HOME.
UUL GH!
AAA AH!
UUR GH!
SO! THE INFAMOUS JOE PINEAPPLES! COME TO KILL ME, HAVE YOU?
WELL, THESE ARE ARMOUR-PIERCING BULLETS, METAL-MAN!
CHAKA!
CHAKA!
BZZZT!... JUST- KRZZZ! - JUST ONE THING, BEFORE I DIE... BZZZT... MCGEE...

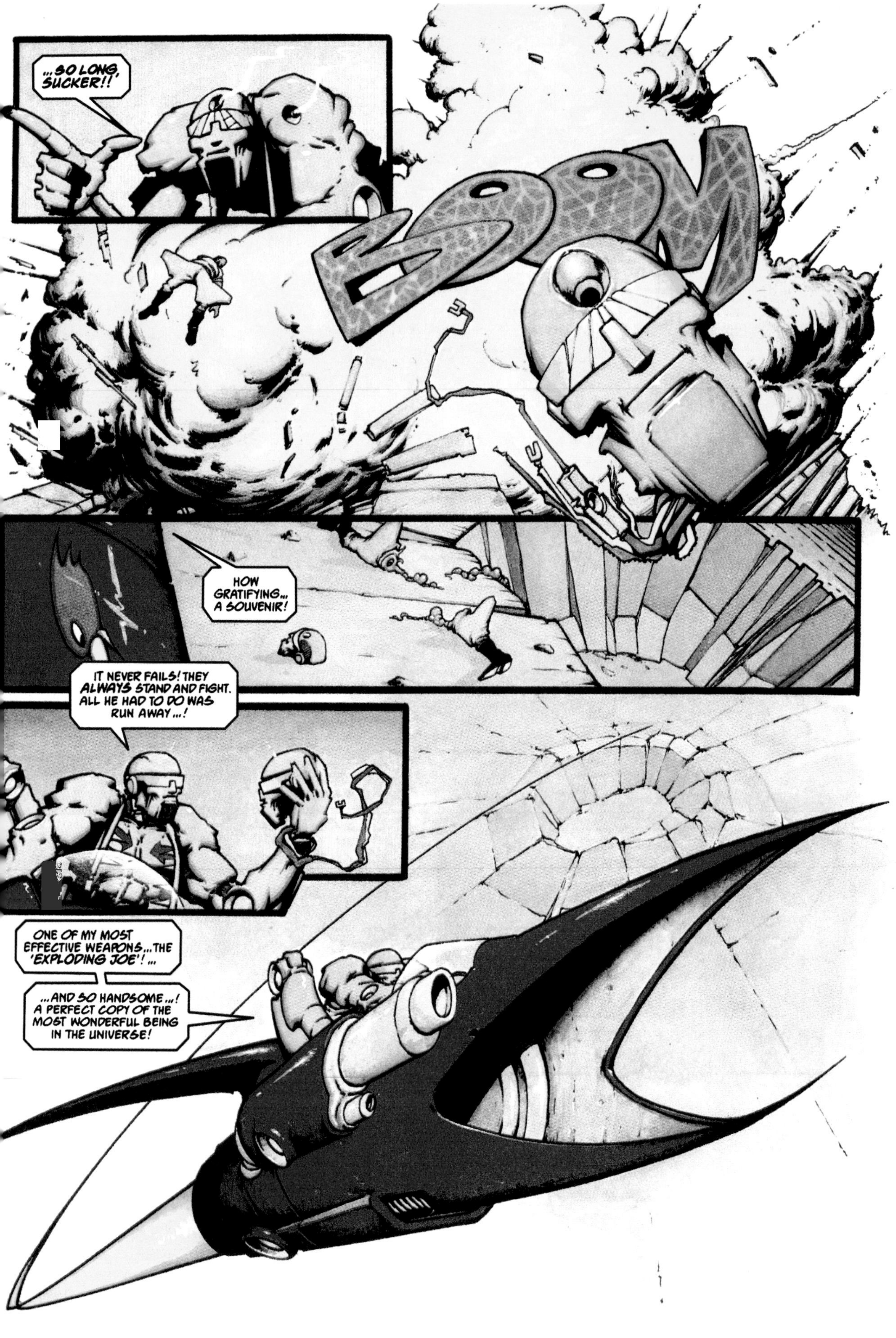
...SO LONG, SUCKER!!'
BOOM
HOW GRATIFYING... A SOUVENIR!
IT NEVER FAILS! THEY ALWAYS STAND AND FIGHT. ALL HE HAD TO DO WAS RUN AWAY...!
ONE OF MY MOST EFFECTIVE WEAPONS... THE 'EXPLODING JOE'!...
...AND SO HANDSOME...! A PERFECT COPY OF THE MOST WONDERFUL BEING IN THE UNIVERSE!

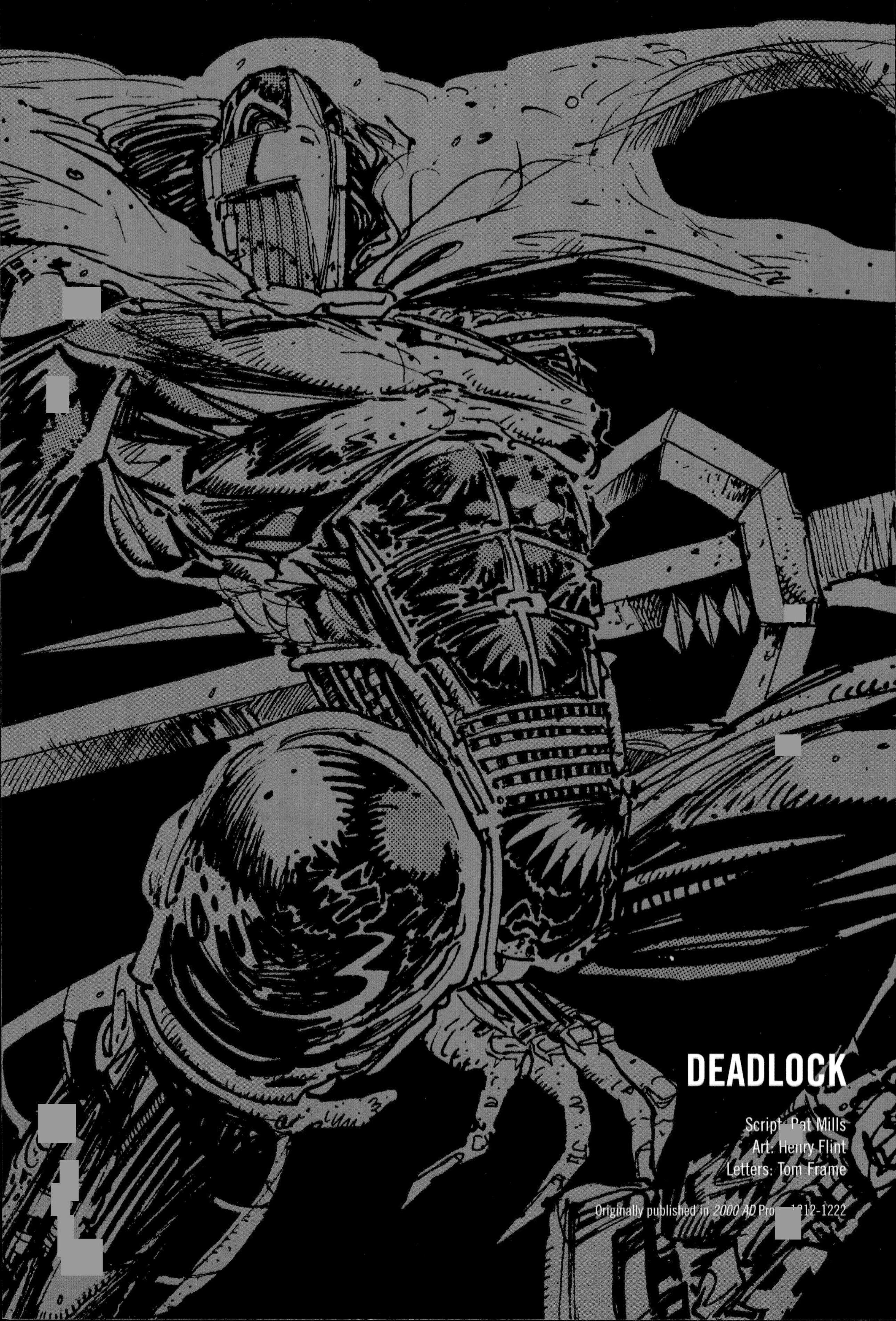

DEADLOCK

Script: Pat Mills
Art: Henry Flint
Letters: Tom Frame

Originally published in *2000 AD* Pro[illegible]212-1222

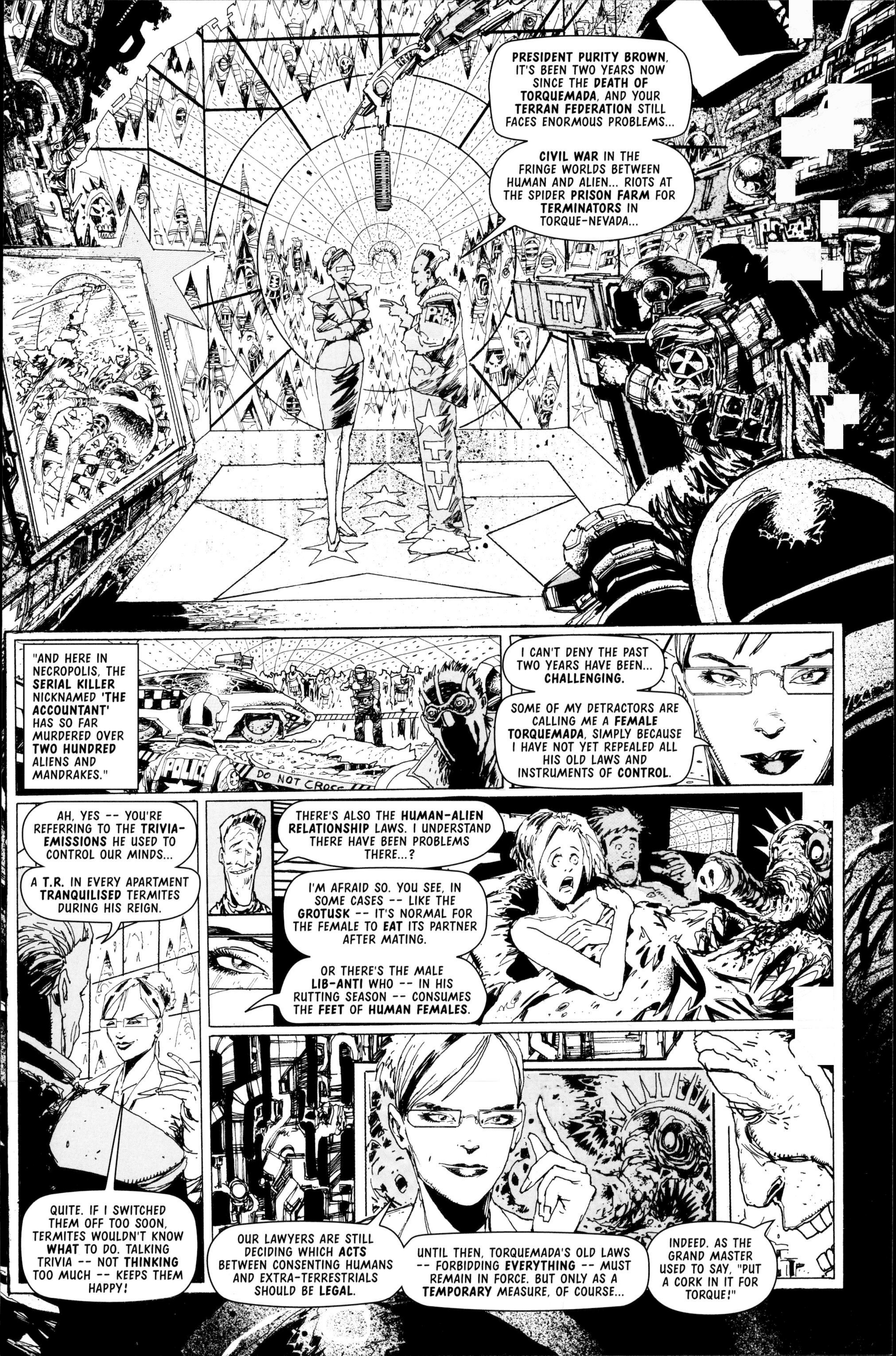
PRESIDENT PURITY BROWN, IT'S BEEN TWO YEARS NOW SINCE THE DEATH OF TORQUEMADA, AND YOUR TERRAN FEDERATION STILL FACES ENORMOUS PROBLEMS...
CIVIL WAR IN THE FRINGE WORLDS BETWEEN HUMAN AND ALIEN... RIOTS AT THE SPIDER PRISON FARM FOR TERMINATORS IN TORQUE-NEVADA...
TTV
TTV
"AND HERE IN NECROPOLIS, THE SERIAL KILLER NICKNAMED 'THE ACCOUNTANT' HAS SO FAR MURDERED OVER TWO HUNDRED ALIENS AND MANDRAKES."
POLICE
DO NOT CROSS
I CAN'T DENY THE PAST TWO YEARS HAVE BEEN... CHALLENGING.
SOME OF MY DETRACTORS ARE CALLING ME A FEMALE TORQUEMADA, SIMPLY BECAUSE I HAVE NOT YET REPEALED ALL HIS OLD LAWS AND INSTRUMENTS OF CONTROL.
AH, YES -- YOU'RE REFERRING TO THE TRIVIA-EMISSIONS HE USED TO CONTROL OUR MINDS...
A T.R. IN EVERY APARTMENT TRANQUILISED TERMITES DURING HIS REIGN.
QUITE. IF I SWITCHED THEM OFF TOO SOON, TERMITES WOULDN'T KNOW WHAT TO DO. TALKING TRIVIA -- NOT THINKING TOO MUCH -- KEEPS THEM HAPPY!
THERE'S ALSO THE HUMAN-ALIEN RELATIONSHIP LAWS. I UNDERSTAND THERE HAVE BEEN PROBLEMS THERE...?
I'M AFRAID SO. YOU SEE, IN SOME CASES -- LIKE THE GROTUSK -- IT'S NORMAL FOR THE FEMALE TO EAT ITS PARTNER AFTER MATING.
OR THERE'S THE MALE LIB-ANTI WHO -- IN HIS RUTTING SEASON -- CONSUMES THE FEET OF HUMAN FEMALES.
OUR LAWYERS ARE STILL DECIDING WHICH ACTS BETWEEN CONSENTING HUMANS AND EXTRA-TERRESTRIALS SHOULD BE LEGAL.
UNTIL THEN, TORQUEMADA'S OLD LAWS -- FORBIDDING EVERYTHING -- MUST REMAIN IN FORCE. BUT ONLY AS A TEMPORARY MEASURE, OF COURSE...
INDEED. AS THE GRAND MASTER USED TO SAY, "PUT A CORK IN IT FOR TORQUE!"

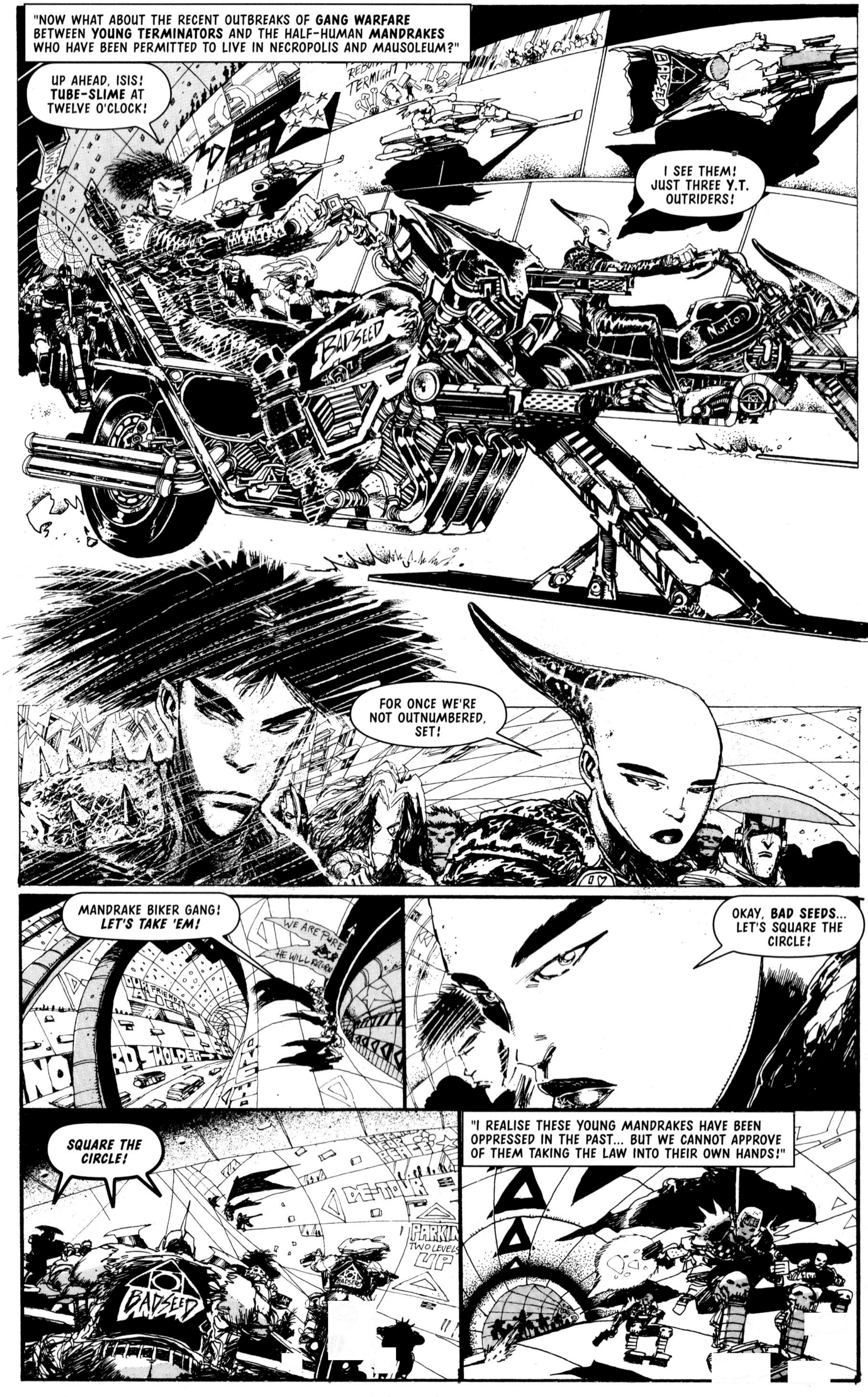
"NOW WHAT ABOUT THE RECENT OUTBREAKS OF GANG WARFARE BETWEEN YOUNG TERMINATORS AND THE HALF-HUMAN MANDRAKES WHO HAVE BEEN PERMITTED TO LIVE IN NECROPOLIS AND MAUSOLEUM?"
UP AHEAD, ISIS! TUBE-SLIME AT TWELVE O'CLOCK!
I SEE THEM! JUST THREE Y.T. OUTRIDERS!
BADSEED
FOR ONCE WE'RE NOT OUTNUMBERED, SET!
MANDRAKE BIKER GANG! LET'S TAKE 'EM!
WE ARE PURE
HE WILL RETURN
OKAY, BAD SEEDS... LET'S SQUARE THE CIRCLE!
SQUARE THE CIRCLE!
"I REALISE THESE YOUNG MANDRAKES HAVE BEEN OPPRESSED IN THE PAST... BUT WE CANNOT APPROVE OF THEM TAKING THE LAW INTO THEIR OWN HANDS!"
DE-TOUR
PARKIN TWO LEVELS UP
BADSEED

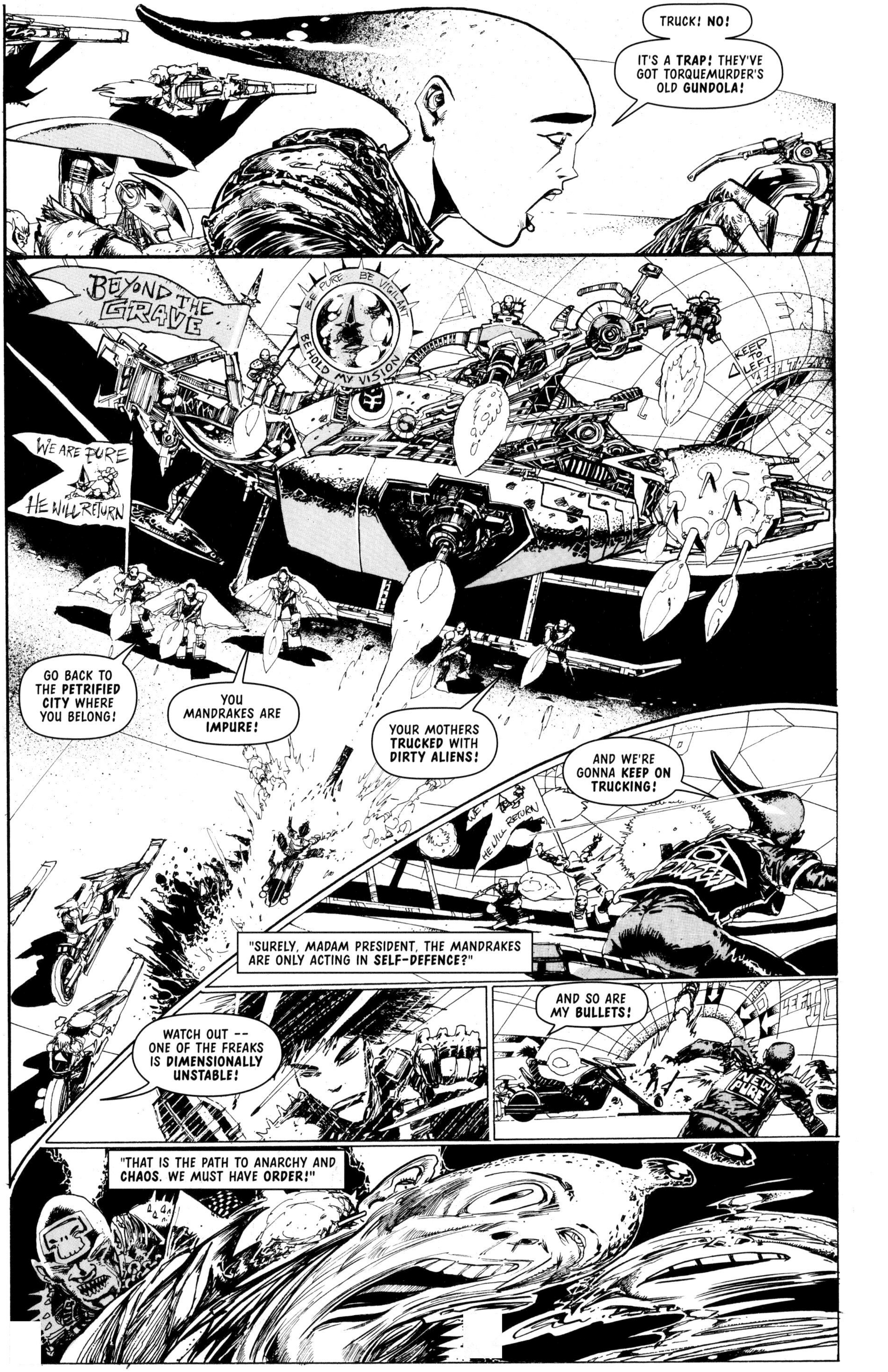

TRUCK! NO!
IT'S A TRAP! THEY'VE GOT TORQUEMURDER'S OLD GUNDOLA!
BEYOND THE GRAVE
BE PURE BE VIGILANT BEHOLD MY VISION
KEEP TO LEFT
WE ARE PURE HE WILL RETURN
GO BACK TO THE PETRIFIED CITY WHERE YOU BELONG!
YOU MANDRAKES ARE IMPURE!
YOUR MOTHERS TRUCKED WITH DIRTY ALIENS!
AND WE'RE GONNA KEEP ON TRUCKING!
HE WILL RETURN
BADSEED
"SURELY, MADAM PRESIDENT, THE MANDRAKES ARE ONLY ACTING IN SELF-DEFENCE?"
WATCH OUT -- ONE OF THE FREAKS IS DIMENSIONALLY UNSTABLE!
AND SO ARE MY BULLETS!
NEW PURE
"THAT IS THE PATH TO ANARCHY AND CHAOS. WE MUST HAVE ORDER!"

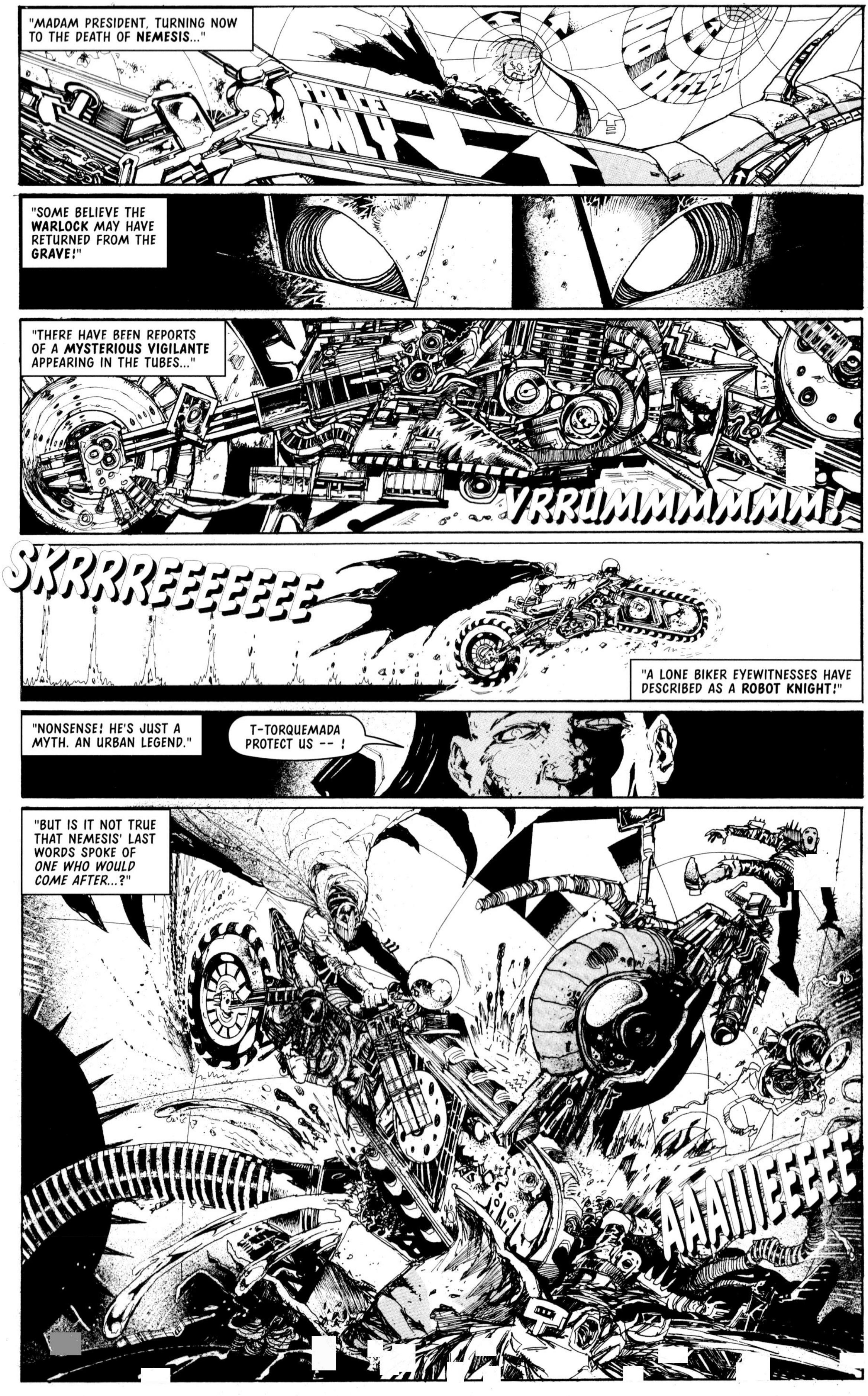
"MADAM PRESIDENT, TURNING NOW TO THE DEATH OF NEMESIS..."
POLICE ONLY
"SOME BELIEVE THE WARLOCK MAY HAVE RETURNED FROM THE GRAVE!"
"THERE HAVE BEEN REPORTS OF A MYSTERIOUS VIGILANTE APPEARING IN THE TUBES..."
VRRUMMMMMMM!
SKRRREEEEEEEE
"A LONE BIKER EYEWITNESSES HAVE DESCRIBED AS A ROBOT KNIGHT!"
"NONSENSE! HE'S JUST A MYTH. AN URBAN LEGEND."
T-TORQUEMADA PROTECT US -- !
"BUT IS IT NOT TRUE THAT NEMESIS' LAST WORDS SPOKE OF ONE WHO WOULD COME AFTER...?"
AAAIIIEEEEE

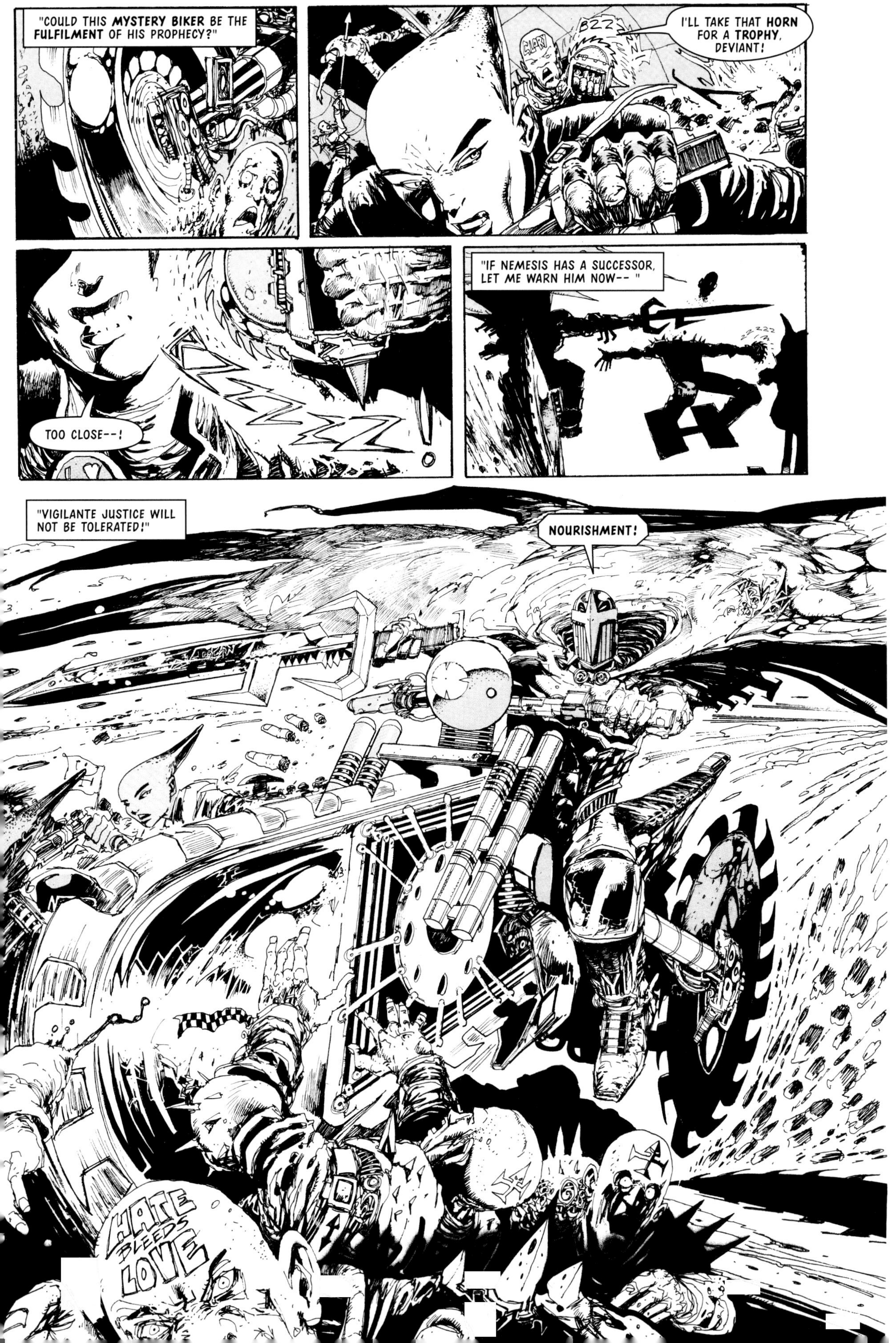
"COULD THIS MYSTERY BIKER BE THE FULFILMENT OF HIS PROPHECY?"
BZZZ
I'LL TAKE THAT HORN FOR A TROPHY, DEVIANT!
TOO CLOSE--!
"IF NEMESIS HAS A SUCCESSOR, LET ME WARN HIM NOW-- "
"VIGILANTE JUSTICE WILL NOT BE TOLERATED!"
NOURISHMENT!
HATE BLEEDS LOVE

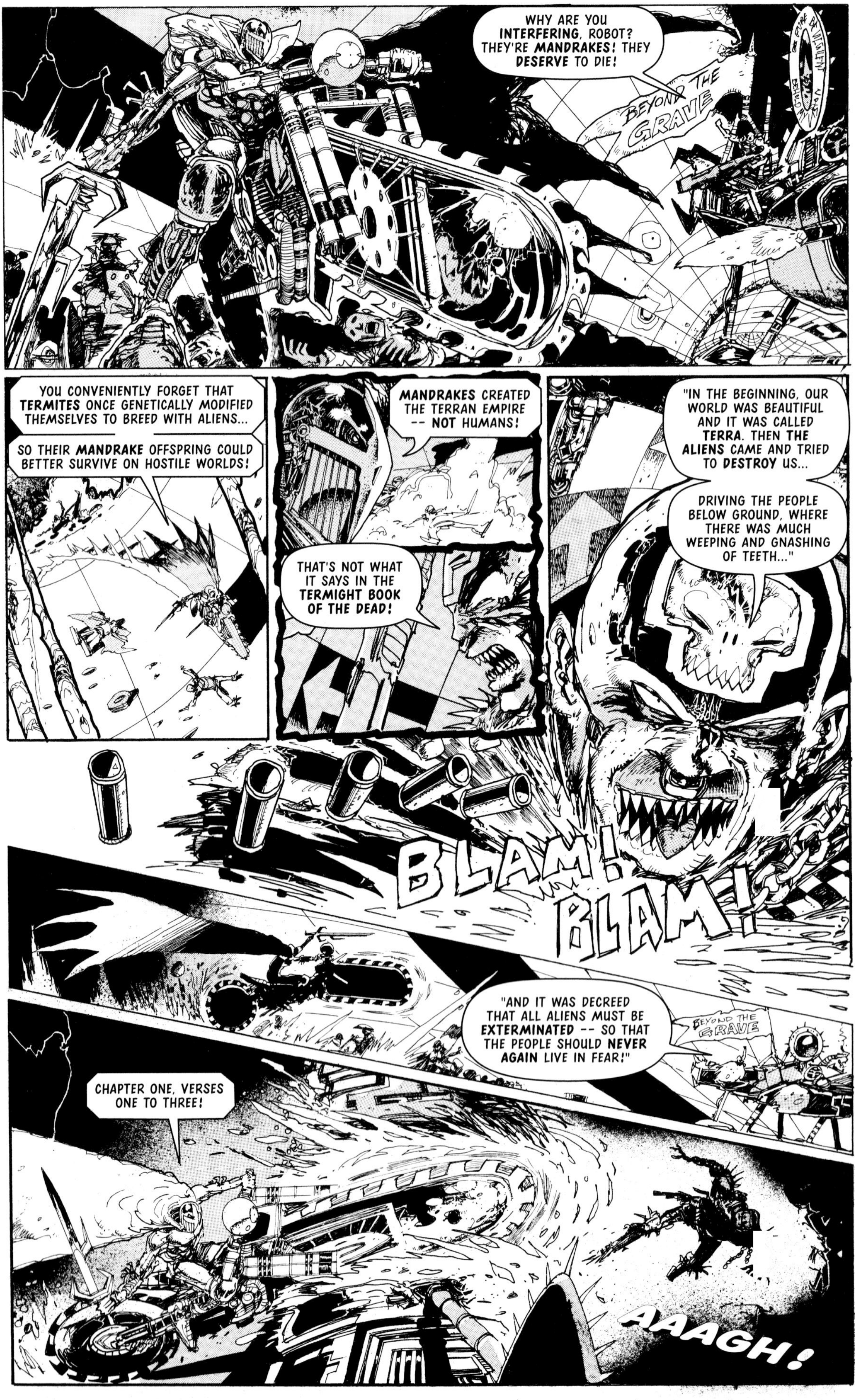
WHY ARE YOU INTERFERING, ROBOT? THEY'RE MANDRAKES! THEY DESERVE TO DIE!
BEYOND THE GRAVE
YOU CONVENIENTLY FORGET THAT TERMITES ONCE GENETICALLY MODIFIED THEMSELVES TO BREED WITH ALIENS...
SO THEIR MANDRAKE OFFSPRING COULD BETTER SURVIVE ON HOSTILE WORLDS!
MANDRAKES CREATED THE TERRAN EMPIRE -- NOT HUMANS!
THAT'S NOT WHAT IT SAYS IN THE TERMIGHT BOOK OF THE DEAD!
"IN THE BEGINNING, OUR WORLD WAS BEAUTIFUL AND IT WAS CALLED TERRA. THEN THE ALIENS CAME AND TRIED TO DESTROY US...
DRIVING THE PEOPLE BELOW GROUND, WHERE THERE WAS MUCH WEEPING AND GNASHING OF TEETH..."
BLAM! BLAM!
"AND IT WAS DECREED THAT ALL ALIENS MUST BE EXTERMINATED -- SO THAT THE PEOPLE SHOULD NEVER AGAIN LIVE IN FEAR!"
BEYOND THE GRAVE
CHAPTER ONE, VERSES ONE TO THREE!
AAAGH!

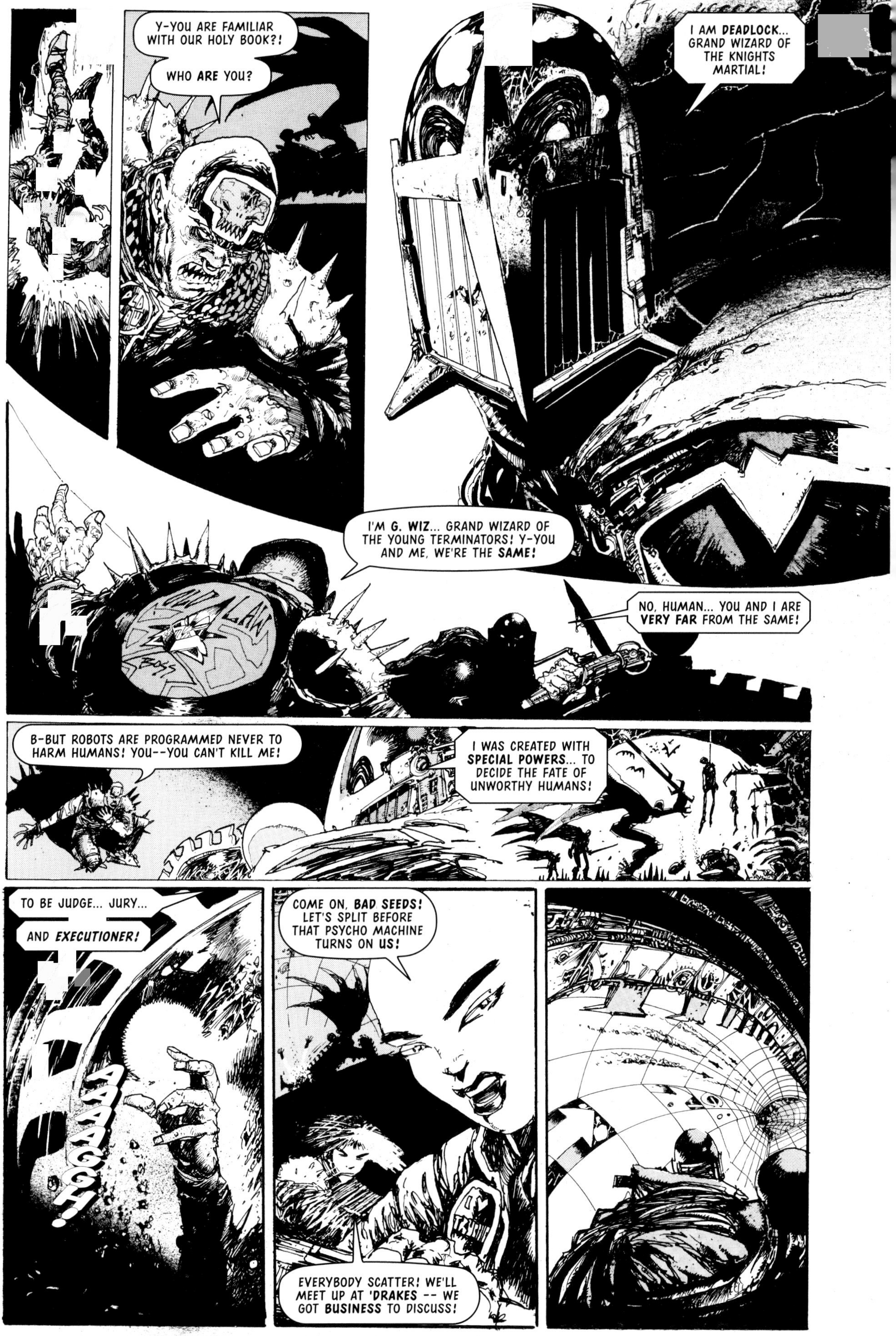

Y-YOU ARE FAMILIAR WITH OUR HOLY BOOK?!
WHO ARE YOU?
I AM DEADLOCK... GRAND WIZARD OF THE KNIGHTS MARTIAL!
I'M G. WIZ... GRAND WIZARD OF THE YOUNG TERMINATORS! Y-YOU AND ME, WE'RE THE SAME!
NO, HUMAN... YOU AND I ARE VERY FAR FROM THE SAME!
B-BUT ROBOTS ARE PROGRAMMED NEVER TO HARM HUMANS! YOU--YOU CAN'T KILL ME!
I WAS CREATED WITH SPECIAL POWERS... TO DECIDE THE FATE OF UNWORTHY HUMANS!
TO BE JUDGE... JURY...
AND EXECUTIONER!
AAAAGGH!
COME ON, BAD SEEDS! LET'S SPLIT BEFORE THAT PSYCHO MACHINE TURNS ON US!
EVERYBODY SCATTER! WE'LL MEET UP AT 'DRAKES -- WE GOT BUSINESS TO DISCUSS!

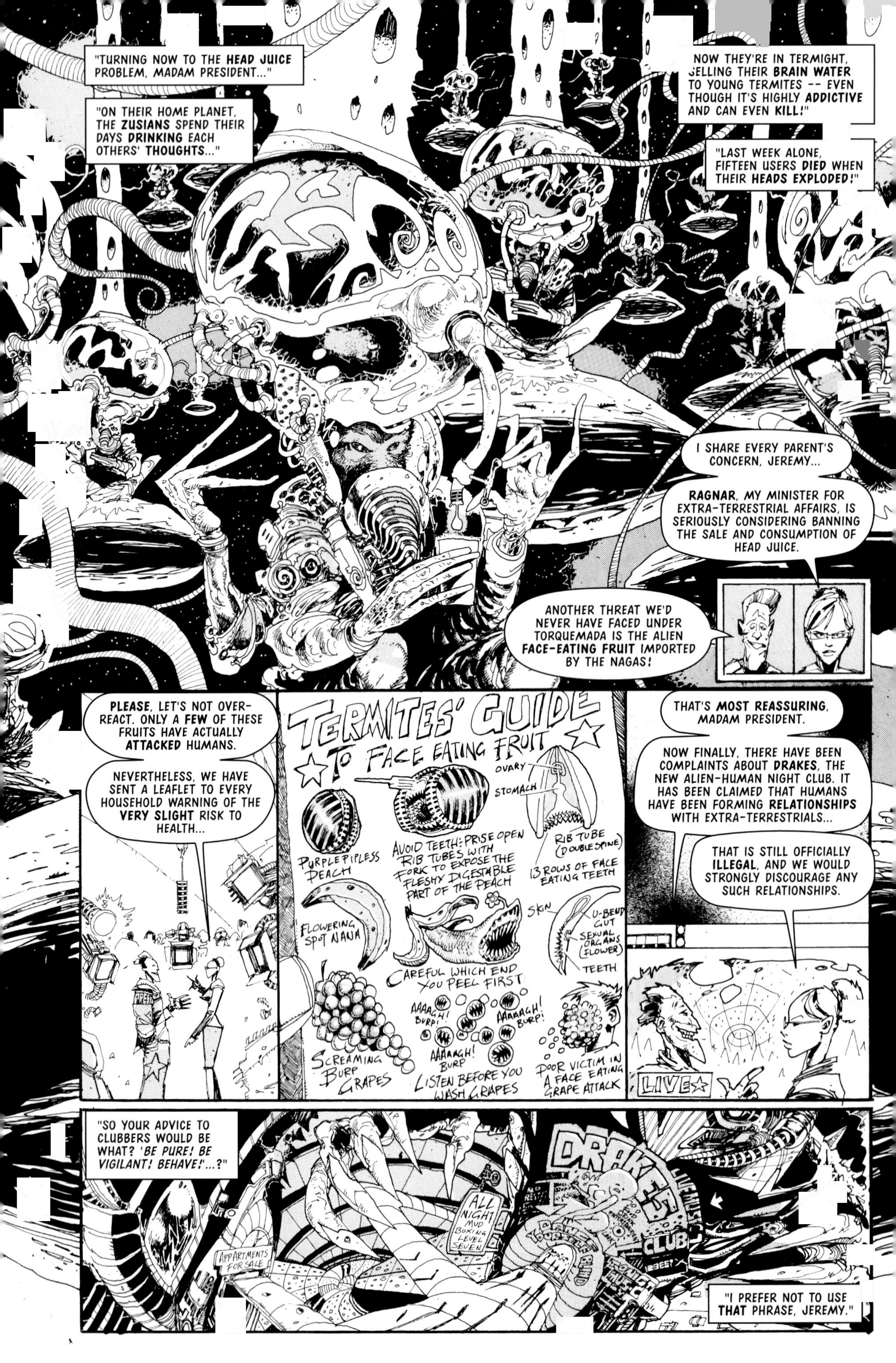
"TURNING NOW TO THE **HEAD JUICE** PROBLEM, MADAM PRESIDENT..."
"ON THEIR HOME PLANET, THE **ZUSIANS** SPEND THEIR DAYS **DRINKING** EACH OTHERS' **THOUGHTS**..."
NOW THEY'RE IN TERMIGHT, SELLING THEIR **BRAIN WATER** TO YOUNG TERMITES -- EVEN THOUGH IT'S HIGHLY **ADDICTIVE** AND CAN EVEN **KILL!**"
"LAST WEEK ALONE, FIFTEEN USERS **DIED** WHEN THEIR **HEADS EXPLODED!**"
I SHARE EVERY PARENT'S CONCERN, JEREMY...
RAGNAR, MY MINISTER FOR EXTRA-TERRESTRIAL AFFAIRS, IS SERIOUSLY CONSIDERING BANNING THE SALE AND CONSUMPTION OF HEAD JUICE.
ANOTHER THREAT WE'D NEVER HAVE FACED UNDER TORQUEMADA IS THE ALIEN **FACE-EATING FRUIT** IMPORTED BY THE NAGAS!
PLEASE, LET'S NOT OVER-REACT. ONLY A **FEW** OF THESE FRUITS HAVE ACTUALLY **ATTACKED** HUMANS.
NEVERTHELESS, WE HAVE SENT A LEAFLET TO EVERY HOUSEHOLD WARNING OF THE **VERY SLIGHT** RISK TO HEALTH...
TERMITES' GUIDE TO FACE EATING FRUIT
OVARY
STOMACH
PURPLE PIPLESS PEACH
AVOID TEETH: PRISE OPEN RIB TUBES WITH FORK TO EXPOSE THE FLESHY DIGESTABLE PART OF THE PEACH
RIB TUBE (DOUBLE SPINE)
13 ROWS OF FACE EATING TEETH
FLOWERING SPOT NANA
SKIN
U-BEND GUT
SEXUAL ORGANS (FLOWER)
TEETH
CAREFUL WHICH END YOU PEEL FIRST
AAAAGH! BURP!
AAAAAGH! BURP!
AAAAAGH! BURP
SCREAMING BURP GRAPES
LISTEN BEFORE YOU WASH GRAPES
POOR VICTIM IN A FACE EATING GRAPE ATTACK
THAT'S **MOST REASSURING**, MADAM PRESIDENT.
NOW FINALLY, THERE HAVE BEEN COMPLAINTS ABOUT **DRAKES**, THE NEW ALIEN-HUMAN NIGHT CLUB. IT HAS BEEN CLAIMED THAT HUMANS HAVE BEEN FORMING **RELATIONSHIPS** WITH EXTRA-TERRESTRIALS...
THAT IS STILL OFFICIALLY **ILLEGAL**, AND WE WOULD STRONGLY DISCOURAGE ANY SUCH RELATIONSHIPS.
LIVE
"SO YOUR ADVICE TO CLUBBERS WOULD BE WHAT? *'BE PURE! BE VIGILANT! BEHAVE!'*...?"
ALL NIGHT MUD BOXING LEVEL SEVEN
APPARTMENTS FOR SALE
DRAKES
CLUB
"I PREFER NOT TO USE **THAT** PHRASE, JEREMY."

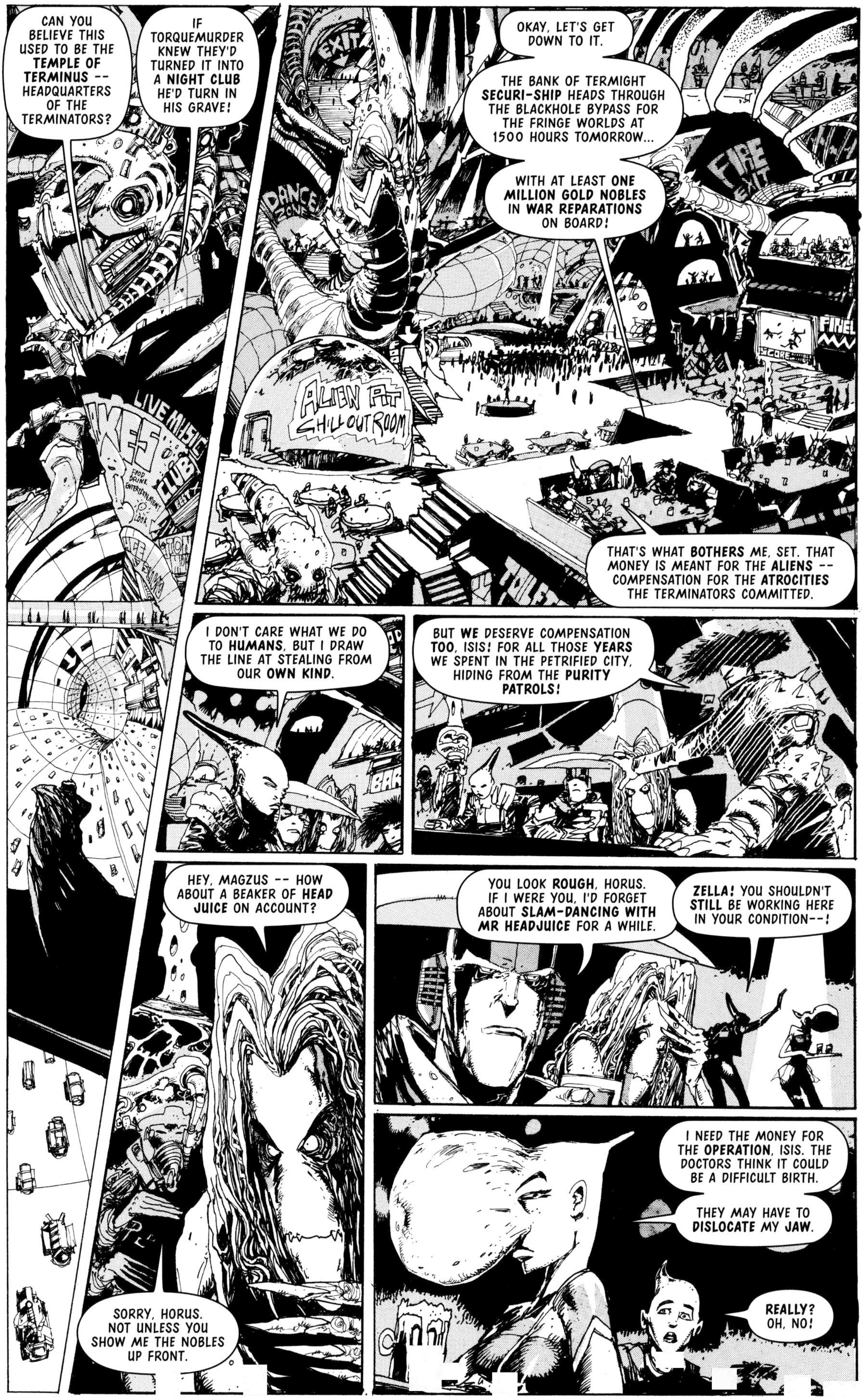
CAN YOU BELIEVE THIS USED TO BE THE **TEMPLE OF TERMINUS** -- HEADQUARTERS OF THE TERMINATORS?
IF TORQUEMURDER KNEW THEY'D TURNED IT INTO A **NIGHT CLUB** HE'D TURN IN HIS GRAVE!
EXIT
OKAY, LET'S GET DOWN TO IT.
THE BANK OF TERMIGHT **SECURI-SHIP** HEADS THROUGH THE BLACKHOLE BYPASS FOR THE FRINGE WORLDS AT 1500 HOURS TOMORROW...
WITH AT LEAST **ONE MILLION GOLD NOBLES** IN **WAR REPARATIONS** ON BOARD!
ALIEN PIT CHILL OUT ROOM
LIVE MUSIC
THAT'S WHAT **BOTHERS ME**, SET. THAT MONEY IS MEANT FOR THE **ALIENS** -- COMPENSATION FOR THE **ATROCITIES** THE TERMINATORS COMMITTED.
I DON'T CARE WHAT WE DO TO **HUMANS**, BUT I DRAW THE LINE AT STEALING FROM OUR **OWN KIND**.
BAR
BUT **WE** DESERVE COMPENSATION **TOO**, ISIS! FOR ALL THOSE **YEARS** WE SPENT IN THE PETRIFIED CITY, HIDING FROM THE **PURITY PATROLS!**
HEY, MAGZUS -- HOW ABOUT A BEAKER OF **HEAD JUICE** ON ACCOUNT?
SORRY, HORUS. NOT UNLESS YOU SHOW ME THE NOBLES UP FRONT.
YOU LOOK **ROUGH**, HORUS. IF I WERE YOU, I'D FORGET ABOUT **SLAM-DANCING WITH MR HEADJUICE** FOR A WHILE.
ZELLA! YOU SHOULDN'T **STILL** BE WORKING HERE IN YOUR CONDITION--!
I NEED THE MONEY FOR THE **OPERATION**, ISIS. THE DOCTORS THINK IT COULD BE A DIFFICULT BIRTH.
THEY MAY HAVE TO **DISLOCATE MY JAW**.
REALLY? OH, NO!

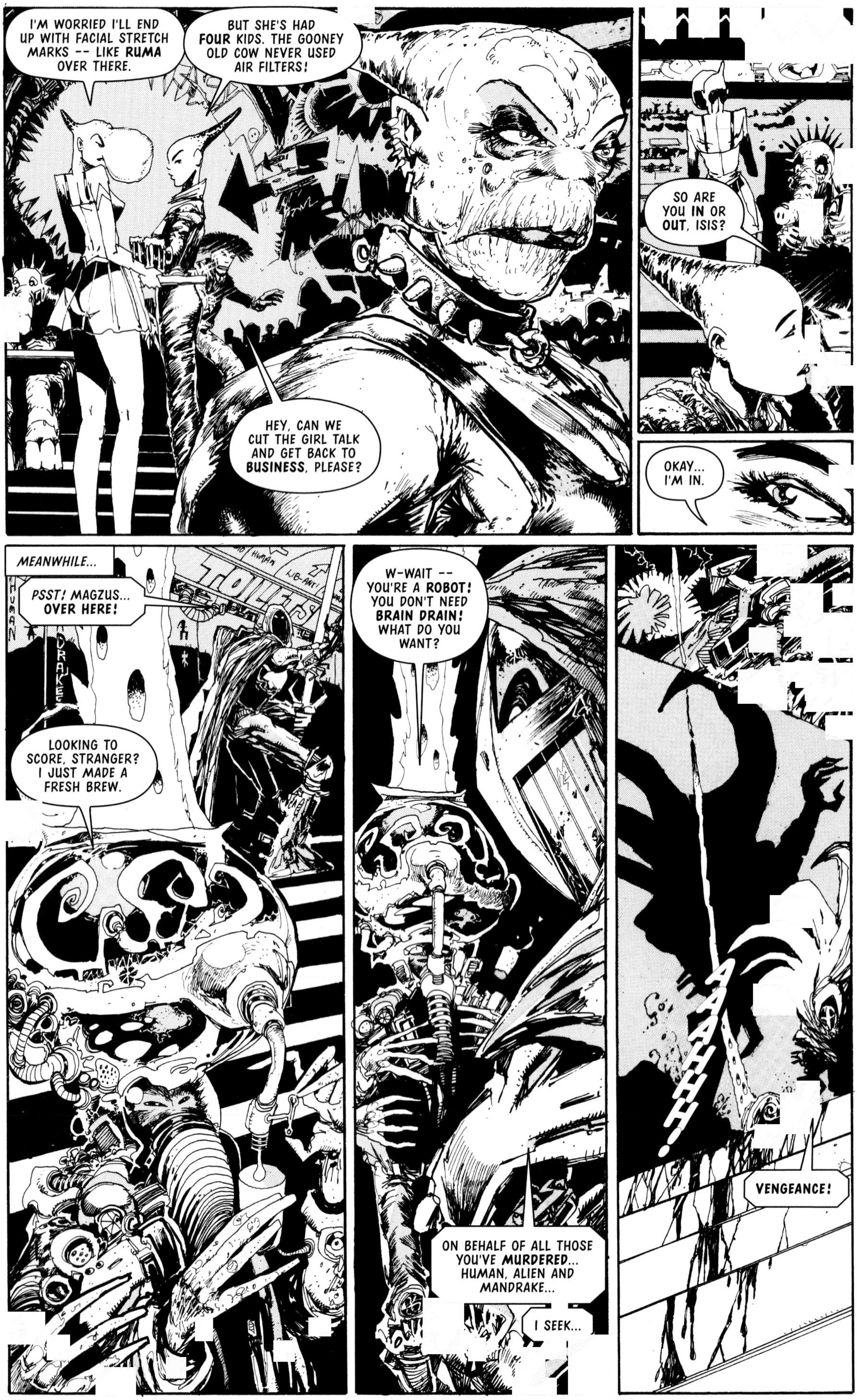
I'M WORRIED I'LL END UP WITH FACIAL STRETCH MARKS -- LIKE RUMA OVER THERE.
BUT SHE'S HAD FOUR KIDS. THE GOONEY OLD COW NEVER USED AIR FILTERS!
HEY, CAN WE CUT THE GIRL TALK AND GET BACK TO BUSINESS, PLEASE?
SO ARE YOU IN OR OUT, ISIS?
OKAY... I'M IN.
MEANWHILE...
PSST! MAGZUS... OVER HERE!
TOILETS
HUMAN
LIB-ANT
DRAKE
LOOKING TO SCORE, STRANGER? I JUST MADE A FRESH BREW.
W-WAIT -- YOU'RE A ROBOT! YOU DON'T NEED BRAIN DRAIN! WHAT DO YOU WANT?
ON BEHALF OF ALL THOSE YOU'VE MURDERED... HUMAN, ALIEN AND MANDRAKE...
I SEEK...
VENGEANCE!
AAAHHHH!

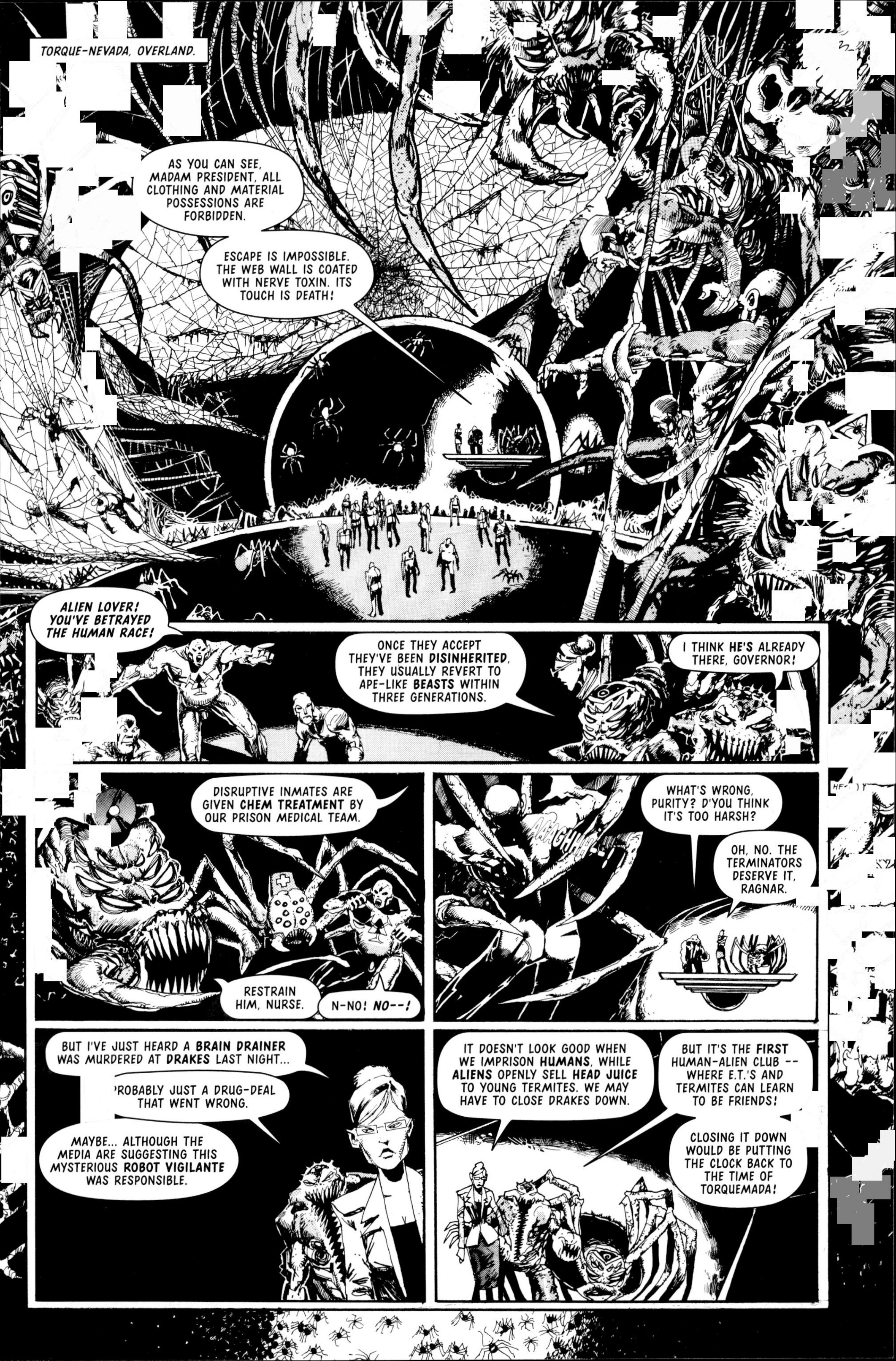

TORQUE-NEVADA, OVERLAND.
AS YOU CAN SEE, MADAM PRESIDENT, ALL CLOTHING AND MATERIAL POSSESSIONS ARE FORBIDDEN.
ESCAPE IS IMPOSSIBLE. THE WEB WALL IS COATED WITH NERVE TOXIN. ITS TOUCH IS DEATH!
ALIEN LOVER! YOU'VE BETRAYED THE HUMAN RACE!
ONCE THEY ACCEPT THEY'VE BEEN DISINHERITED, THEY USUALLY REVERT TO APE-LIKE BEASTS WITHIN THREE GENERATIONS.
I THINK HE'S ALREADY THERE, GOVERNOR!
DISRUPTIVE INMATES ARE GIVEN CHEM TREATMENT BY OUR PRISON MEDICAL TEAM.
RESTRAIN HIM, NURSE.
N-NO! NO--!
WHAT'S WRONG, PURITY? D'YOU THINK IT'S TOO HARSH?
OH, NO. THE TERMINATORS DESERVE IT, RAGNAR.
BUT I'VE JUST HEARD A BRAIN DRAINER WAS MURDERED AT DRAKES LAST NIGHT...
PROBABLY JUST A DRUG-DEAL THAT WENT WRONG.
MAYBE... ALTHOUGH THE MEDIA ARE SUGGESTING THIS MYSTERIOUS ROBOT VIGILANTE WAS RESPONSIBLE.
IT DOESN'T LOOK GOOD WHEN WE IMPRISON HUMANS, WHILE ALIENS OPENLY SELL HEAD JUICE TO YOUNG TERMITES. WE MAY HAVE TO CLOSE DRAKES DOWN.
BUT IT'S THE FIRST HUMAN-ALIEN CLUB -- WHERE E.T.'S AND TERMITES CAN LEARN TO BE FRIENDS!
CLOSING IT DOWN WOULD BE PUTTING THE CLOCK BACK TO THE TIME OF TORQUEMADA!

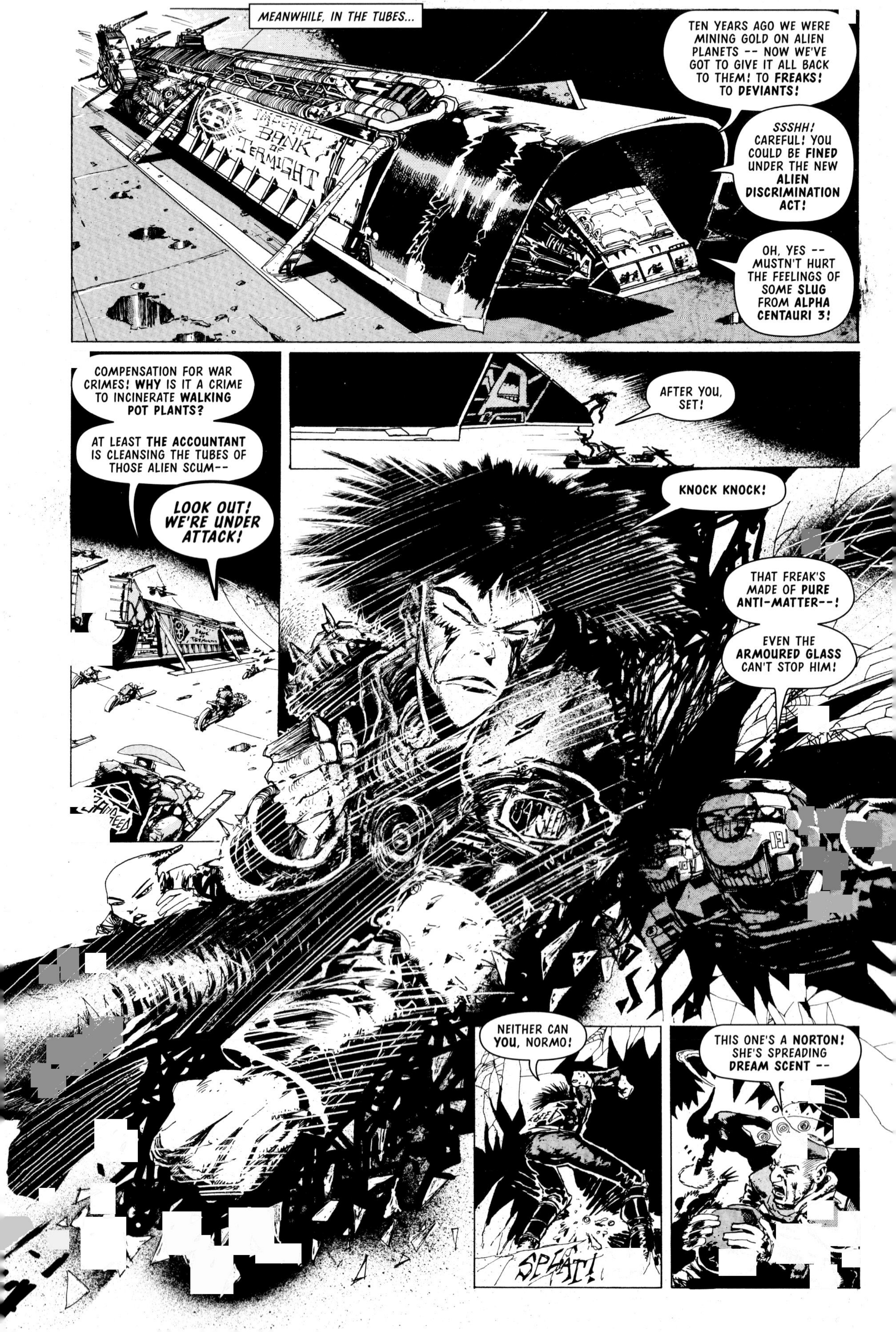
MEANWHILE, IN THE TUBES...
IMPERIAL BANK OF TERMIGHT
TEN YEARS AGO WE WERE MINING GOLD ON ALIEN PLANETS -- NOW WE'VE GOT TO GIVE IT ALL BACK TO THEM! TO FREAKS! TO DEVIANTS!
SSSHH! CAREFUL! YOU COULD BE FINED UNDER THE NEW ALIEN DISCRIMINATION ACT!
OH, YES -- MUSTN'T HURT THE FEELINGS OF SOME SLUG FROM ALPHA CENTAURI 3!
COMPENSATION FOR WAR CRIMES! WHY IS IT A CRIME TO INCINERATE WALKING POT PLANTS?
AT LEAST THE ACCOUNTANT IS CLEANSING THE TUBES OF THOSE ALIEN SCUM--
LOOK OUT! WE'RE UNDER ATTACK!
AFTER YOU, SET!
KNOCK KNOCK!
THAT FREAK'S MADE OF PURE ANTI-MATTER--!
EVEN THE ARMOURED GLASS CAN'T STOP HIM!
NEITHER CAN YOU, NORMO!
SPLAT!
THIS ONE'S A NORTON! SHE'S SPREADING DREAM SCENT --

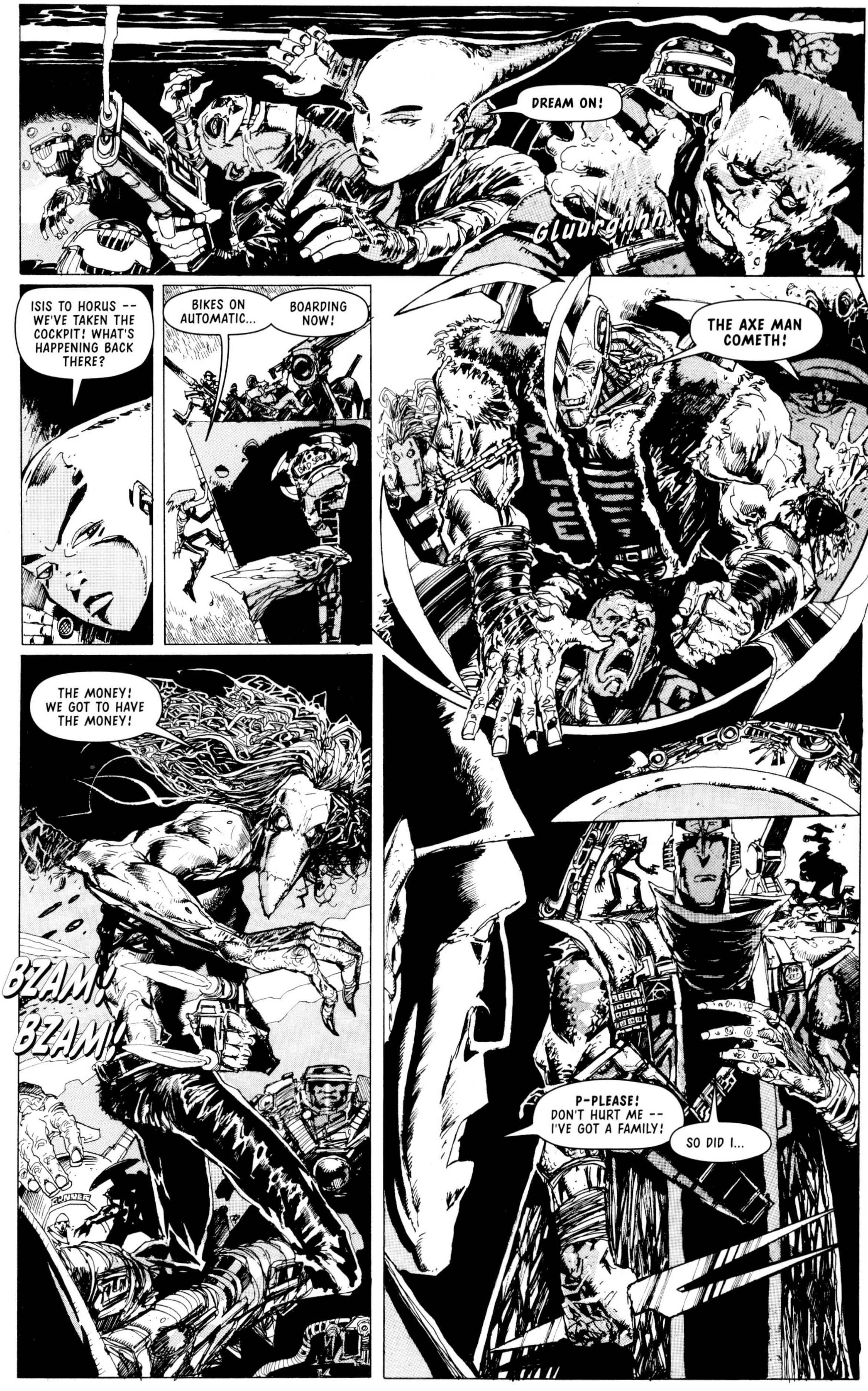
DREAM ON!
Gluurghhh...
ISIS TO HORUS -- WE'VE TAKEN THE COCKPIT! WHAT'S HAPPENING BACK THERE?
BIKES ON AUTOMATIC...
BOARDING NOW!
THE AXE MAN COMETH!
THE MONEY! WE GOT TO HAVE THE MONEY!
BZAM! BZAM!
P-PLEASE! DON'T HURT ME -- I'VE GOT A FAMILY!
SO DID I...

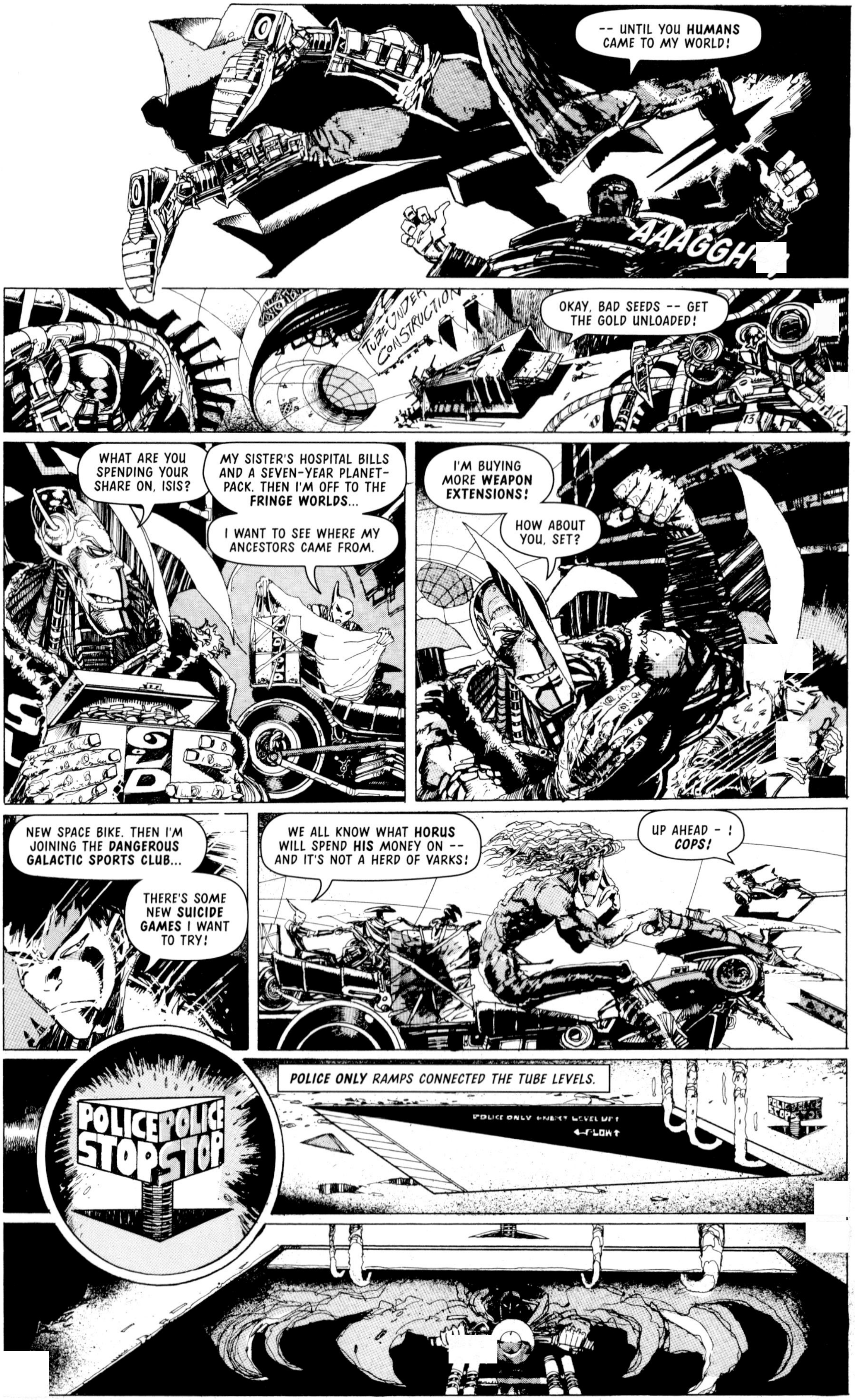
-- UNTIL YOU **HUMANS** CAME TO MY WORLD!
AAAGGH
TUBE UNDER CONSTRUCTION
OKAY, BAD SEEDS -- GET THE GOLD UNLOADED!
WHAT ARE YOU SPENDING YOUR SHARE ON, ISIS?
MY SISTER'S HOSPITAL BILLS AND A SEVEN-YEAR PLANET-PACK. THEN I'M OFF TO THE **FRINGE WORLDS**...
I WANT TO SEE WHERE MY ANCESTORS CAME FROM.
I'M BUYING MORE **WEAPON EXTENSIONS!**
HOW ABOUT YOU, SET?
NEW SPACE BIKE. THEN I'M JOINING THE **DANGEROUS GALACTIC SPORTS CLUB**...
THERE'S SOME NEW **SUICIDE GAMES** I WANT TO TRY!
WE ALL KNOW WHAT **HORUS** WILL SPEND **HIS** MONEY ON -- AND IT'S NOT A HERD OF VARKS!
UP AHEAD - ! ***COPS!***
POLICE POLICE
STOP STOP
POLICE ONLY *RAMPS CONNECTED THE TUBE LEVELS.*

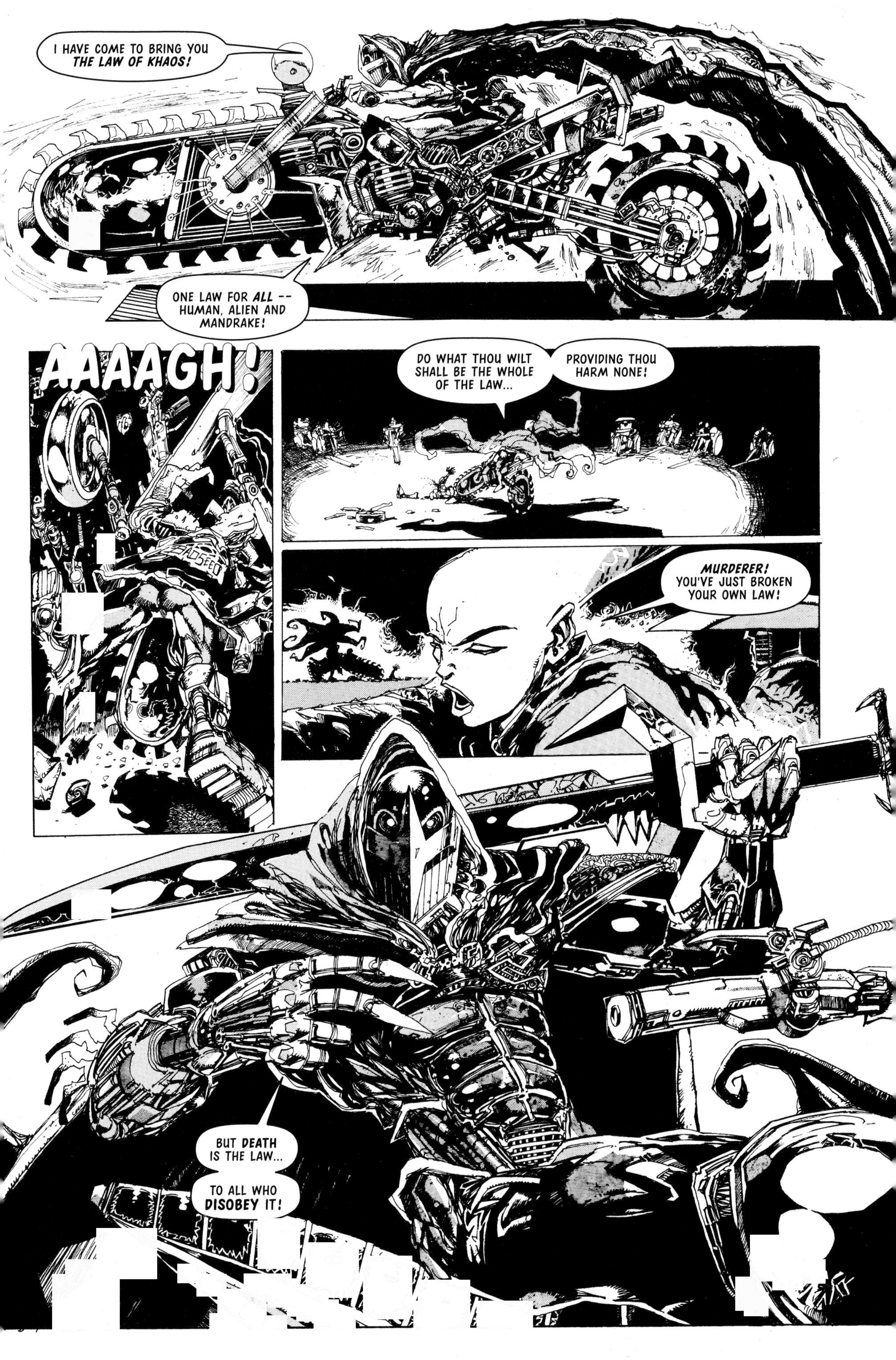
I HAVE COME TO BRING YOU THE LAW OF KHAOS!
ONE LAW FOR ALL -- HUMAN, ALIEN AND MANDRAKE!
AAAAGH!
DO WHAT THOU WILT SHALL BE THE WHOLE OF THE LAW...
PROVIDING THOU HARM NONE!
MURDERER! YOU'VE JUST BROKEN YOUR OWN LAW!
BUT DEATH IS THE LAW...
TO ALL WHO DISOBEY IT!

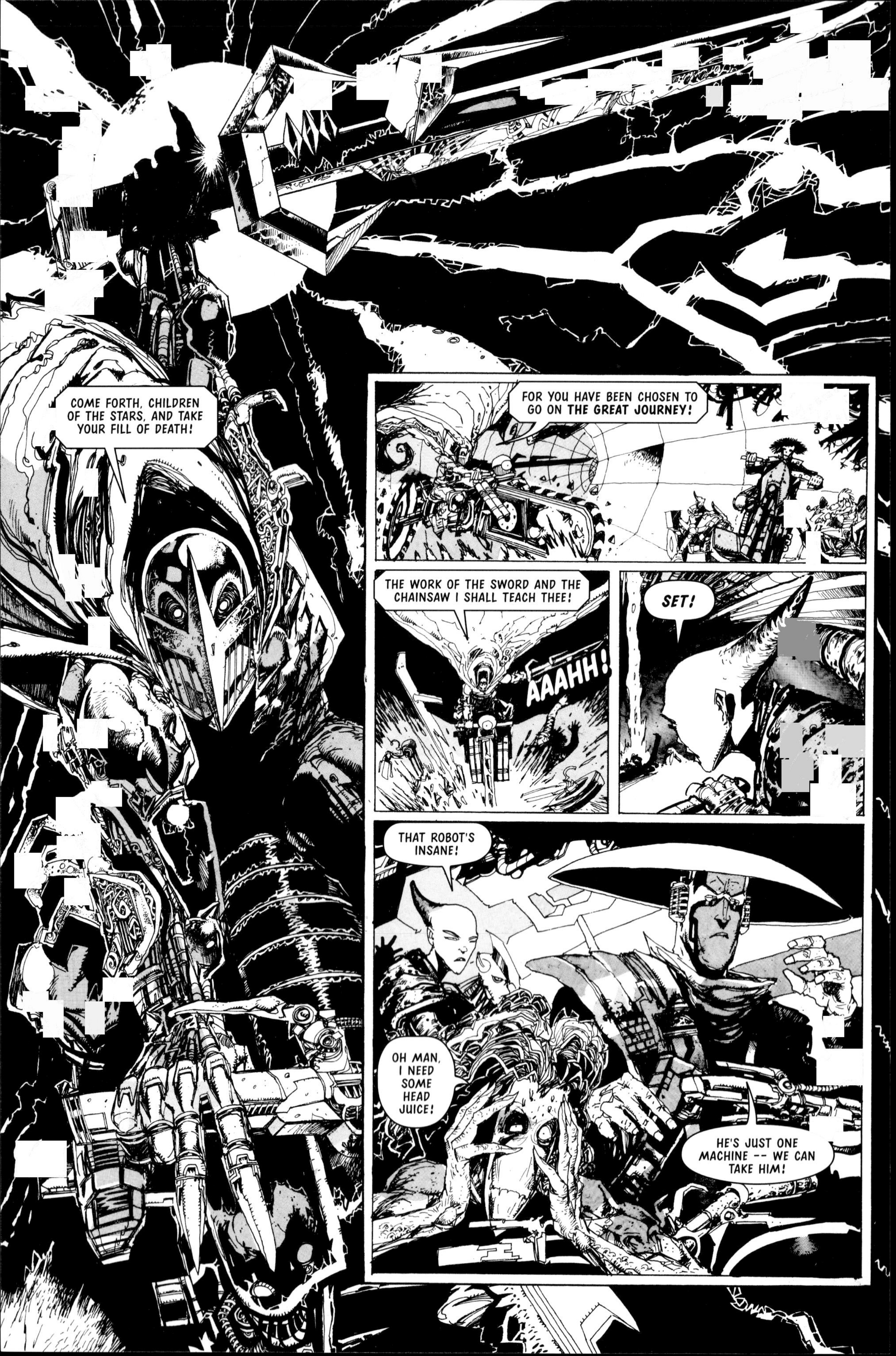
COME FORTH, CHILDREN OF THE STARS, AND TAKE YOUR FILL OF DEATH!
FOR YOU HAVE BEEN CHOSEN TO GO ON THE GREAT JOURNEY!
THE WORK OF THE SWORD AND THE CHAINSAW I SHALL TEACH THEE!
AAAHH!
SET!
THAT ROBOT'S INSANE!
OH MAN, I NEED SOME HEAD JUICE!
HE'S JUST ONE MACHINE -- WE CAN TAKE HIM!

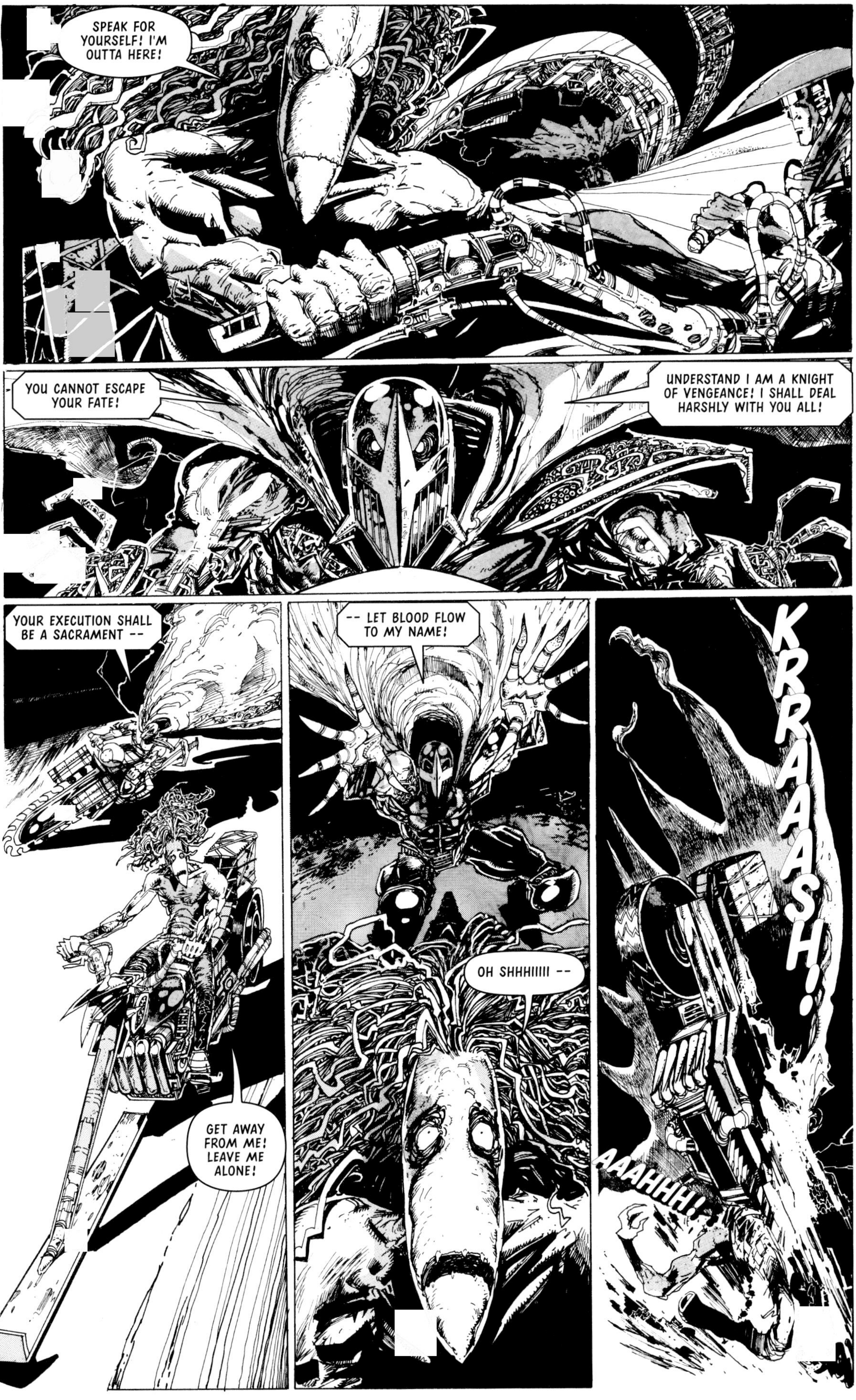
SPEAK FOR YOURSELF! I'M OUTTA HERE!
YOU CANNOT ESCAPE YOUR FATE!
UNDERSTAND I AM A KNIGHT OF VENGEANCE! I SHALL DEAL HARSHLY WITH YOU ALL!
YOUR EXECUTION SHALL BE A SACRAMENT --
GET AWAY FROM ME! LEAVE ME ALONE!
-- LET BLOOD FLOW TO MY NAME!
OH SHHHIIIII --
KRRAAASH!!
AAAHHH!

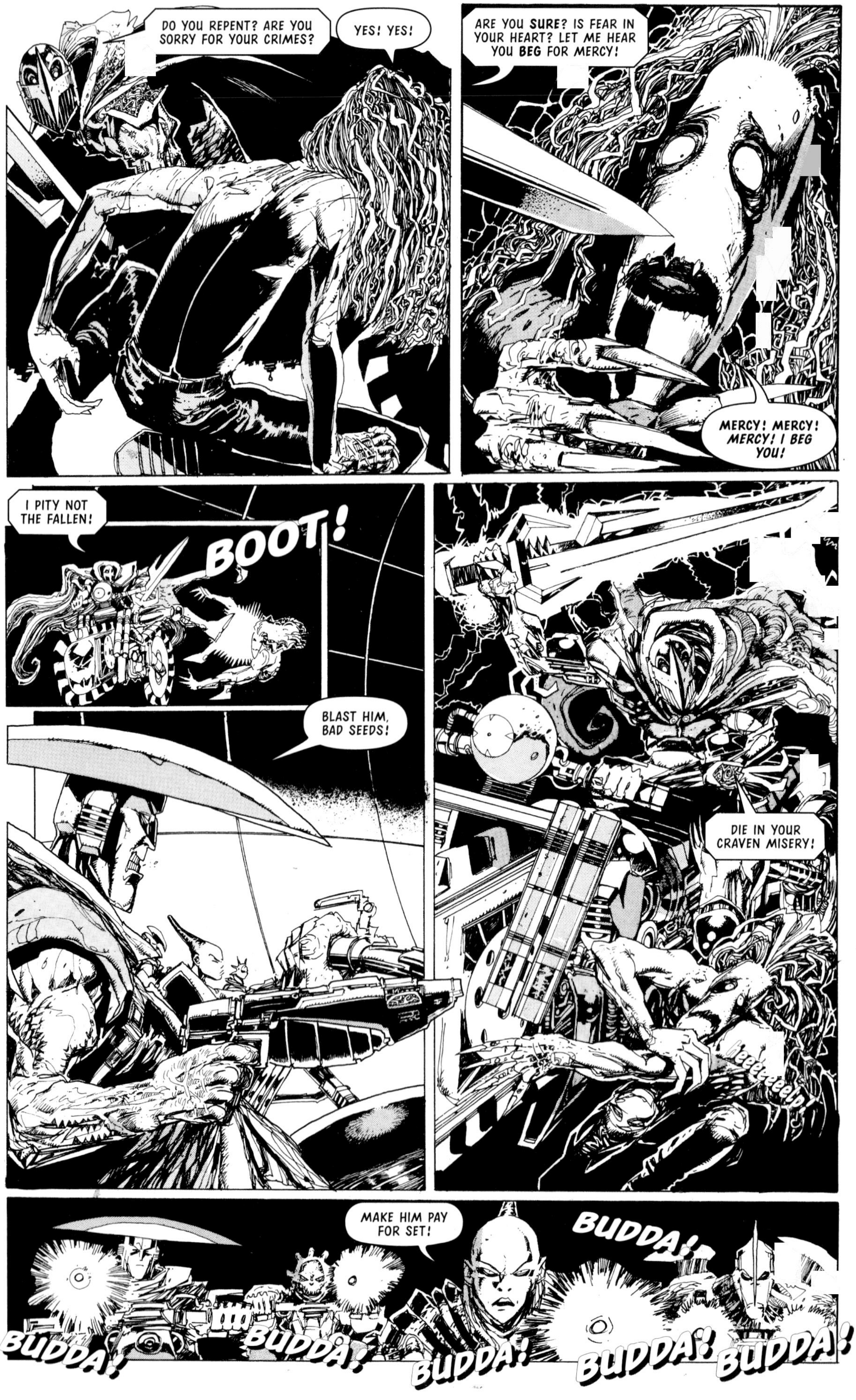
DO YOU REPENT? ARE YOU SORRY FOR YOUR CRIMES?
YES! YES!
ARE YOU SURE? IS FEAR IN YOUR HEART? LET ME HEAR YOU BEG FOR MERCY!
MERCY! MERCY! MERCY! I BEG YOU!
I PITY NOT THE FALLEN!
BOOT!
BLAST HIM, BAD SEEDS!
DIE IN YOUR CRAVEN MISERY!
MAKE HIM PAY FOR SET!
BUDDA!
BUDDA!
BUDDA!
BUDDA!
BUDDA!
BUDDA!

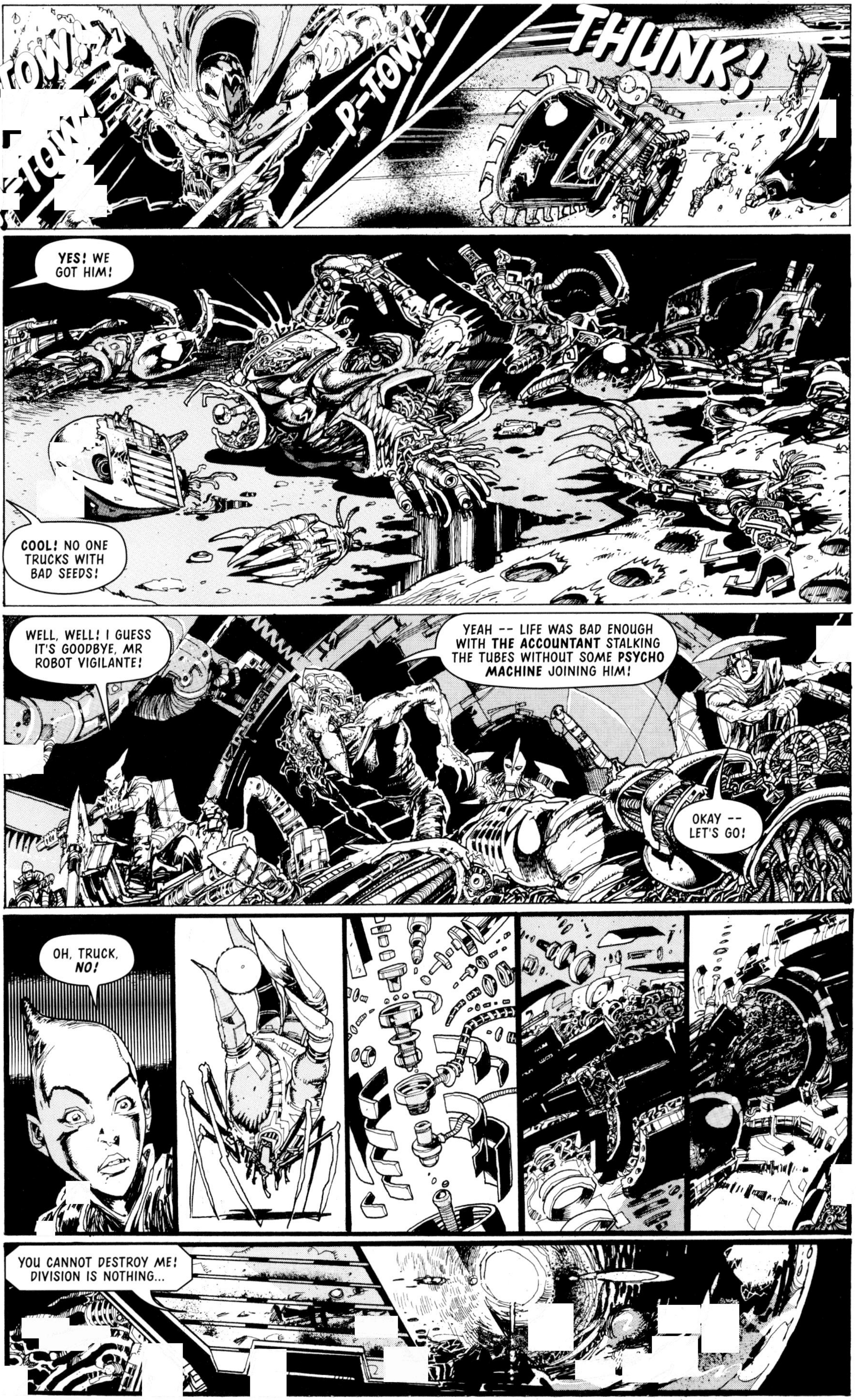

P-TOW!
P-TOW!
P-TOW!
P-TOW!
THUNK!
YES! WE GOT HIM!
COOL! NO ONE TRUCKS WITH BAD SEEDS!
WELL, WELL! I GUESS IT'S GOODBYE, MR ROBOT VIGILANTE!
YEAH -- LIFE WAS BAD ENOUGH WITH THE ACCOUNTANT STALKING THE TUBES WITHOUT SOME PSYCHO MACHINE JOINING HIM!
OKAY -- LET'S GO!
OH, TRUCK, NO!
YOU CANNOT DESTROY ME! DIVISION IS NOTHING...

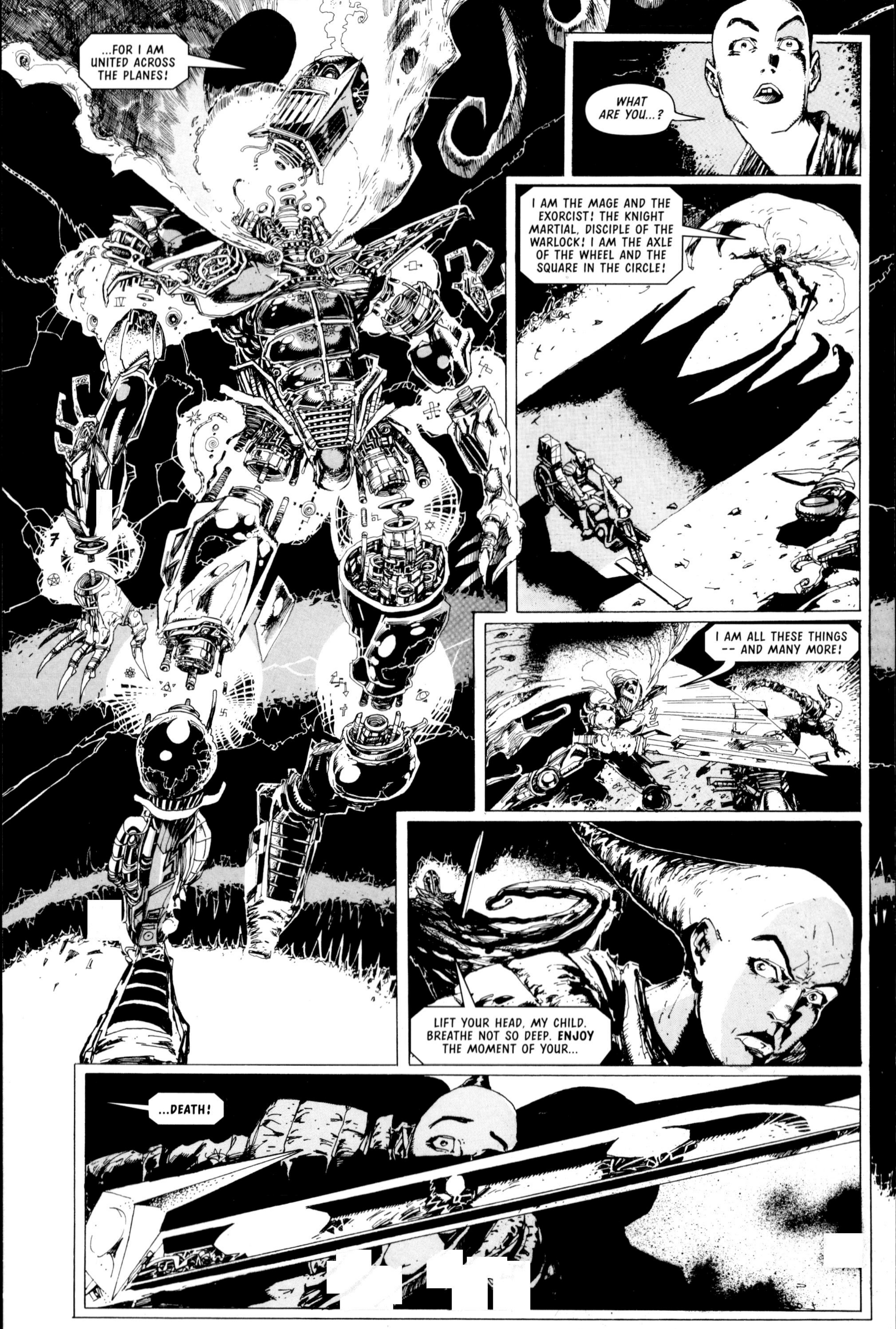
...FOR I AM UNITED ACROSS THE PLANES!
WHAT ARE YOU...?
I AM THE MAGE AND THE EXORCIST! THE KNIGHT MARTIAL, DISCIPLE OF THE WARLOCK! I AM THE AXLE OF THE WHEEL AND THE SQUARE IN THE CIRCLE!
I AM ALL THESE THINGS -- AND MANY MORE!
LIFT YOUR HEAD, MY CHILD. BREATHE NOT SO DEEP. ENJOY THE MOMENT OF YOUR...
...DEATH!

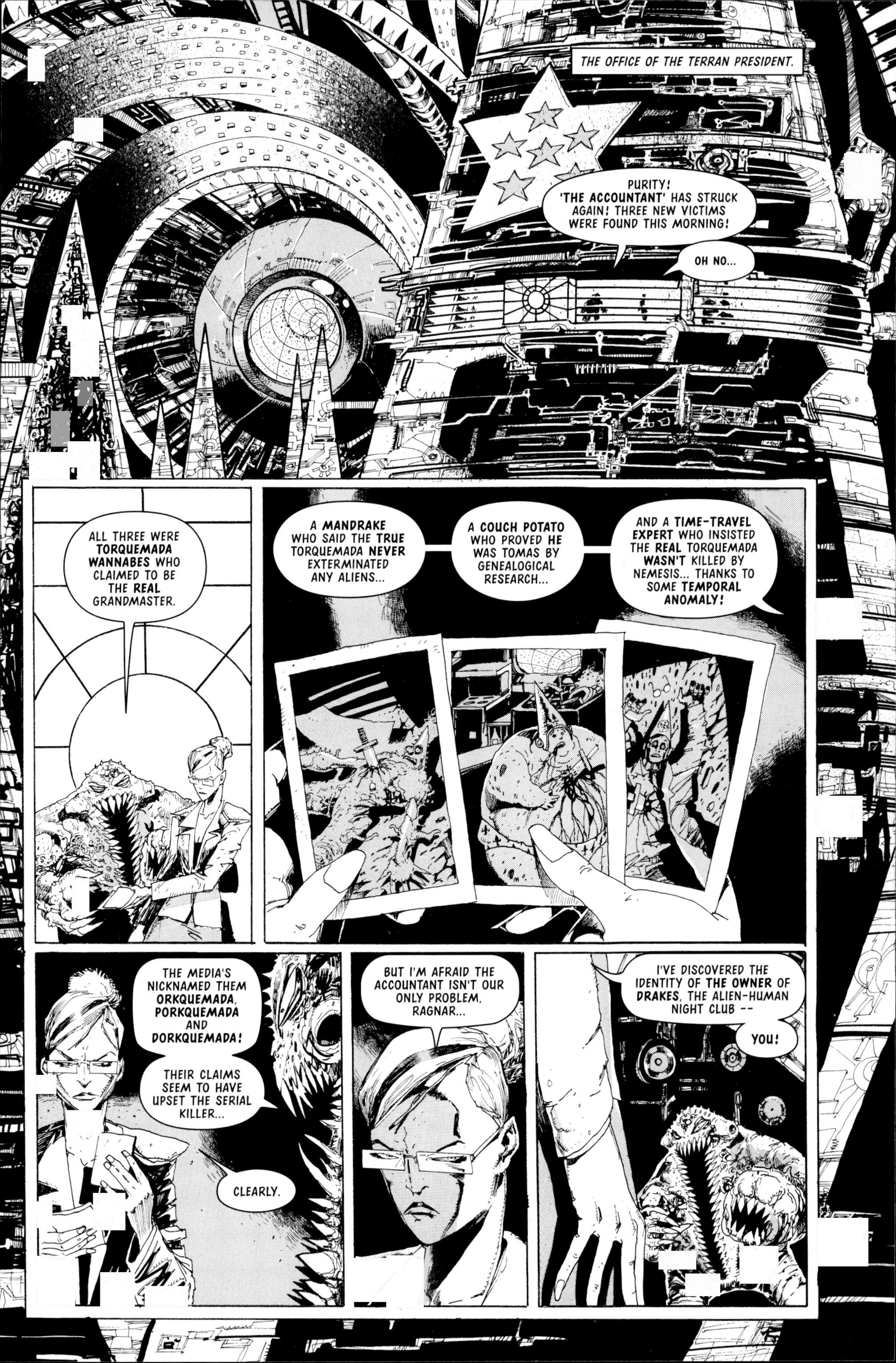
THE OFFICE OF THE TERRAN PRESIDENT.
PURITY! 'THE ACCOUNTANT' HAS STRUCK AGAIN! THREE NEW VICTIMS WERE FOUND THIS MORNING!
OH NO...
ALL THREE WERE TORQUEMADA WANNABES WHO CLAIMED TO BE THE REAL GRANDMASTER.
A MANDRAKE WHO SAID THE TRUE TORQUEMADA NEVER EXTERMINATED ANY ALIENS...
A COUCH POTATO WHO PROVED HE WAS TOMAS BY GENEALOGICAL RESEARCH...
AND A TIME-TRAVEL EXPERT WHO INSISTED THE REAL TORQUEMADA WASN'T KILLED BY NEMESIS... THANKS TO SOME TEMPORAL ANOMALY!
THE MEDIA'S NICKNAMED THEM ORKQUEMADA, PORKQUEMADA AND DORKQUEMADA!
THEIR CLAIMS SEEM TO HAVE UPSET THE SERIAL KILLER...
CLEARLY.
BUT I'M AFRAID THE ACCOUNTANT ISN'T OUR ONLY PROBLEM, RAGNAR...
I'VE DISCOVERED THE IDENTITY OF THE OWNER OF DRAKES, THE ALIEN-HUMAN NIGHT CLUB --
YOU!

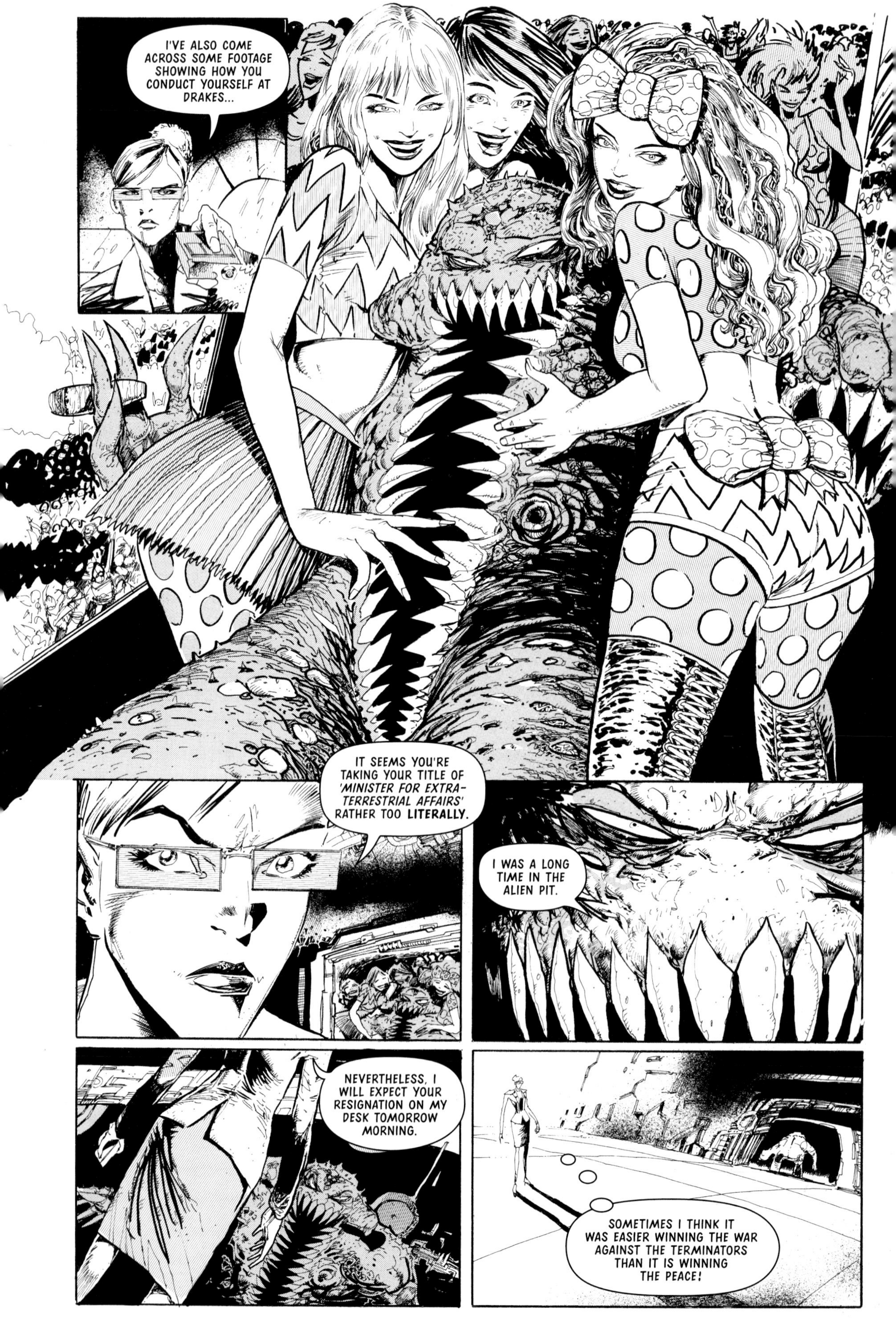

I'VE ALSO COME ACROSS SOME FOOTAGE SHOWING HOW YOU CONDUCT YOURSELF AT DRAKES...
IT SEEMS YOU'RE TAKING YOUR TITLE OF *'MINISTER FOR EXTRA-TERRESTRIAL AFFAIRS'* RATHER TOO **LITERALLY**.
I WAS A LONG TIME IN THE ALIEN PIT.
NEVERTHELESS, I WILL EXPECT YOUR RESIGNATION ON MY DESK TOMORROW MORNING.
SOMETIMES I THINK IT WAS EASIER WINNING THE WAR AGAINST THE TERMINATORS THAN IT IS WINNING THE PEACE!

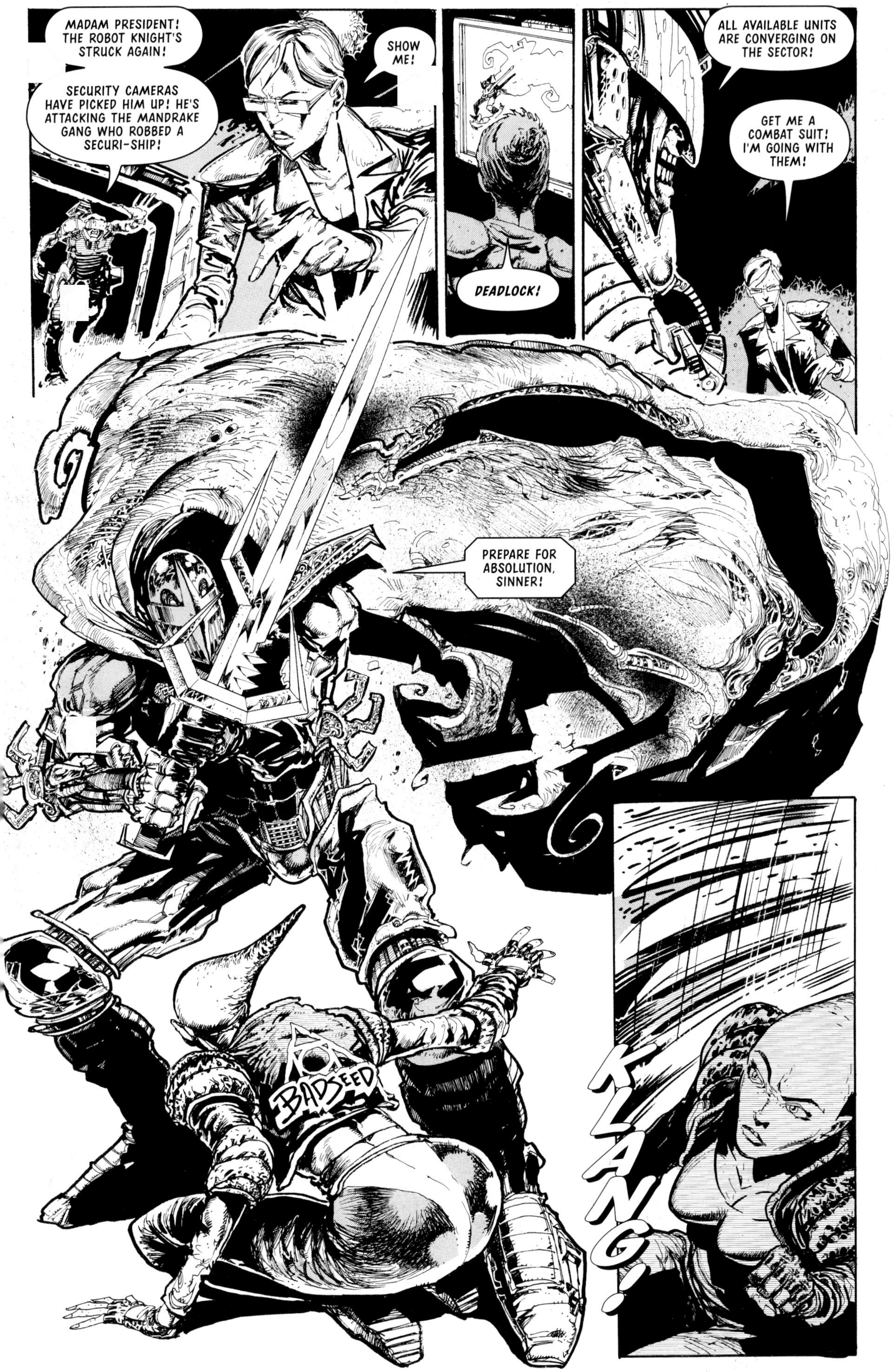
MADAM PRESIDENT! THE ROBOT KNIGHT'S STRUCK AGAIN!
SECURITY CAMERAS HAVE PICKED HIM UP! HE'S ATTACKING THE MANDRAKE GANG WHO ROBBED A SECURI-SHIP!
SHOW ME!
DEADLOCK!
ALL AVAILABLE UNITS ARE CONVERGING ON THE SECTOR!
GET ME A COMBAT SUIT! I'M GOING WITH THEM!
PREPARE FOR ABSOLUTION, SINNER!
BADSEED
KLANG!

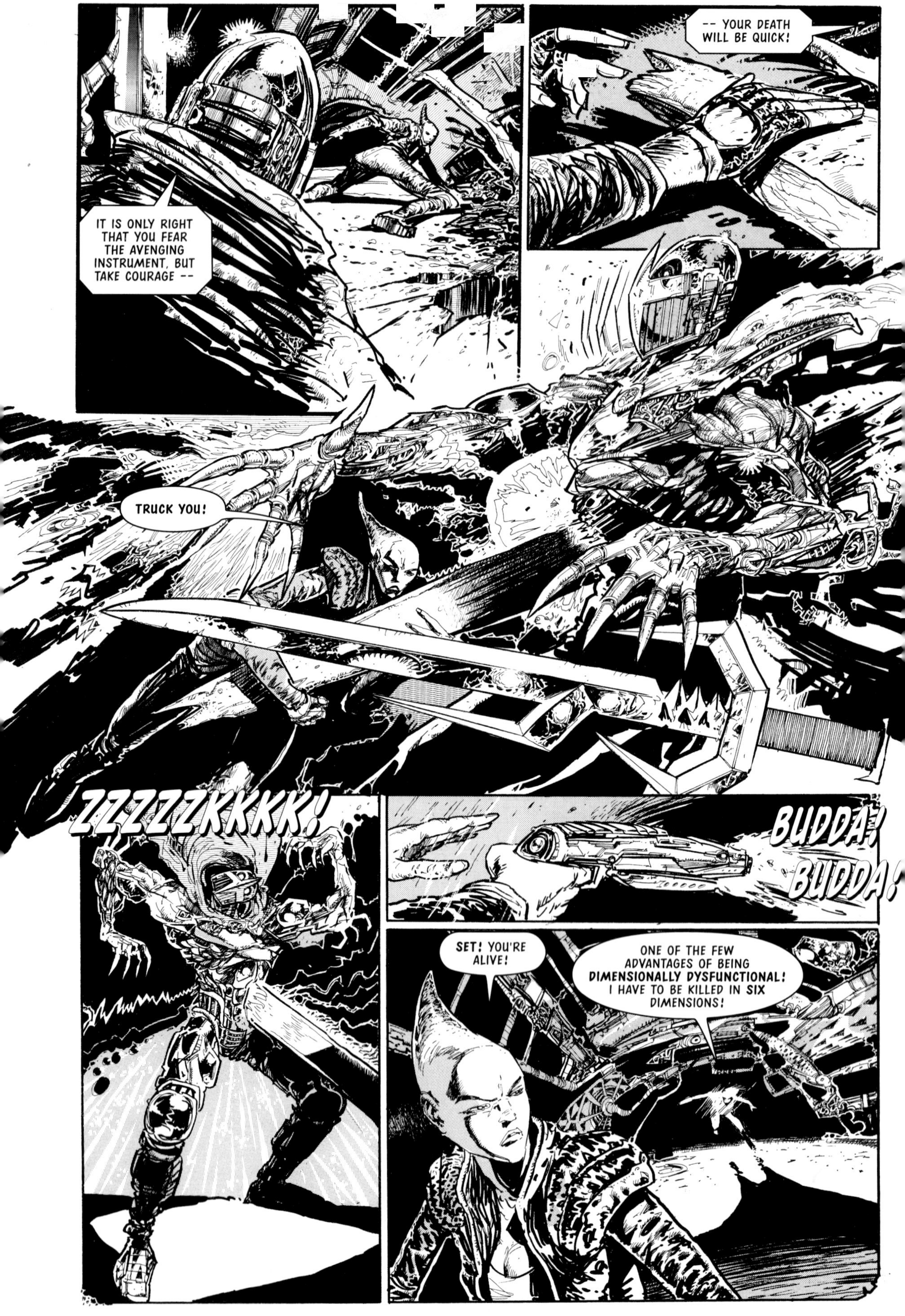
IT IS ONLY RIGHT THAT YOU FEAR THE AVENGING INSTRUMENT, BUT TAKE COURAGE --
-- YOUR DEATH WILL BE QUICK!
TRUCK YOU!
ZZZZZZKKKK!
BUDDA! BUDDA!
SET! YOU'RE ALIVE!
ONE OF THE FEW ADVANTAGES OF BEING **DIMENSIONALLY DYSFUNCTIONAL!** I HAVE TO BE KILLED IN **SIX** DIMENSIONS!

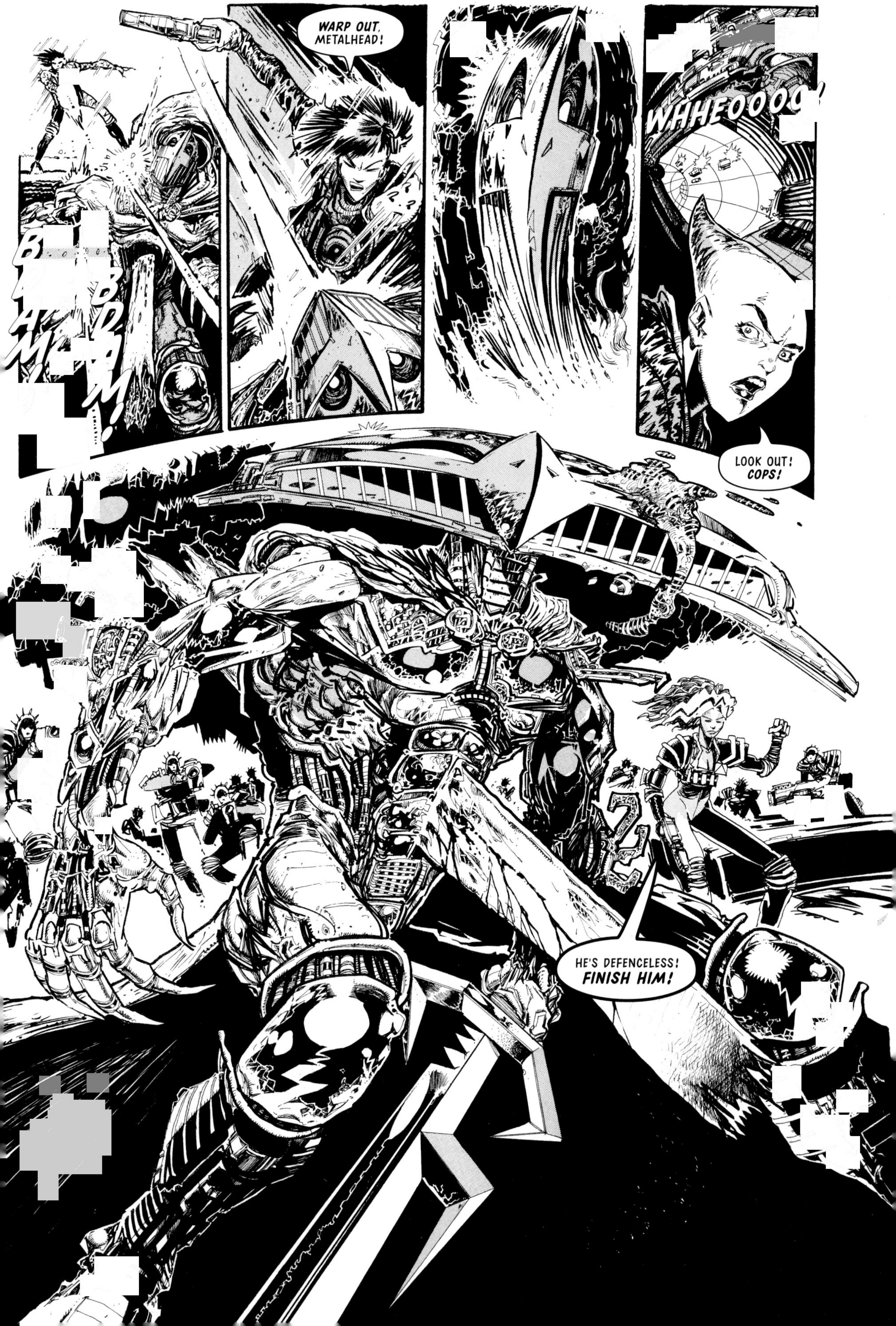
WARP OUT, METALHEAD!
WHHEOOOO
LOOK OUT! COPS!
HE'S DEFENCELESS! FINISH HIM!

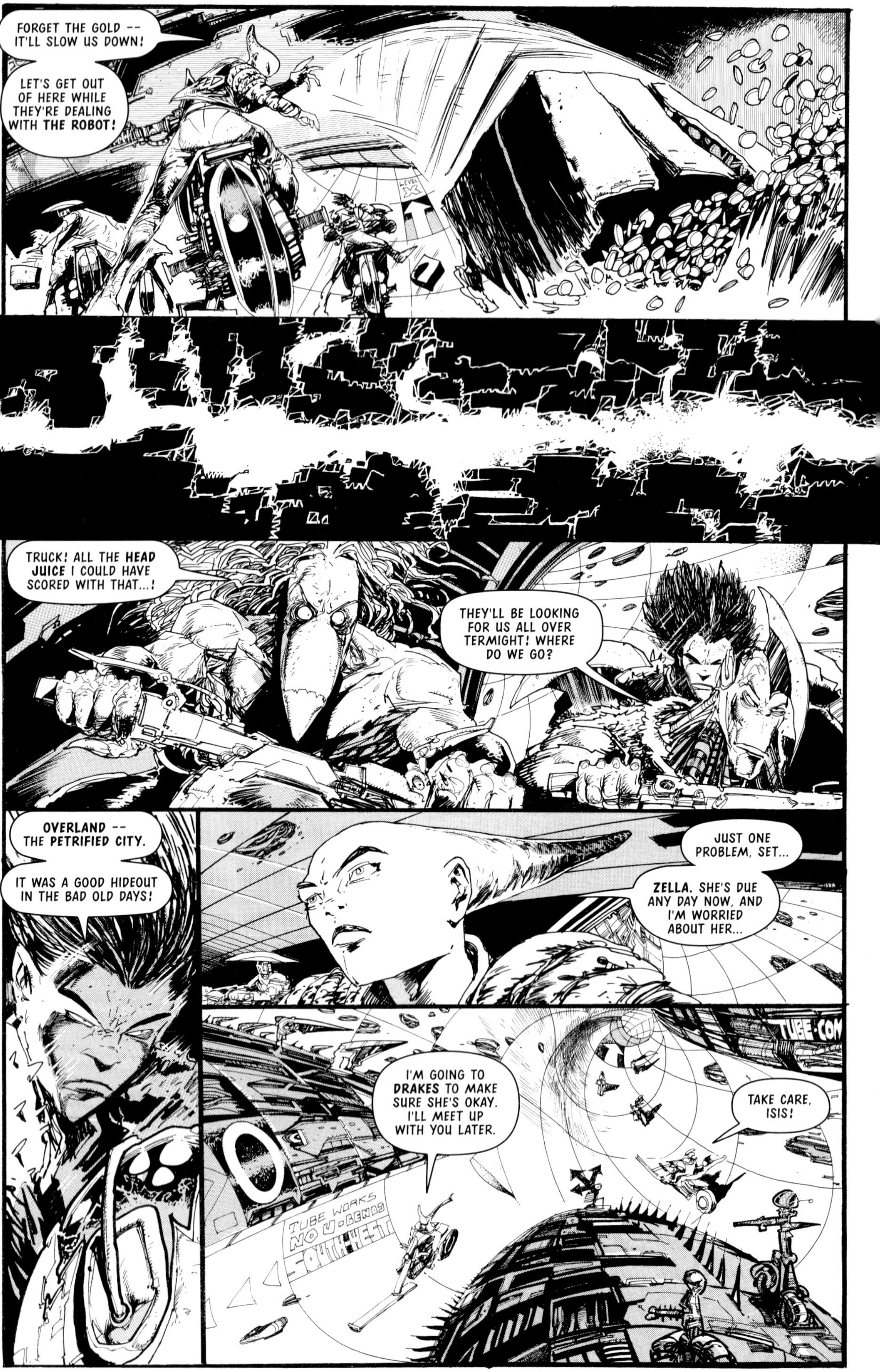
FORGET THE GOLD -- IT'LL SLOW US DOWN!
LET'S GET OUT OF HERE WHILE THEY'RE DEALING WITH **THE ROBOT!**
LEVEL X
TRUCK! ALL THE **HEAD JUICE** I COULD HAVE SCORED WITH THAT...!
THEY'LL BE LOOKING FOR US ALL OVER TERMIGHT! WHERE DO WE GO?
OVERLAND -- THE **PETRIFIED CITY.**
IT WAS A GOOD HIDEOUT IN THE BAD OLD DAYS!
JUST ONE PROBLEM, SET...
ZELLA. SHE'S DUE ANY DAY NOW, AND I'M WORRIED ABOUT HER...
TUBE-COM
I'M GOING TO **DRAKES** TO MAKE SURE SHE'S OKAY. I'LL MEET UP WITH YOU LATER.
TAKE CARE, ISIS!
TUBE WORKS
NO U-BENDS
SOUTH-WEST

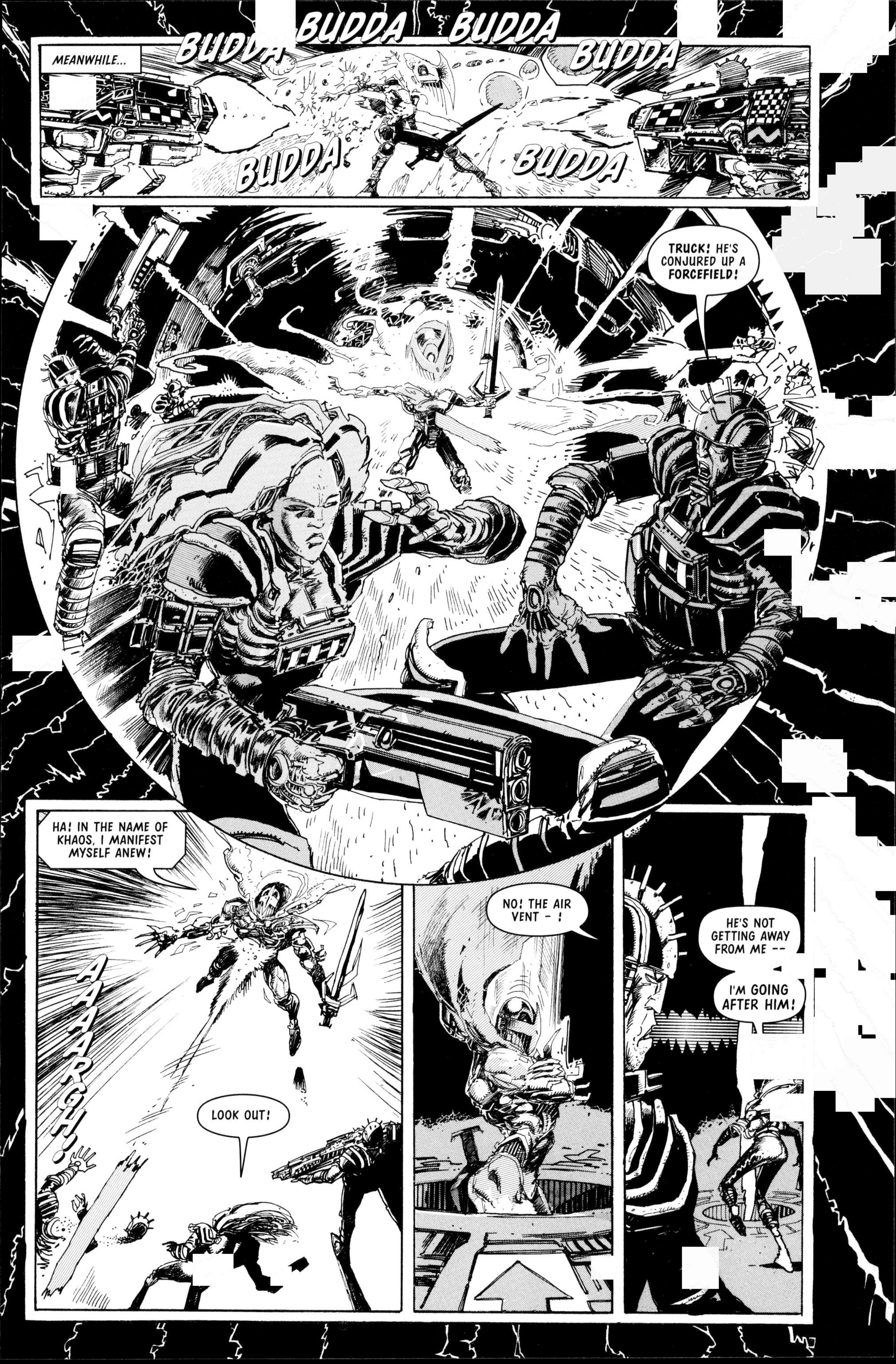
MEANWHILE...
BUDDA
BUDDA
BUDDA
BUDDA
BUDDA
BUDDA
TRUCK! HE'S CONJURED UP A FORCEFIELD!
HA! IN THE NAME OF KHAOS, I MANIFEST MYSELF ANEW!
AAAAARGH!!
LOOK OUT!
NO! THE AIR VENT - !
HE'S NOT GETTING AWAY FROM ME --
I'M GOING AFTER HIM!

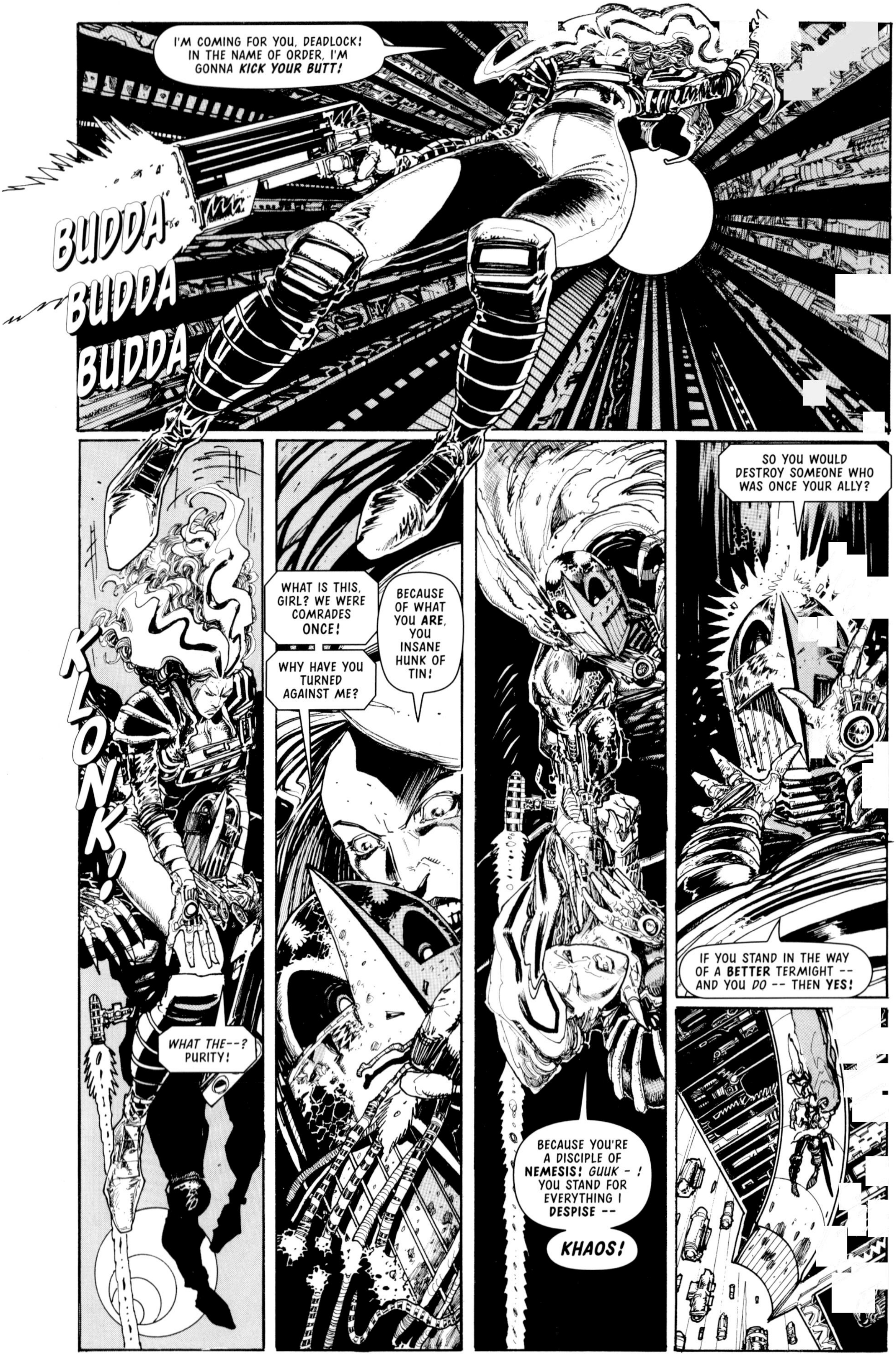
I'M COMING FOR YOU, DEADLOCK! IN THE NAME OF ORDER, I'M GONNA KICK YOUR BUTT!
BUDDA BUDDA BUDDA
KLONK!
WHAT THE--? PURITY!
WHAT IS THIS, GIRL? WE WERE COMRADES ONCE!
WHY HAVE YOU TURNED AGAINST ME?
BECAUSE OF WHAT YOU ARE, YOU INSANE HUNK OF TIN!
BECAUSE YOU'RE A DISCIPLE OF NEMESIS! GUUK - ! YOU STAND FOR EVERYTHING I DESPISE --
KHAOS!
SO YOU WOULD DESTROY SOMEONE WHO WAS ONCE YOUR ALLY?
IF YOU STAND IN THE WAY OF A BETTER TERMIGHT -- AND YOU DO -- THEN YES!

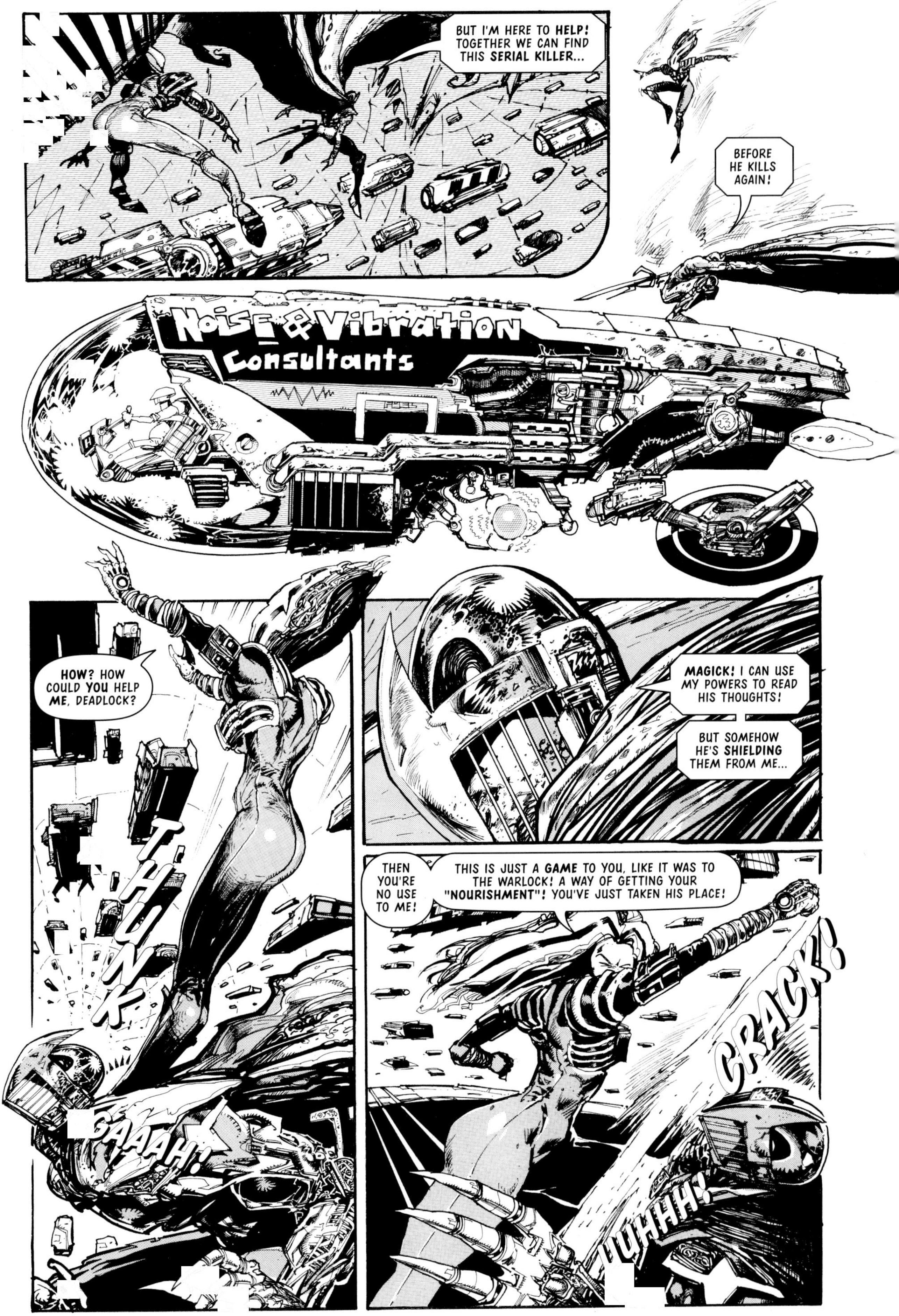
BUT I'M HERE TO HELP! TOGETHER WE CAN FIND THIS SERIAL KILLER...
BEFORE HE KILLS AGAIN!
Noise & Vibration Consultants
HOW? HOW COULD YOU HELP ME, DEADLOCK?
THUNK
GAAAH!
MAGICK! I CAN USE MY POWERS TO READ HIS THOUGHTS!
BUT SOMEHOW HE'S SHIELDING THEM FROM ME...
THEN YOU'RE NO USE TO ME!
THIS IS JUST A GAME TO YOU, LIKE IT WAS TO THE WARLOCK! A WAY OF GETTING YOUR "NOURISHMENT"! YOU'VE JUST TAKEN HIS PLACE!
CRACK!
UHHH!

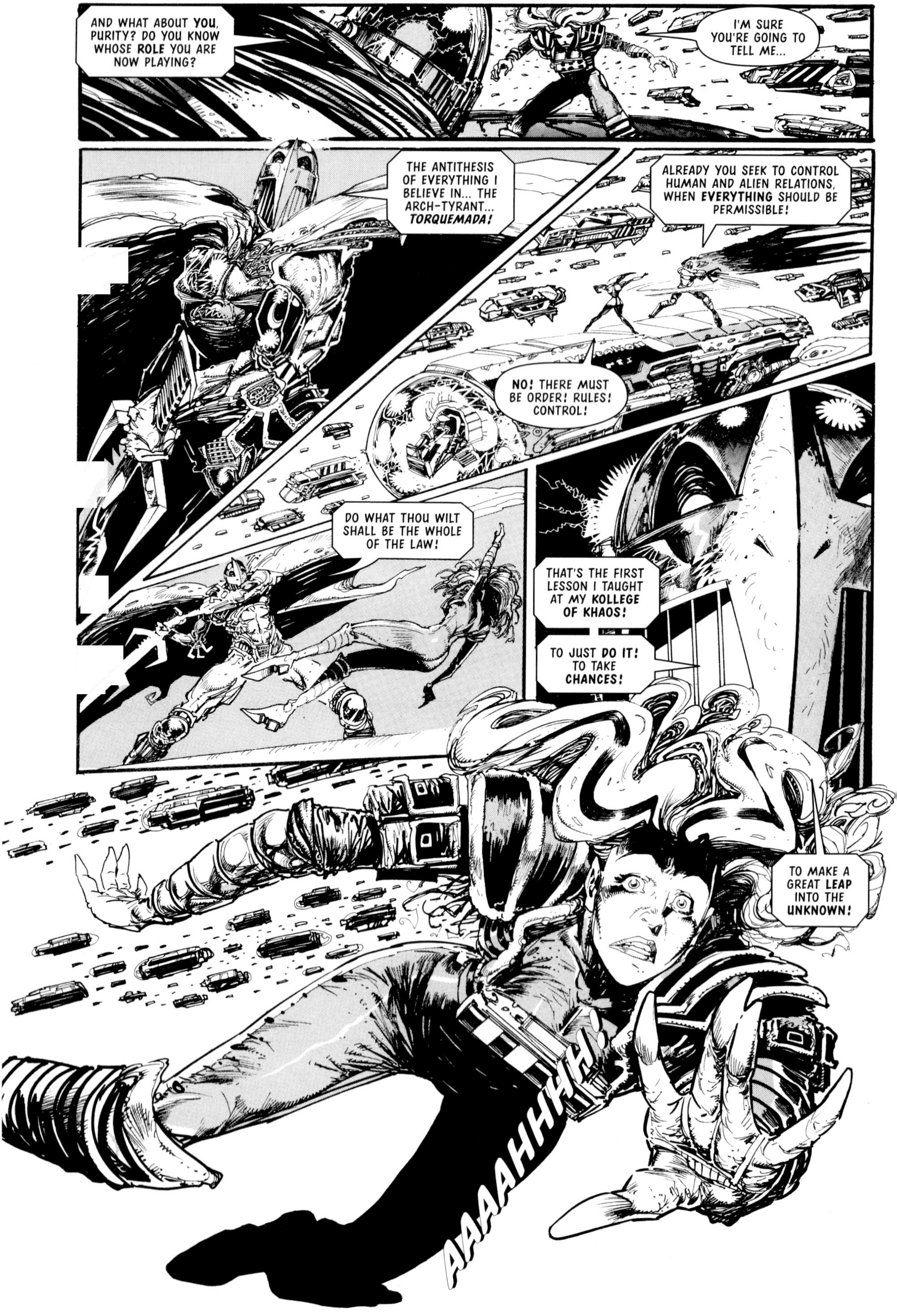
AND WHAT ABOUT **YOU**, PURITY? DO YOU KNOW WHOSE **ROLE** YOU ARE NOW PLAYING?
I'M SURE YOU'RE GOING TO TELL ME...
THE ANTITHESIS OF EVERYTHING I BELIEVE IN... THE ARCH-TYRANT... ***TORQUEMADA!***
ALREADY YOU SEEK TO CONTROL HUMAN AND ALIEN RELATIONS, WHEN **EVERYTHING** SHOULD BE PERMISSIBLE!
NO! THERE MUST BE ORDER! RULES! CONTROL!
DO WHAT THOU WILT SHALL BE THE WHOLE OF THE LAW!
THAT'S THE FIRST LESSON I TAUGHT AT MY **KOLLEGE OF KHAOS!**
TO JUST **DO IT!** TO TAKE **CHANCES!**
TO MAKE A GREAT **LEAP** INTO THE **UNKNOWN!**
AAAAHHHH!

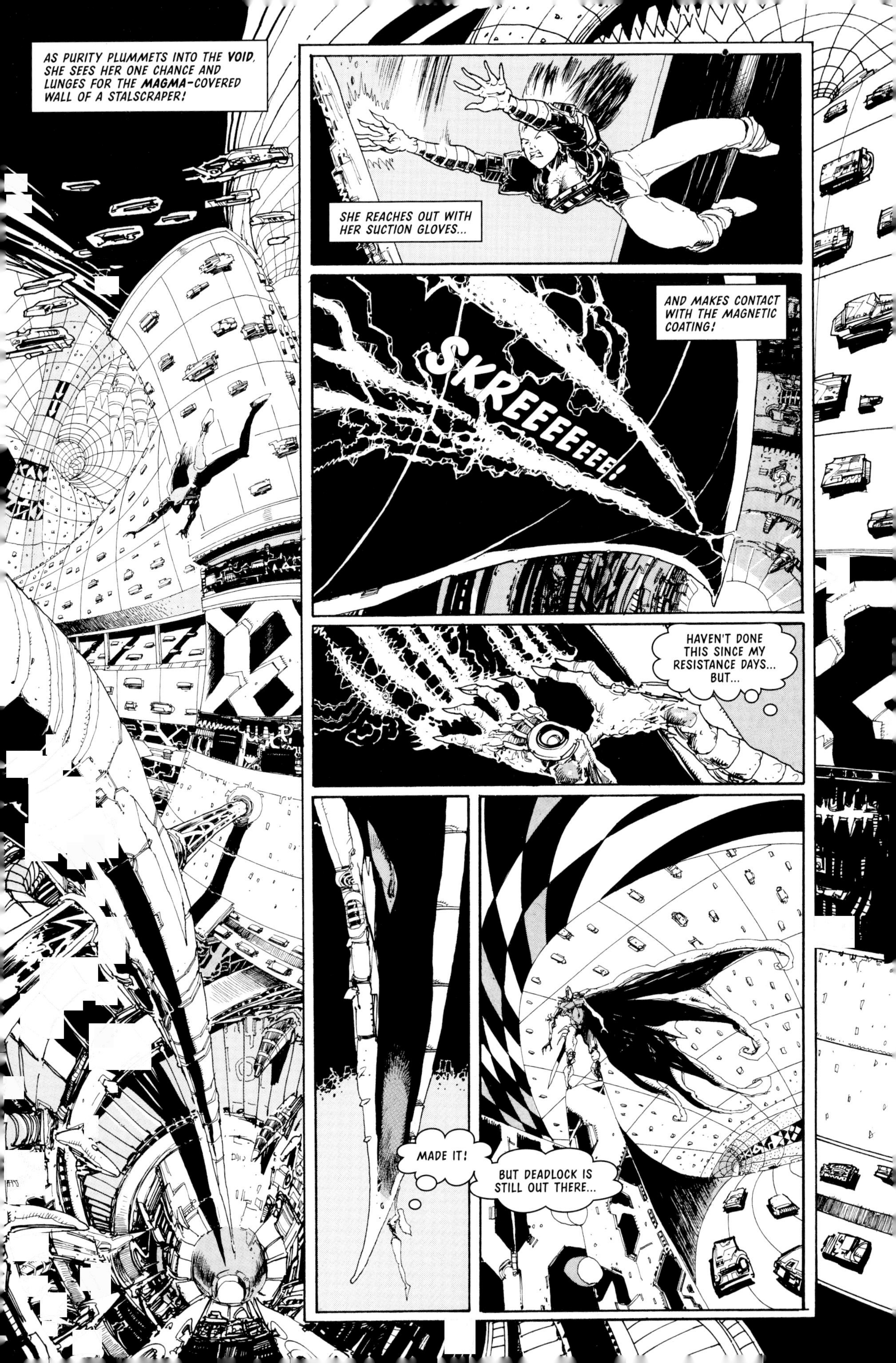
AS PURITY PLUMMETS INTO THE VOID, SHE SEES HER ONE CHANCE AND LUNGES FOR THE MAGMA-COVERED WALL OF A STALSCRAPER!
SHE REACHES OUT WITH HER SUCTION GLOVES...
AND MAKES CONTACT WITH THE MAGNETIC COATING!
SKREEEEEEEE!
HAVEN'T DONE THIS SINCE MY RESISTANCE DAYS... BUT...
MADE IT!
BUT DEADLOCK IS STILL OUT THERE...

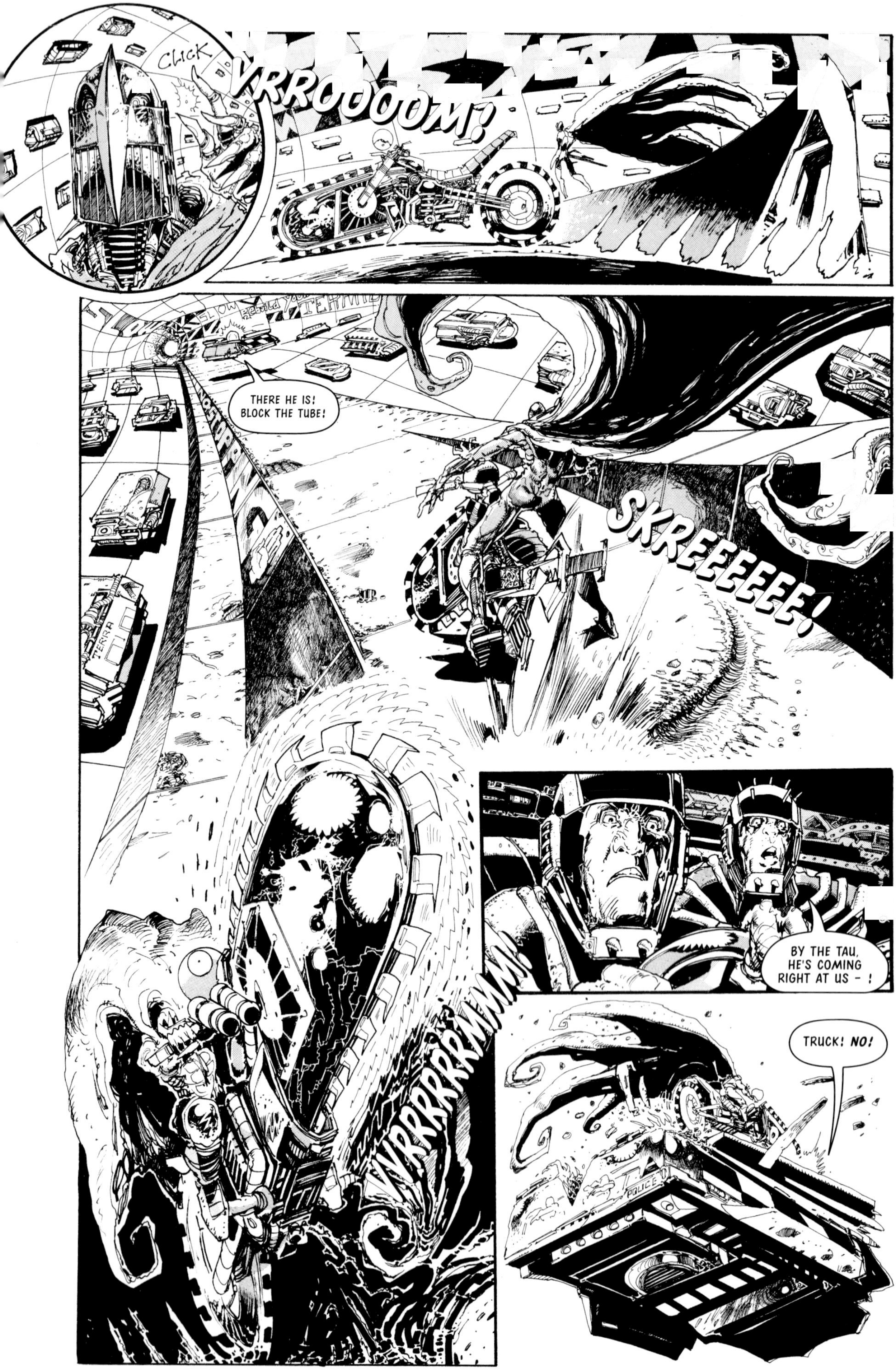
CLICK
VRROOOOOM!
THERE HE IS! BLOCK THE TUBE!
SKREEEEEEE!
TERRA
BY THE TAU, HE'S COMING RIGHT AT US – !
VVRRRRRRMMM!
TRUCK! NO!
POLICE

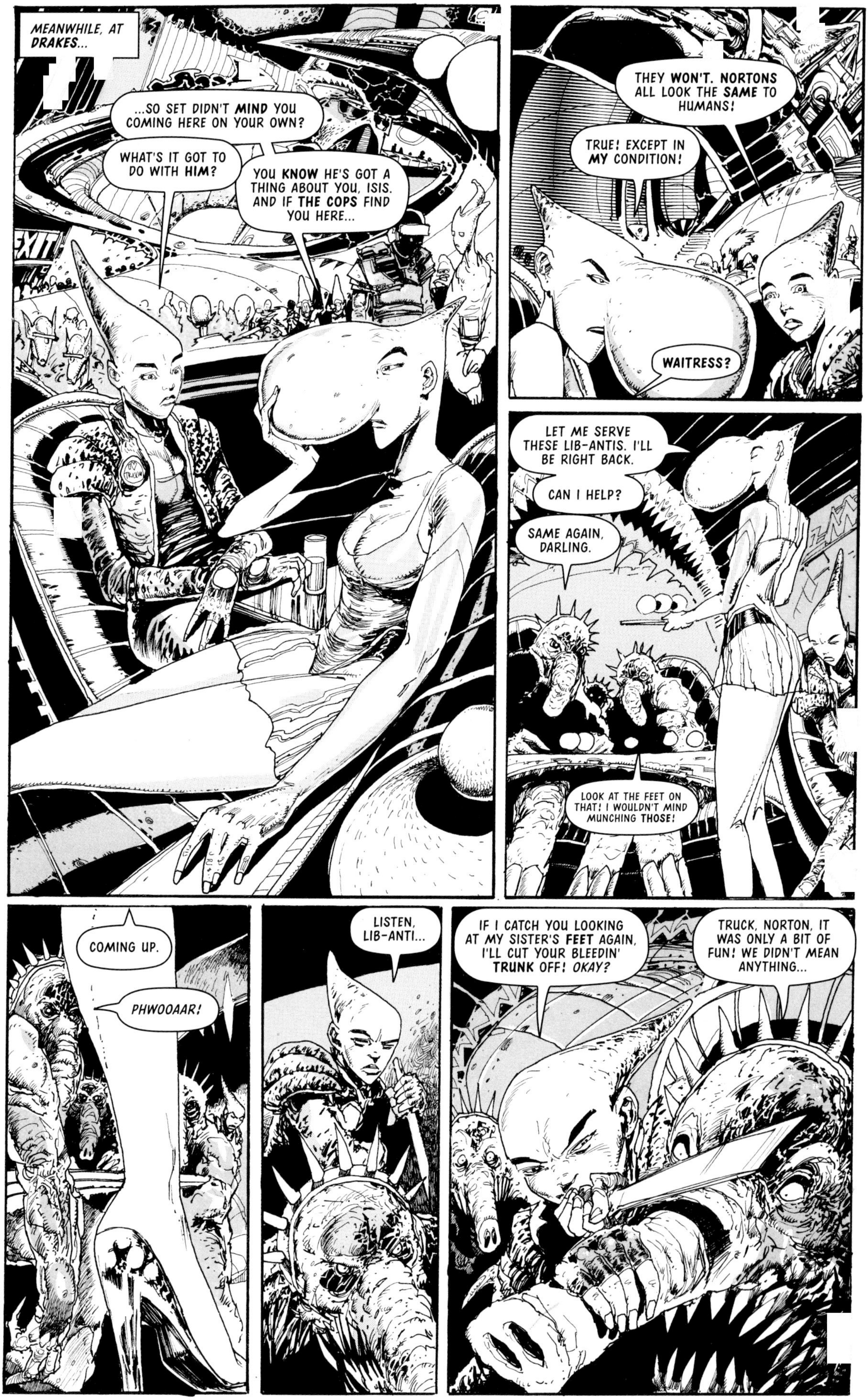
MEANWHILE, AT DRAKES...
...SO SET DIDN'T MIND YOU COMING HERE ON YOUR OWN?
WHAT'S IT GOT TO DO WITH HIM?
YOU KNOW HE'S GOT A THING ABOUT YOU, ISIS. AND IF THE COPS FIND YOU HERE...
THEY WON'T. NORTONS ALL LOOK THE SAME TO HUMANS!
TRUE! EXCEPT IN MY CONDITION!
WAITRESS?
LET ME SERVE THESE LIB-ANTIS. I'LL BE RIGHT BACK.
CAN I HELP?
SAME AGAIN, DARLING.
LOOK AT THE FEET ON THAT! I WOULDN'T MIND MUNCHING THOSE!
COMING UP.
PHWOOAAR!
LISTEN, LIB-ANTI...
IF I CATCH YOU LOOKING AT MY SISTER'S FEET AGAIN, I'LL CUT YOUR BLEEDIN' TRUNK OFF! OKAY?
TRUCK, NORTON, IT WAS ONLY A BIT OF FUN! WE DIDN'T MEAN ANYTHING...

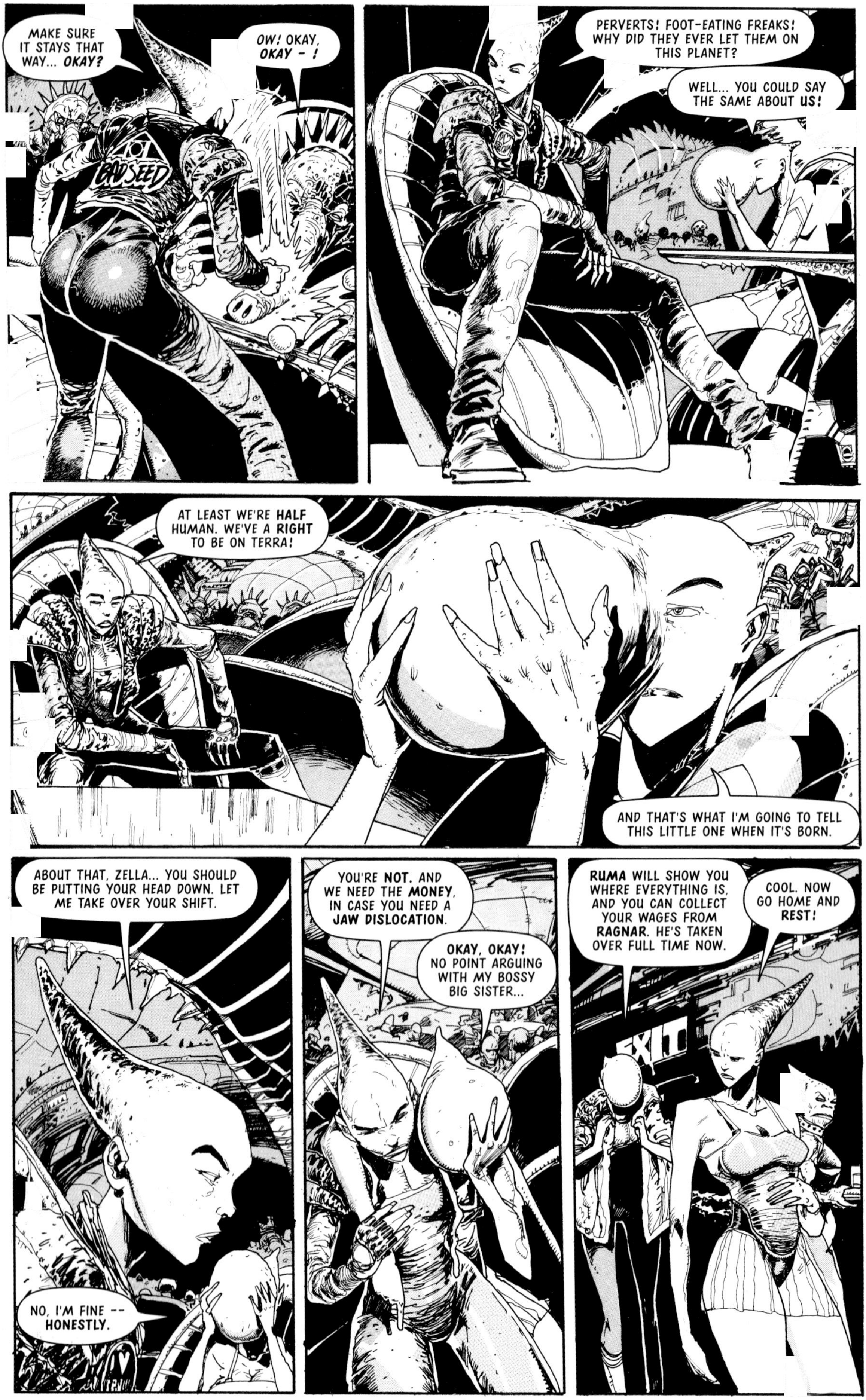
MAKE SURE IT STAYS THAT WAY... OKAY?
OW! OKAY, OKAY - !
BAD SEED
PERVERTS! FOOT-EATING FREAKS! WHY DID THEY EVER LET THEM ON THIS PLANET?
WELL... YOU COULD SAY THE SAME ABOUT US!
AT LEAST WE'RE HALF HUMAN. WE'VE A RIGHT TO BE ON TERRA!
AND THAT'S WHAT I'M GOING TO TELL THIS LITTLE ONE WHEN IT'S BORN.
ABOUT THAT, ZELLA... YOU SHOULD BE PUTTING YOUR HEAD DOWN. LET ME TAKE OVER YOUR SHIFT.
NO, I'M FINE -- HONESTLY.
YOU'RE NOT. AND WE NEED THE MONEY, IN CASE YOU NEED A JAW DISLOCATION.
OKAY, OKAY! NO POINT ARGUING WITH MY BOSSY BIG SISTER...
RUMA WILL SHOW YOU WHERE EVERYTHING IS, AND YOU CAN COLLECT YOUR WAGES FROM RAGNAR. HE'S TAKEN OVER FULL TIME NOW.
COOL. NOW GO HOME AND REST!
EXIT

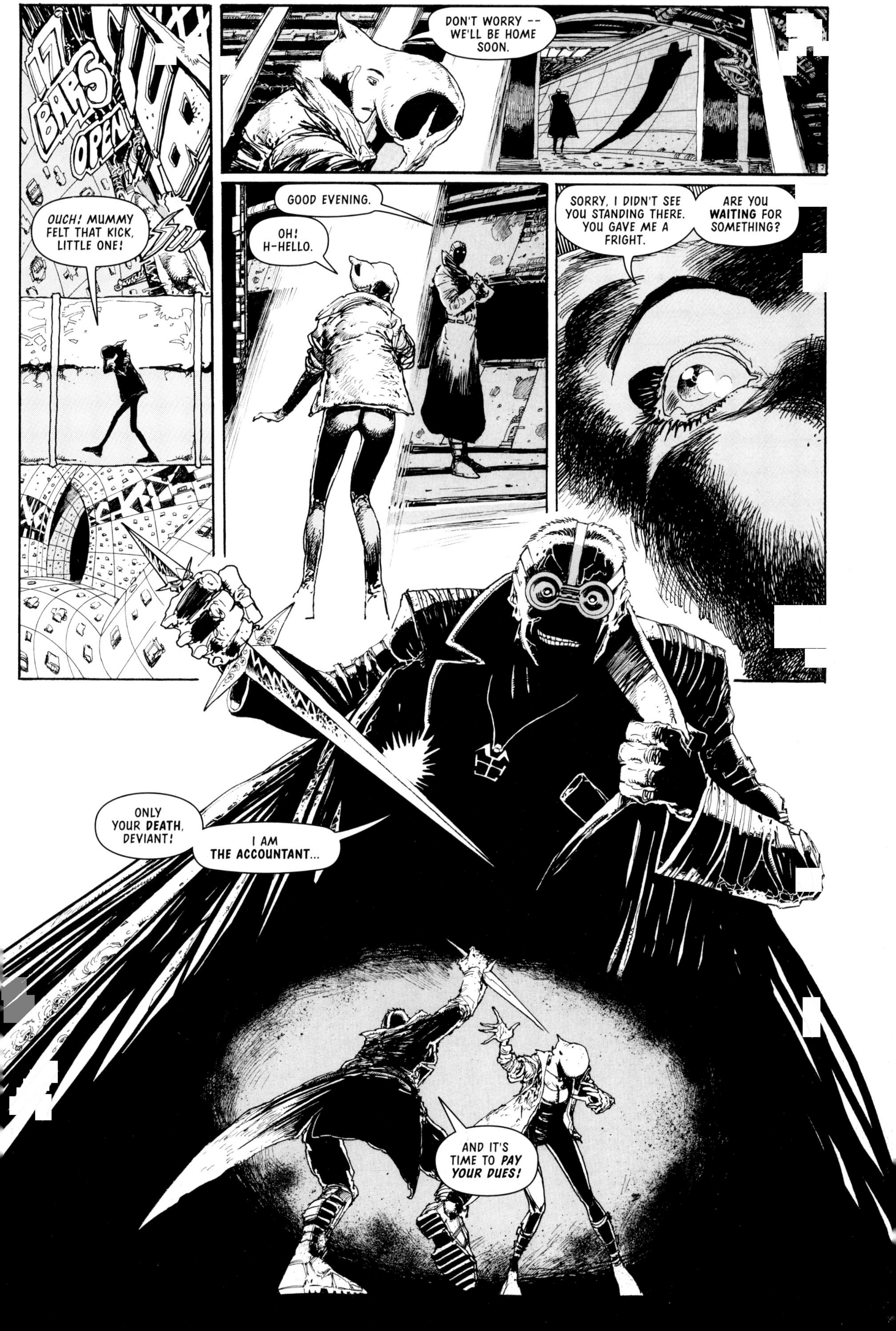
17 BARS OPEN
OUCH! MUMMY FELT THAT KICK, LITTLE ONE!
DON'T WORRY -- WE'LL BE HOME SOON.
GOOD EVENING.
OH! H-HELLO.
SORRY, I DIDN'T SEE YOU STANDING THERE. YOU GAVE ME A FRIGHT.
ARE YOU WAITING FOR SOMETHING?
ONLY YOUR DEATH, DEVIANT!
I AM THE ACCOUNTANT...
AND IT'S TIME TO PAY YOUR DUES!

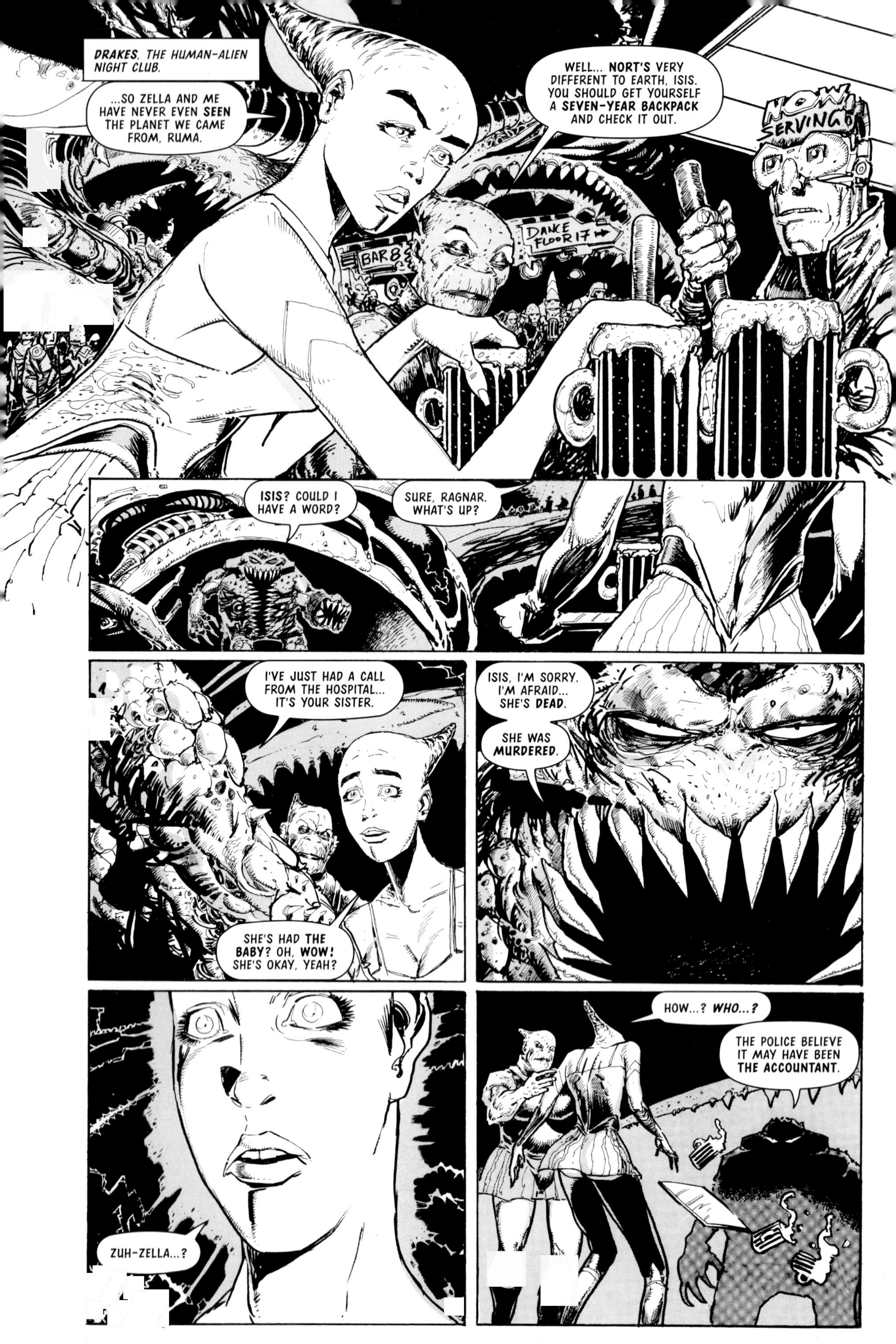
DRAKES, THE HUMAN-ALIEN NIGHT CLUB.
...SO ZELLA AND ME HAVE NEVER EVEN SEEN THE PLANET WE CAME FROM, RUMA.
WELL... NORT'S VERY DIFFERENT TO EARTH, ISIS. YOU SHOULD GET YOURSELF A SEVEN-YEAR BACKPACK AND CHECK IT OUT.
NOW SERVING
DANCE FLOOR 17
BAR 8
ISIS? COULD I HAVE A WORD?
SURE, RAGNAR. WHAT'S UP?
I'VE JUST HAD A CALL FROM THE HOSPITAL... IT'S YOUR SISTER.
SHE'S HAD THE BABY? OH, WOW! SHE'S OKAY, YEAH?
ISIS, I'M SORRY. I'M AFRAID... SHE'S DEAD.
SHE WAS MURDERED.
ZUH-ZELLA...?
HOW...? WHO...?
THE POLICE BELIEVE IT MAY HAVE BEEN THE ACCOUNTANT.

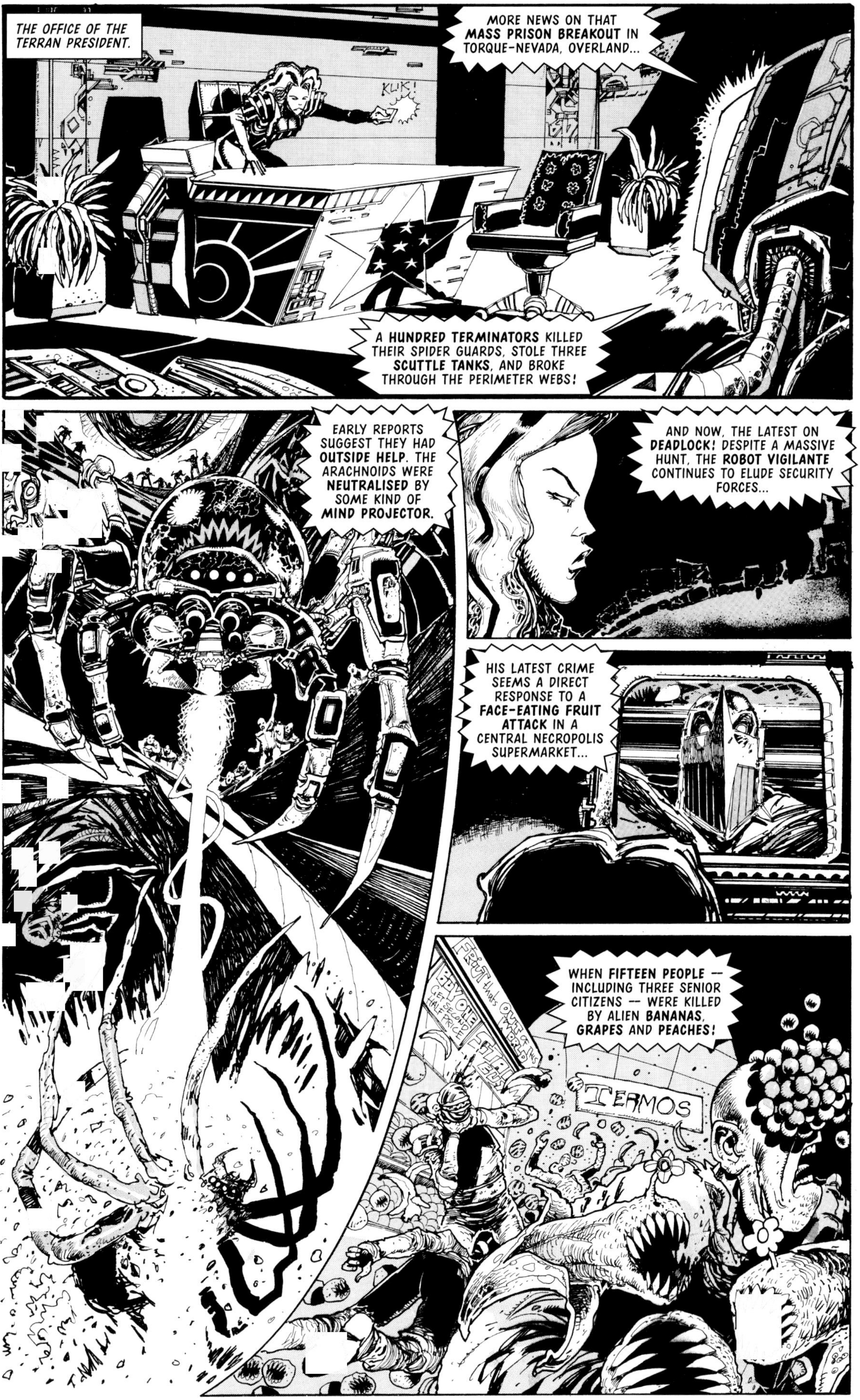
THE OFFICE OF THE TERRAN PRESIDENT.
MORE NEWS ON THAT MASS PRISON BREAKOUT IN TORQUE-NEVADA, OVERLAND...
KLIK!
A HUNDRED TERMINATORS KILLED THEIR SPIDER GUARDS, STOLE THREE SCUTTLE TANKS, AND BROKE THROUGH THE PERIMETER WEBS!
EARLY REPORTS SUGGEST THEY HAD OUTSIDE HELP. THE ARACHNOIDS WERE NEUTRALISED BY SOME KIND OF MIND PROJECTOR.
AND NOW, THE LATEST ON DEADLOCK! DESPITE A MASSIVE HUNT, THE ROBOT VIGILANTE CONTINUES TO ELUDE SECURITY FORCES...
HIS LATEST CRIME SEEMS A DIRECT RESPONSE TO A FACE-EATING FRUIT ATTACK IN A CENTRAL NECROPOLIS SUPERMARKET...
WHEN FIFTEEN PEOPLE -- INCLUDING THREE SENIOR CITIZENS -- WERE KILLED BY ALIEN BANANAS, GRAPES AND PEACHES!
TERMOS

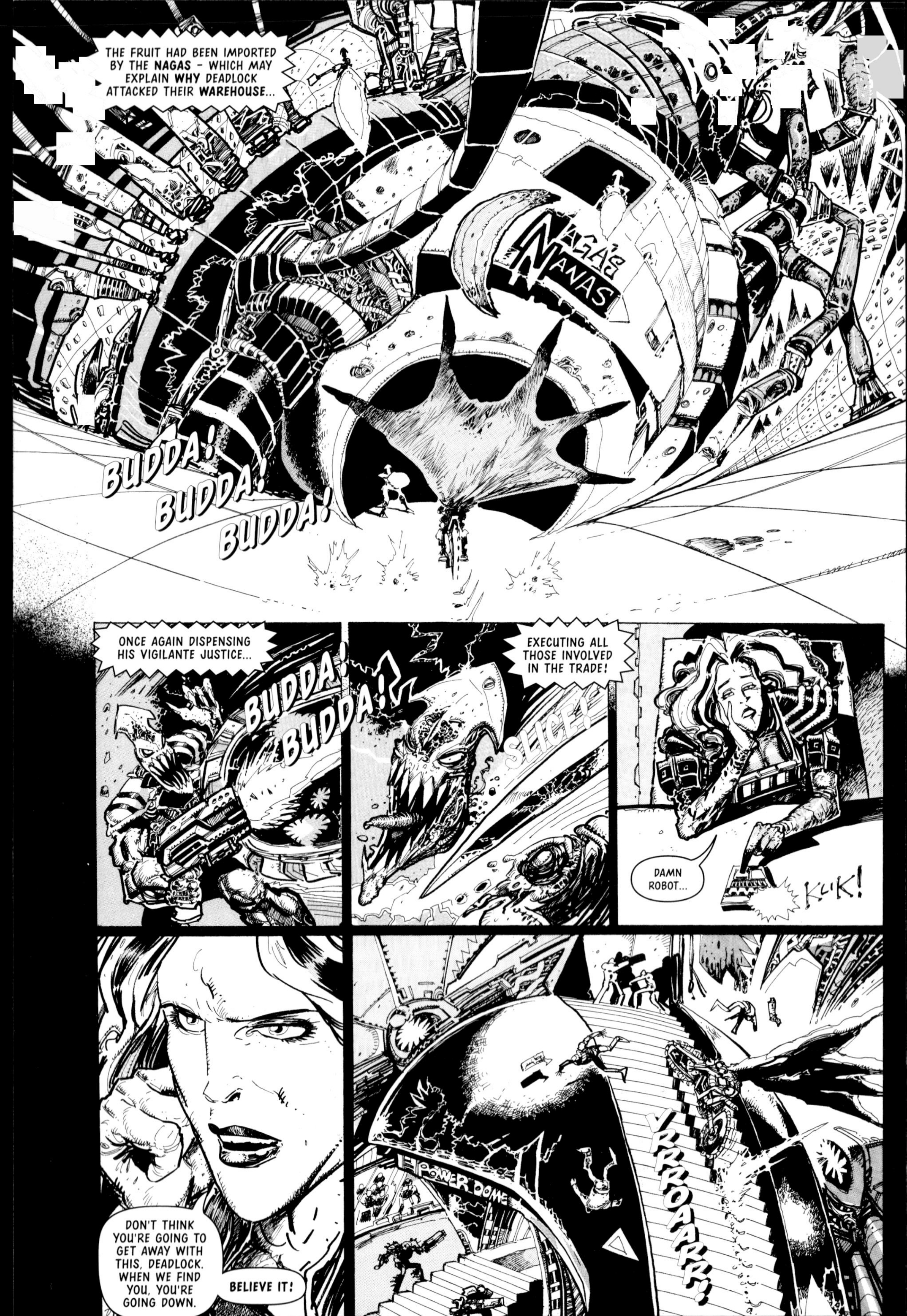
THE FRUIT HAD BEEN IMPORTED BY THE NAGAS - WHICH MAY EXPLAIN WHY DEADLOCK ATTACKED THEIR WAREHOUSE...
NAGA'S NANAS
BUDDA! BUDDA! BUDDA!
ONCE AGAIN DISPENSING HIS VIGILANTE JUSTICE...
BUDDA! BUDDA!
EXECUTING ALL THOSE INVOLVED IN THE TRADE!
SLICE!
DAMN ROBOT...
K'LIK!
DON'T THINK YOU'RE GOING TO GET AWAY WITH THIS, DEADLOCK. WHEN WE FIND YOU, YOU'RE GOING DOWN.
BELIEVE IT!
POWER DOME
VRRROAARR!

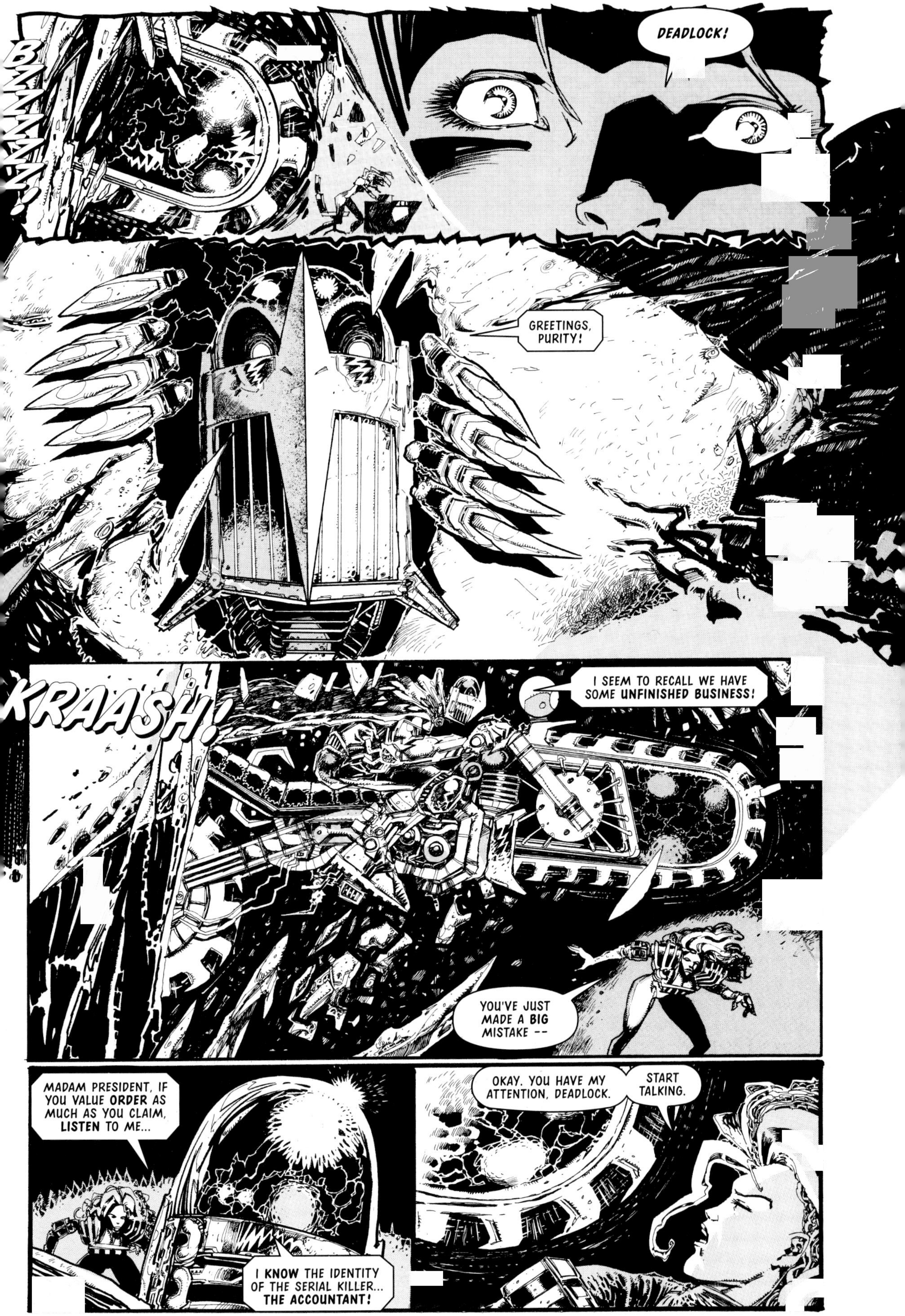
BZZZZZT!
DEADLOCK!
GREETINGS, PURITY!
KRAASH!
I SEEM TO RECALL WE HAVE SOME UNFINISHED BUSINESS!
YOU'VE JUST MADE A BIG MISTAKE --
MADAM PRESIDENT, IF YOU VALUE ORDER AS MUCH AS YOU CLAIM, LISTEN TO ME...
I KNOW THE IDENTITY OF THE SERIAL KILLER... THE ACCOUNTANT!
OKAY. YOU HAVE MY ATTENTION, DEADLOCK.
START TALKING.

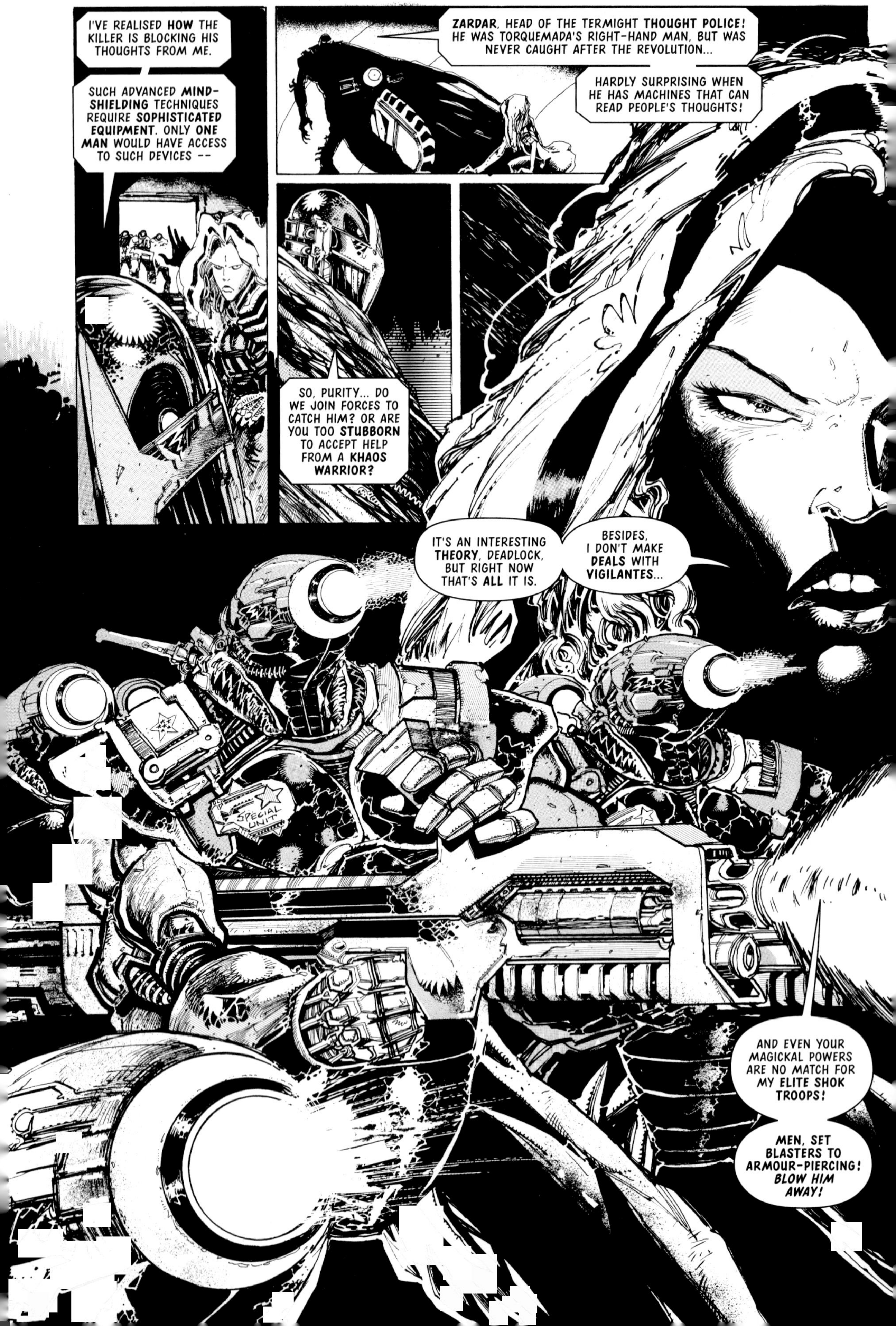
I'VE REALISED HOW THE KILLER IS BLOCKING HIS THOUGHTS FROM ME.
SUCH ADVANCED MIND-SHIELDING TECHNIQUES REQUIRE SOPHISTICATED EQUIPMENT. ONLY ONE MAN WOULD HAVE ACCESS TO SUCH DEVICES --
ZARDAR, HEAD OF THE TERMIGHT THOUGHT POLICE! HE WAS TORQUEMADA'S RIGHT-HAND MAN, BUT WAS NEVER CAUGHT AFTER THE REVOLUTION...
HARDLY SURPRISING WHEN HE HAS MACHINES THAT CAN READ PEOPLE'S THOUGHTS!
SO, PURITY... DO WE JOIN FORCES TO CATCH HIM? OR ARE YOU TOO STUBBORN TO ACCEPT HELP FROM A KHAOS WARRIOR?
IT'S AN INTERESTING THEORY, DEADLOCK, BUT RIGHT NOW THAT'S ALL IT IS.
BESIDES, I DON'T MAKE DEALS WITH VIGILANTES...
SPECIAL UNIT
AND EVEN YOUR MAGICKAL POWERS ARE NO MATCH FOR MY ELITE SHOK TROOPS!
MEN, SET BLASTERS TO ARMOUR-PIERCING! BLOW HIM AWAY!

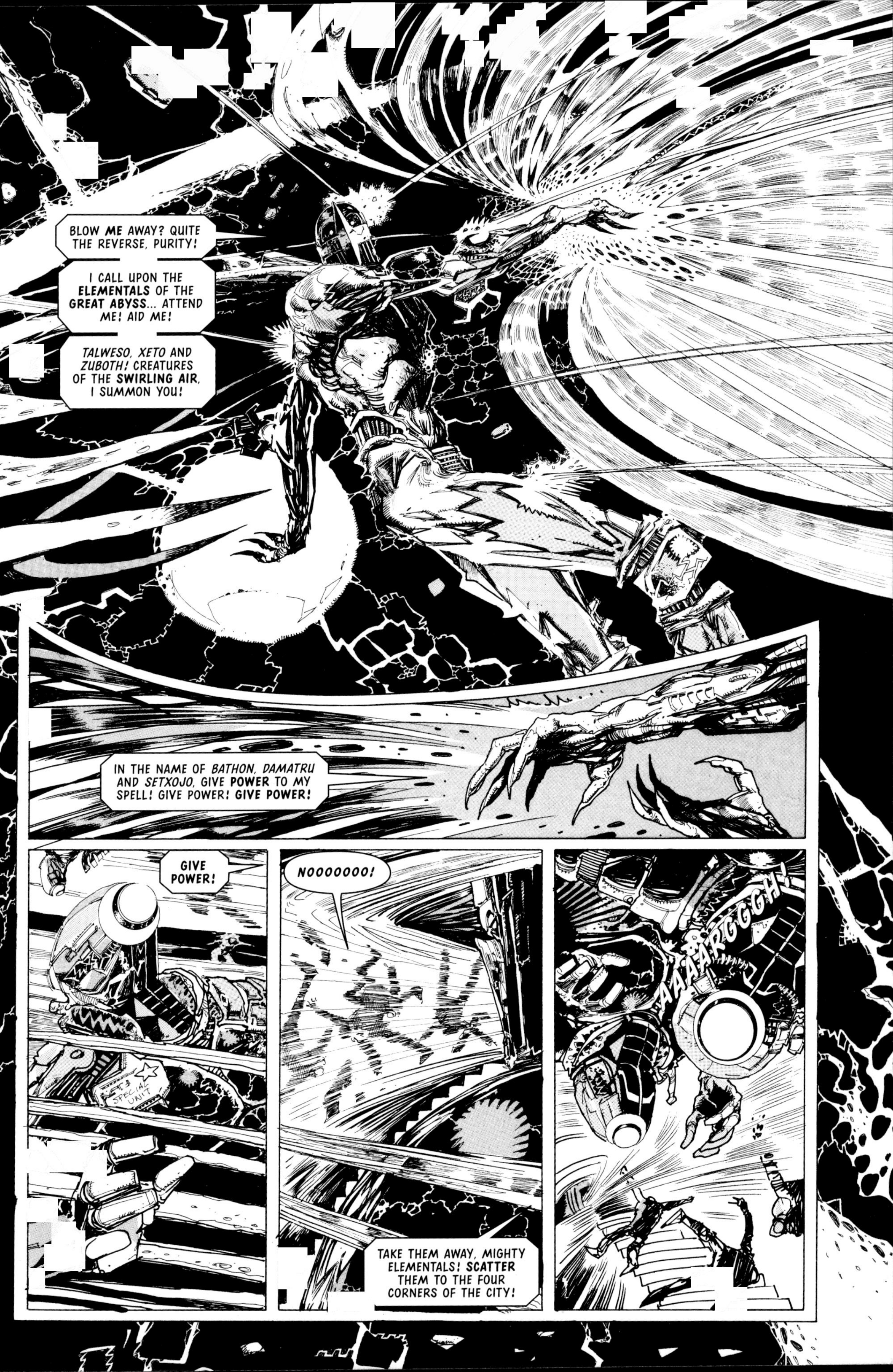
BLOW ME AWAY? QUITE THE REVERSE, PURITY!
I CALL UPON THE ELEMENTALS OF THE GREAT ABYSS... ATTEND ME! AID ME!
TALWESO, XETO AND ZUBOTH! CREATURES OF THE SWIRLING AIR, I SUMMON YOU!
IN THE NAME OF BATHON, DAMATRU AND SETXOJO, GIVE POWER TO MY SPELL! GIVE POWER! GIVE POWER!
GIVE POWER!
SPECIAL UNIT
NOOOOOOO!
TAKE THEM AWAY, MIGHTY ELEMENTALS! SCATTER THEM TO THE FOUR CORNERS OF THE CITY!
AAARGGGH!

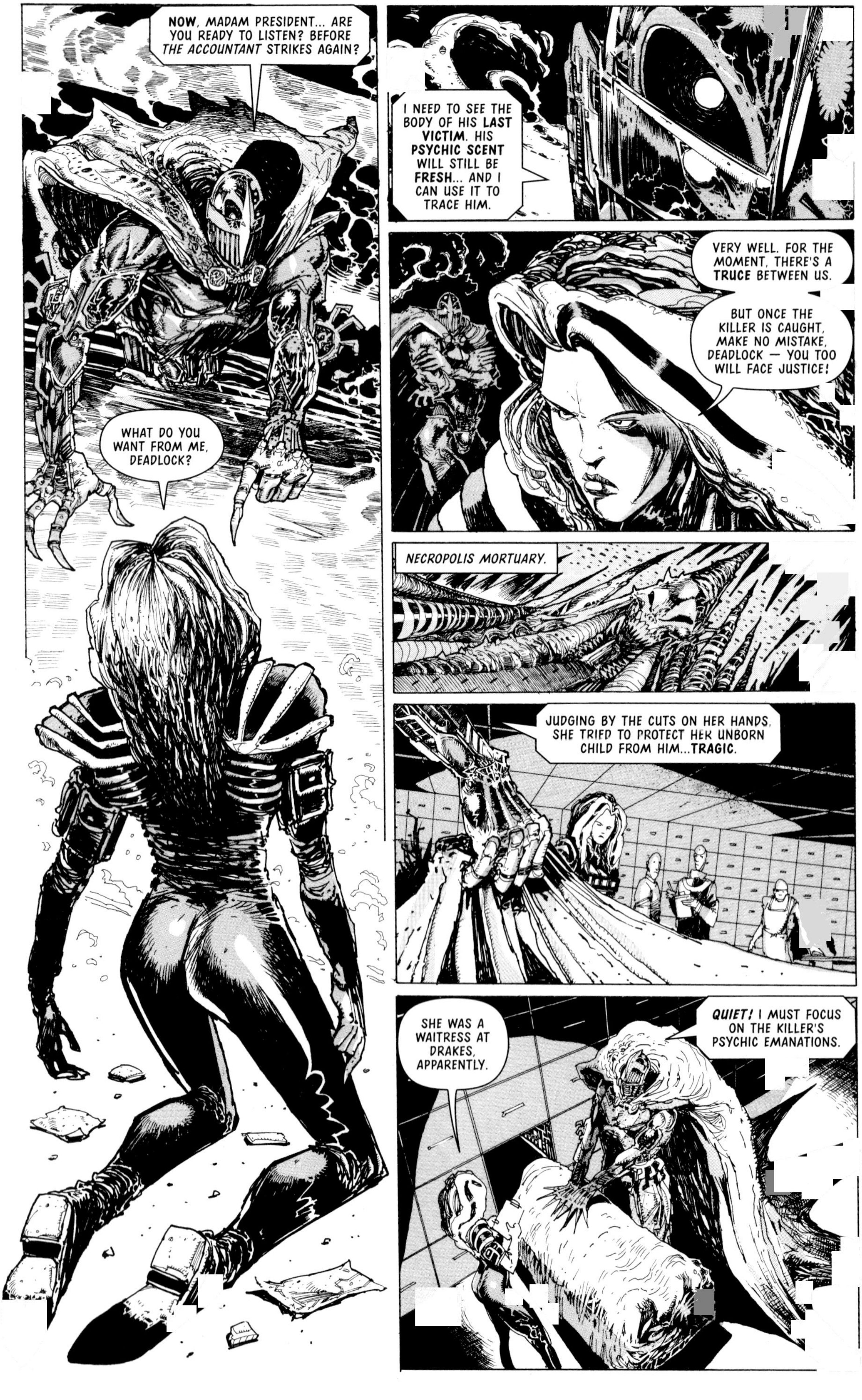
NOW, MADAM PRESIDENT... ARE YOU READY TO LISTEN? BEFORE THE ACCOUNTANT STRIKES AGAIN?
WHAT DO YOU WANT FROM ME, DEADLOCK?
I NEED TO SEE THE BODY OF HIS LAST VICTIM. HIS PSYCHIC SCENT WILL STILL BE FRESH... AND I CAN USE IT TO TRACE HIM.
VERY WELL. FOR THE MOMENT, THERE'S A TRUCE BETWEEN US.
BUT ONCE THE KILLER IS CAUGHT, MAKE NO MISTAKE, DEADLOCK — YOU TOO WILL FACE JUSTICE!
NECROPOLIS MORTUARY.
JUDGING BY THE CUTS ON HER HANDS, SHE TRIED TO PROTECT HER UNBORN CHILD FROM HIM...TRAGIC.
SHE WAS A WAITRESS AT DRAKES, APPARENTLY.
QUIET! I MUST FOCUS ON THE KILLER'S PSYCHIC EMANATIONS.

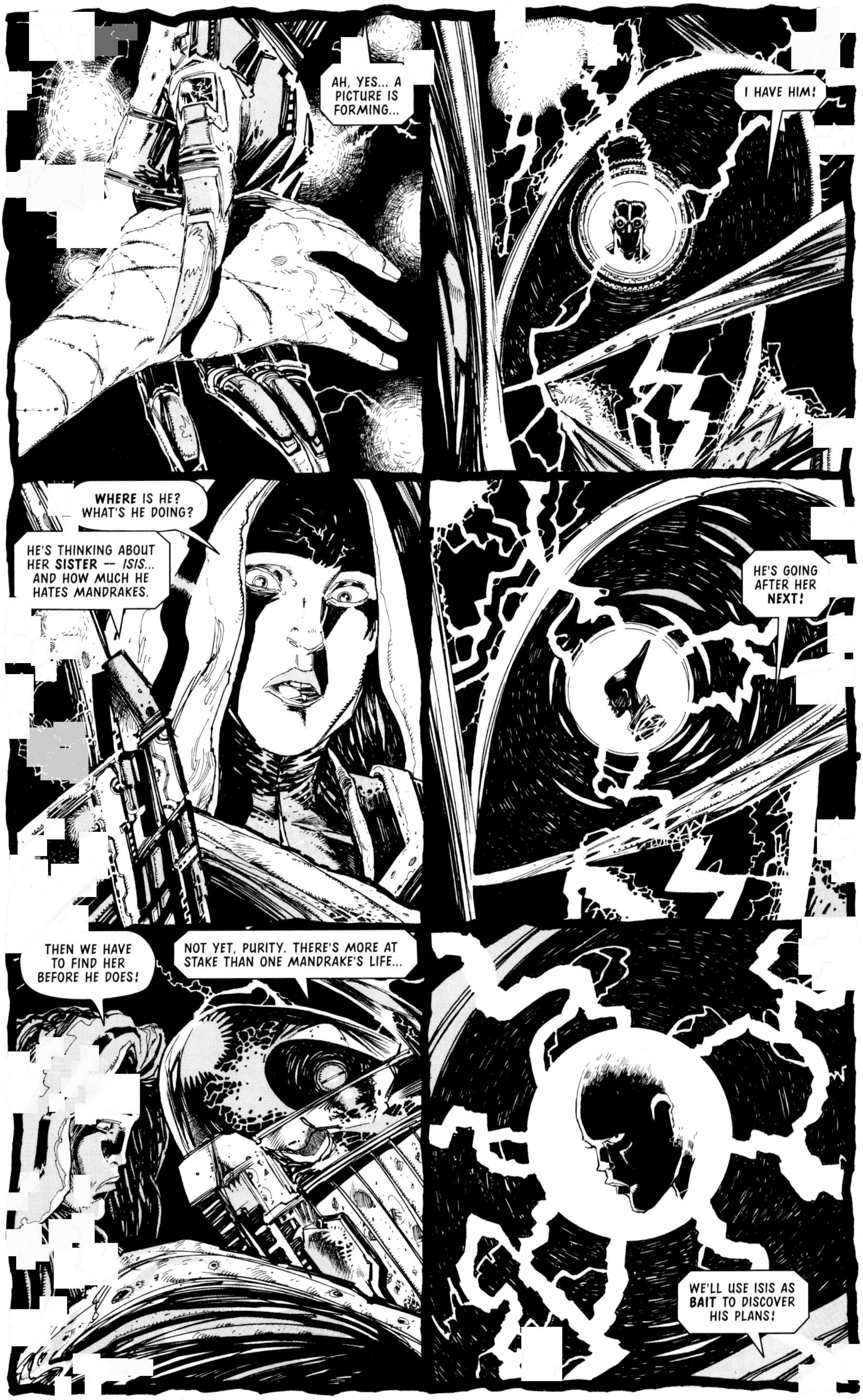
AH, YES... A PICTURE IS FORMING...
I HAVE HIM!
WHERE IS HE? WHAT'S HE DOING?
HE'S THINKING ABOUT HER SISTER -- ISIS... AND HOW MUCH HE HATES MANDRAKES.
HE'S GOING AFTER HER NEXT!
THEN WE HAVE TO FIND HER BEFORE HE DOES!
NOT YET, PURITY. THERE'S MORE AT STAKE THAN ONE MANDRAKE'S LIFE...
WE'LL USE ISIS AS BAIT TO DISCOVER HIS PLANS!

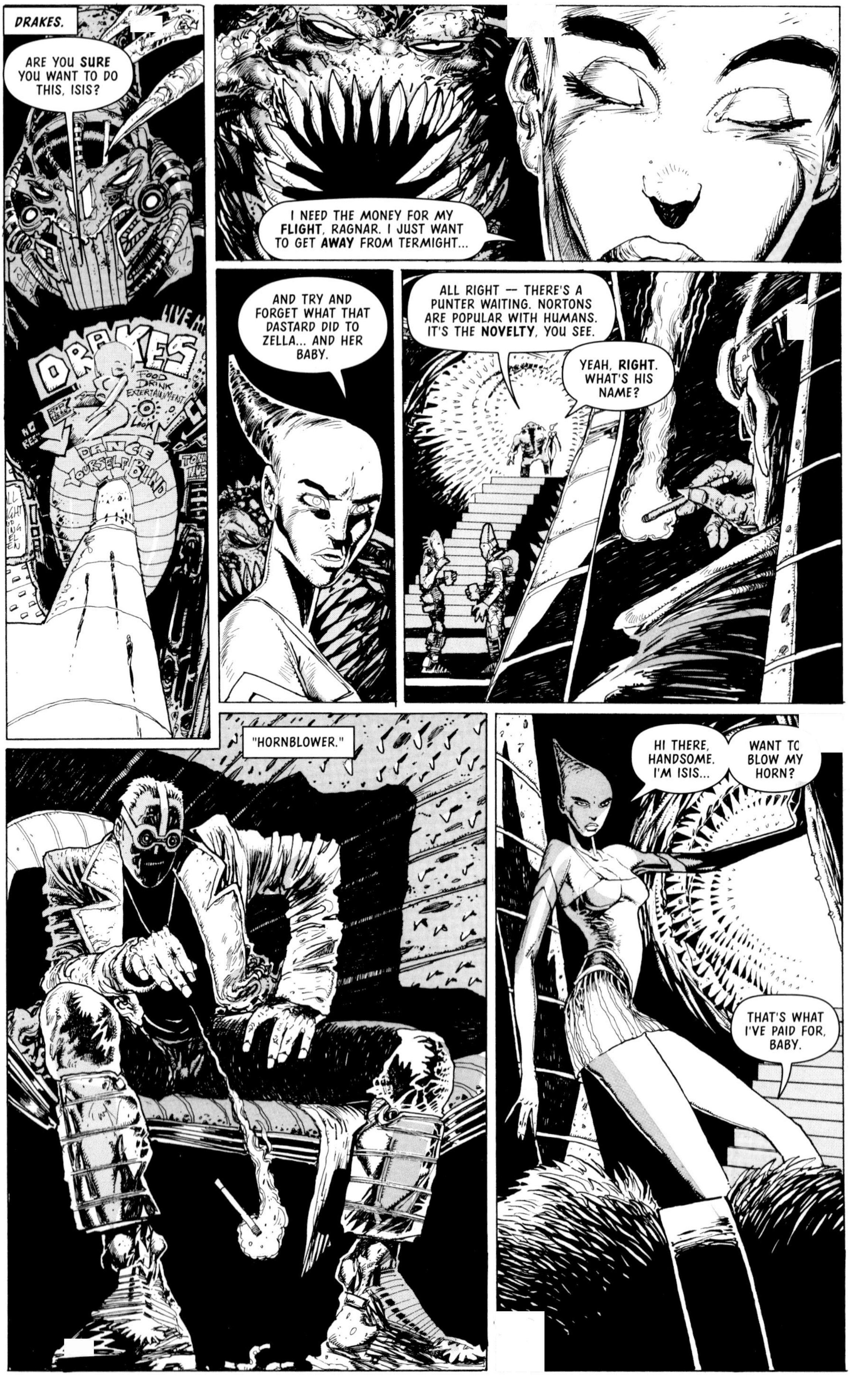

DRAKES.
ARE YOU SURE YOU WANT TO DO THIS, ISIS?
DRAKES
FOOD DRINK ENTERTAINMENT
DANCE YOURSELF BLIND
I NEED THE MONEY FOR MY FLIGHT, RAGNAR. I JUST WANT TO GET AWAY FROM TERMIGHT...
AND TRY AND FORGET WHAT THAT DASTARD DID TO ZELLA... AND HER BABY.
ALL RIGHT — THERE'S A PUNTER WAITING. NORTONS ARE POPULAR WITH HUMANS. IT'S THE NOVELTY, YOU SEE.
YEAH, RIGHT. WHAT'S HIS NAME?
"HORNBLOWER."
HI THERE, HANDSOME. I'M ISIS...
WANT TO BLOW MY HORN?
THAT'S WHAT I'VE PAID FOR, BABY.

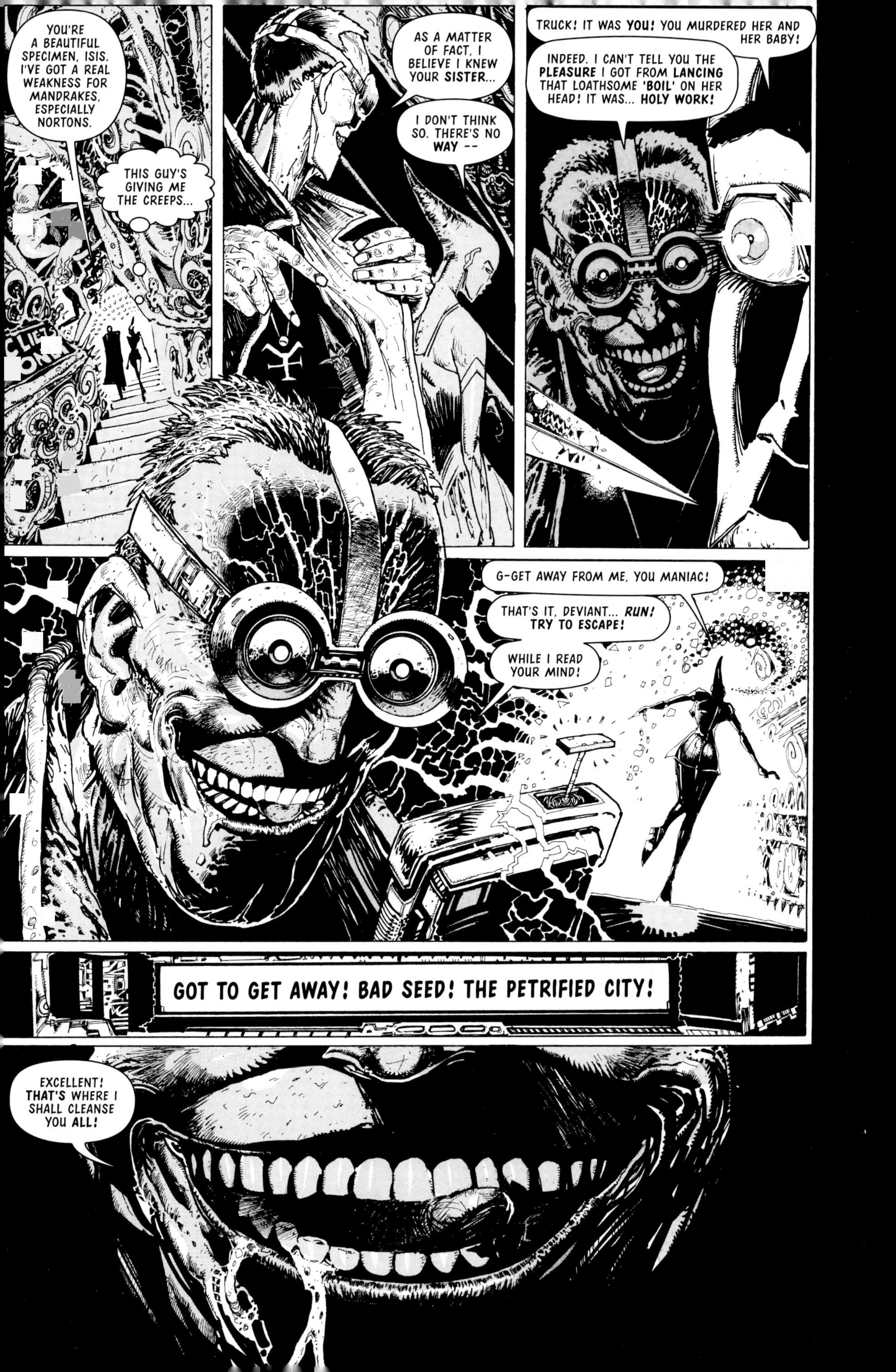

YOU'RE A BEAUTIFUL SPECIMEN, ISIS. I'VE GOT A REAL WEAKNESS FOR MANDRAKES, ESPECIALLY NORTONS.
THIS GUY'S GIVING ME THE CREEPS...
AS A MATTER OF FACT, I BELIEVE I KNEW YOUR SISTER...
I DON'T THINK SO. THERE'S NO WAY --
TRUCK! IT WAS YOU! YOU MURDERED HER AND HER BABY!
INDEED. I CAN'T TELL YOU THE PLEASURE I GOT FROM LANCING THAT LOATHSOME 'BOIL' ON HER HEAD! IT WAS... HOLY WORK!
G-GET AWAY FROM ME, YOU MANIAC!
THAT'S IT, DEVIANT... RUN! TRY TO ESCAPE!
WHILE I READ YOUR MIND!
GOT TO GET AWAY! BAD SEED! THE PETRIFIED CITY!
EXCELLENT! THAT'S WHERE I SHALL CLEANSE YOU ALL!

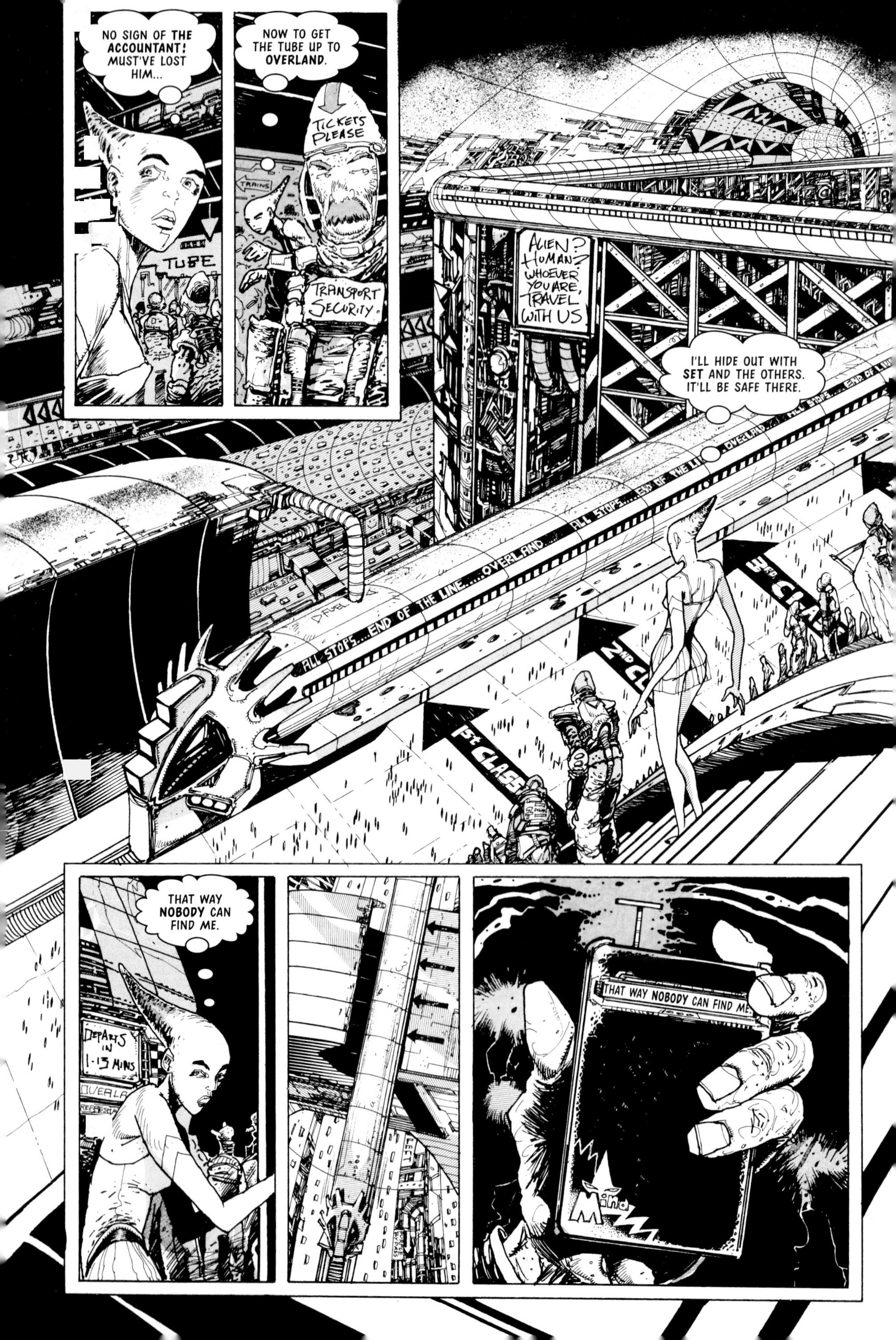

NO SIGN OF THE ACCOUNTANT! MUST'VE LOST HIM...
TUBE
NOW TO GET THE TUBE UP TO OVERLAND.
TICKETS PLEASE
TRAINS
TRANSPORT SECURITY
ALIEN? HUMAN? WHOEVER YOU ARE, TRAVEL WITH US
I'LL HIDE OUT WITH SET AND THE OTHERS. IT'LL BE SAFE THERE.
ALL STOPS....END OF THE LINE....OVERLAND
1st CLASS
2ND CL
3RD CLA
THAT WAY NOBODY CAN FIND ME.
DEPARTS IN 1.13 MINS
THAT WAY NOBODY CAN FIND ME

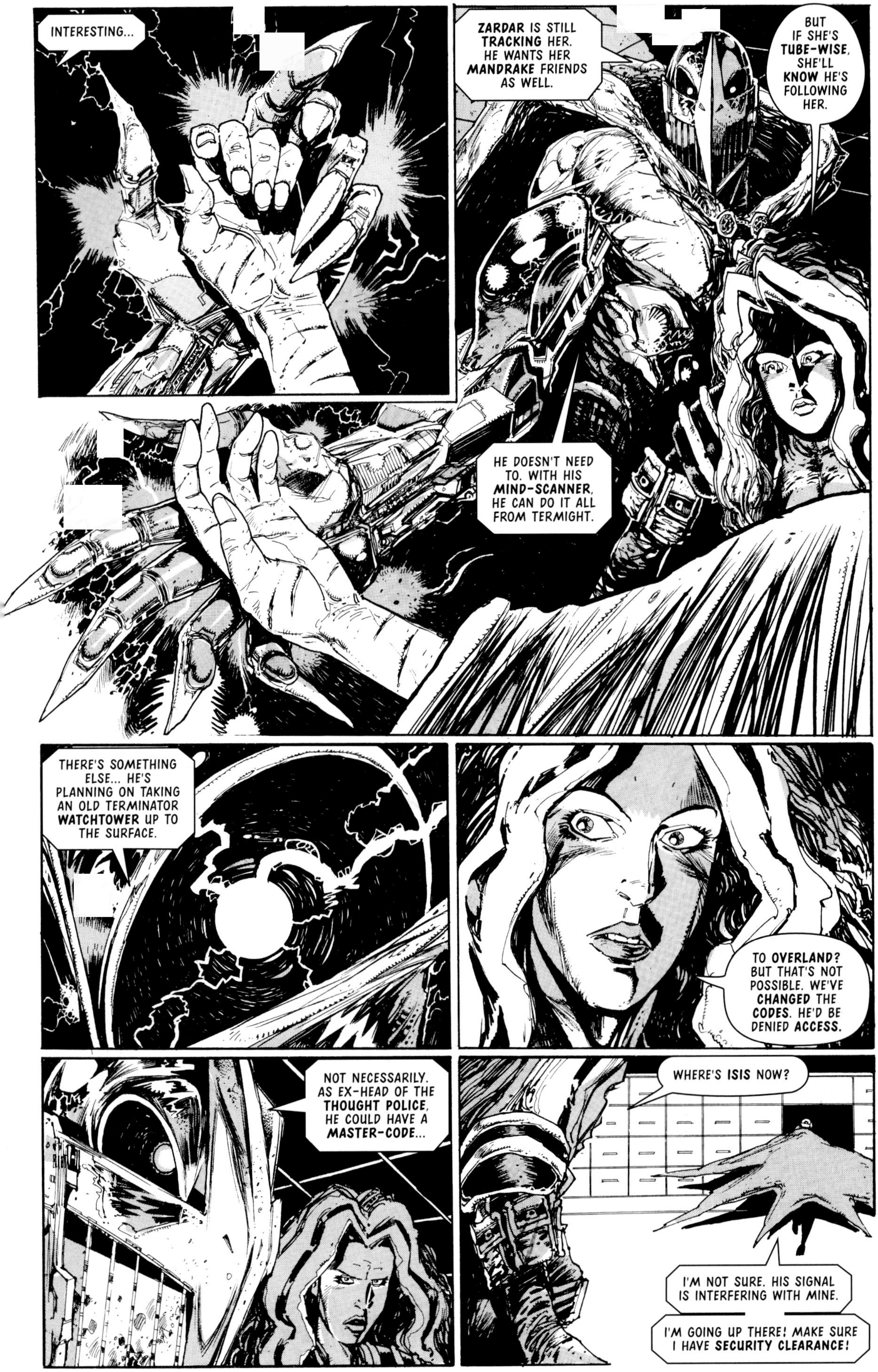
INTERESTING...
ZARDAR IS STILL TRACKING HER. HE WANTS HER MANDRAKE FRIENDS AS WELL.
BUT IF SHE'S TUBE-WISE, SHE'LL KNOW HE'S FOLLOWING HER.
HE DOESN'T NEED TO. WITH HIS MIND-SCANNER, HE CAN DO IT ALL FROM TERMIGHT.
THERE'S SOMETHING ELSE... HE'S PLANNING ON TAKING AN OLD TERMINATOR WATCHTOWER UP TO THE SURFACE.
TO OVERLAND? BUT THAT'S NOT POSSIBLE. WE'VE CHANGED THE CODES. HE'D BE DENIED ACCESS.
NOT NECESSARILY. AS EX-HEAD OF THE THOUGHT POLICE, HE COULD HAVE A MASTER-CODE...
WHERE'S ISIS NOW?
I'M NOT SURE. HIS SIGNAL IS INTERFERING WITH MINE.
I'M GOING UP THERE! MAKE SURE I HAVE SECURITY CLEARANCE!

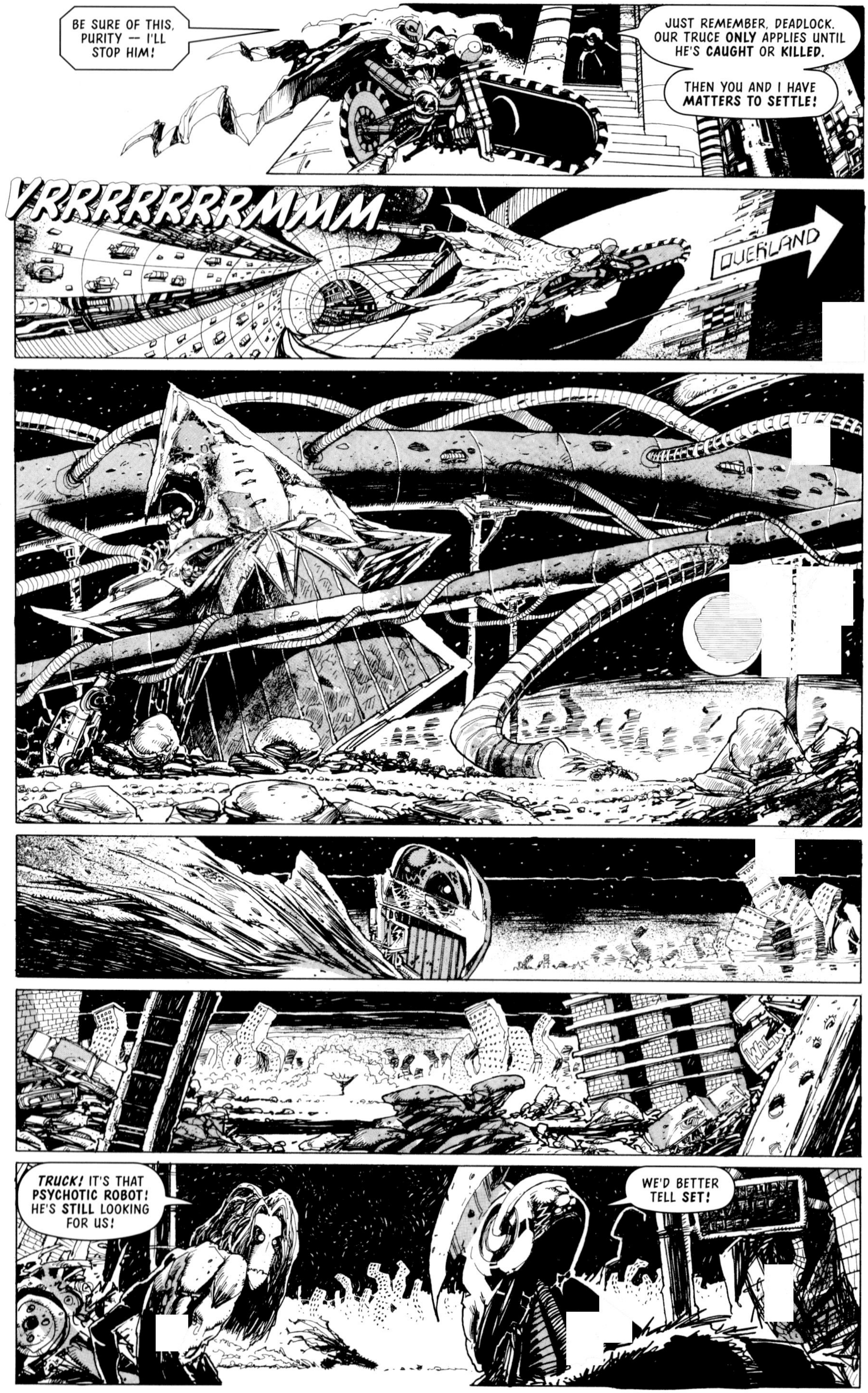
BE SURE OF THIS, PURITY -- I'LL STOP HIM!
JUST REMEMBER, DEADLOCK. OUR TRUCE **ONLY** APPLIES UNTIL HE'S **CAUGHT** OR **KILLED.**
THEN YOU AND I HAVE **MATTERS TO SETTLE!**
VRRRRRRRRMMMM
OVERLAND
TRUCK! IT'S THAT **PSYCHOTIC ROBOT!** HE'S **STILL** LOOKING FOR US!
WE'D BETTER TELL **SET!**

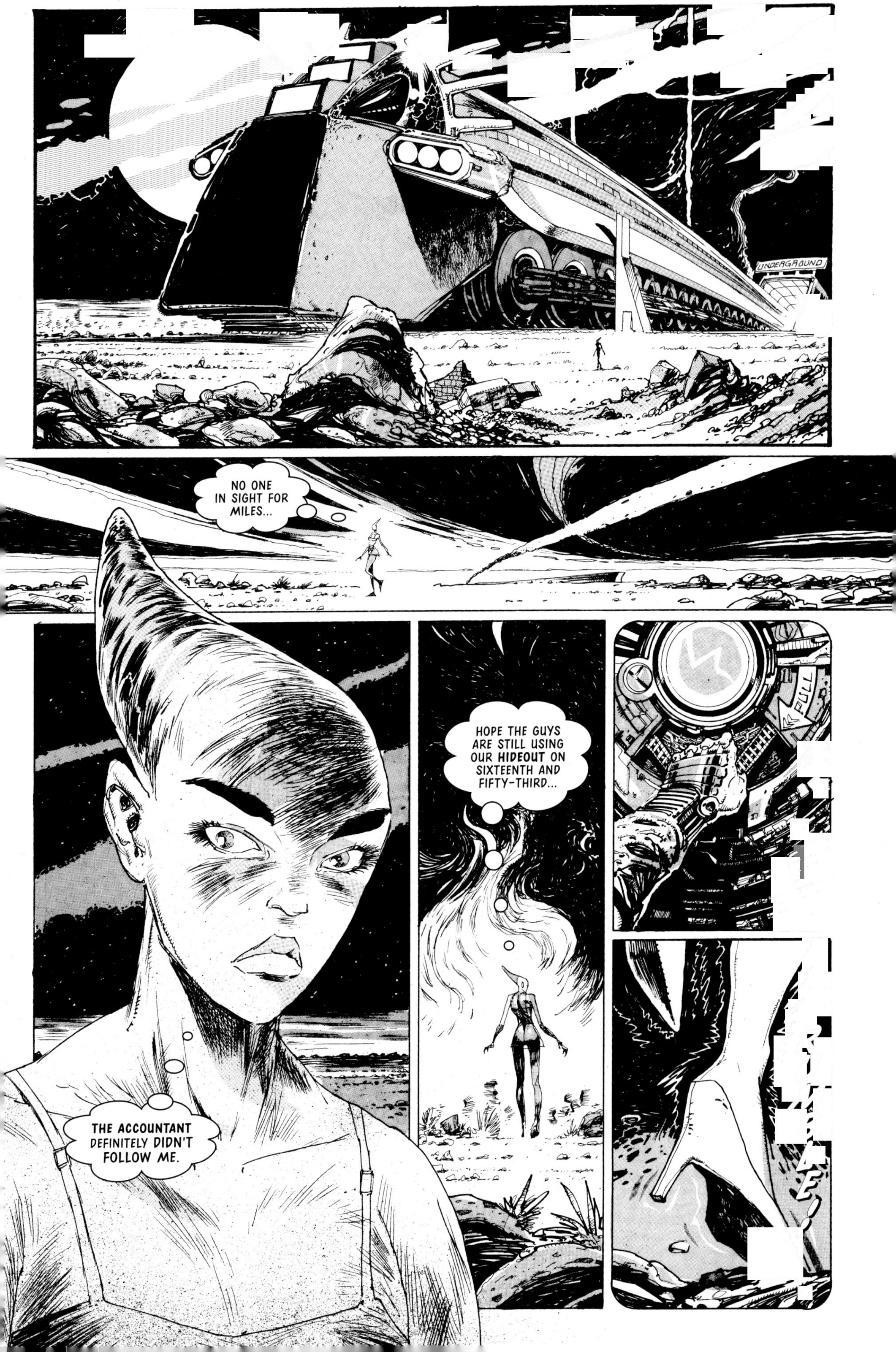
UNDERGROUND
NO ONE IN SIGHT FOR MILES...
THE ACCOUNTANT DEFINITELY DIDN'T FOLLOW ME.
HOPE THE GUYS ARE STILL USING OUR **HIDEOUT** ON SIXTEENTH AND FIFTY-THIRD...
PULL

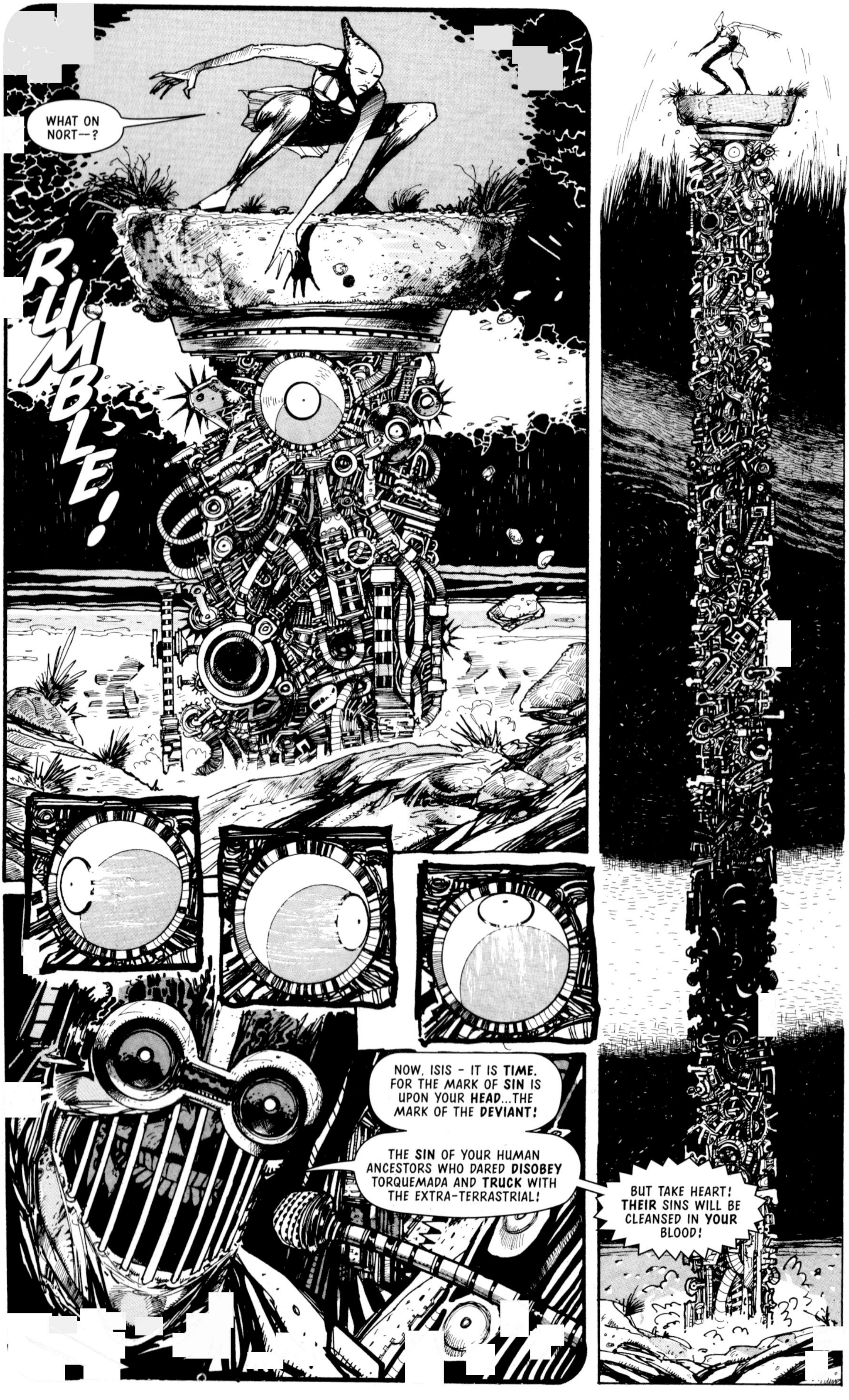
WHAT ON NORT--?
RUMBLE!
NOW, ISIS - IT IS TIME. FOR THE MARK OF SIN IS UPON YOUR HEAD...THE MARK OF THE DEVIANT!
THE SIN OF YOUR HUMAN ANCESTORS WHO DARED DISOBEY TORQUEMADA AND TRUCK WITH THE EXTRA-TERRASTRIAL!
BUT TAKE HEART! THEIR SINS WILL BE CLEANSED IN YOUR BLOOD!

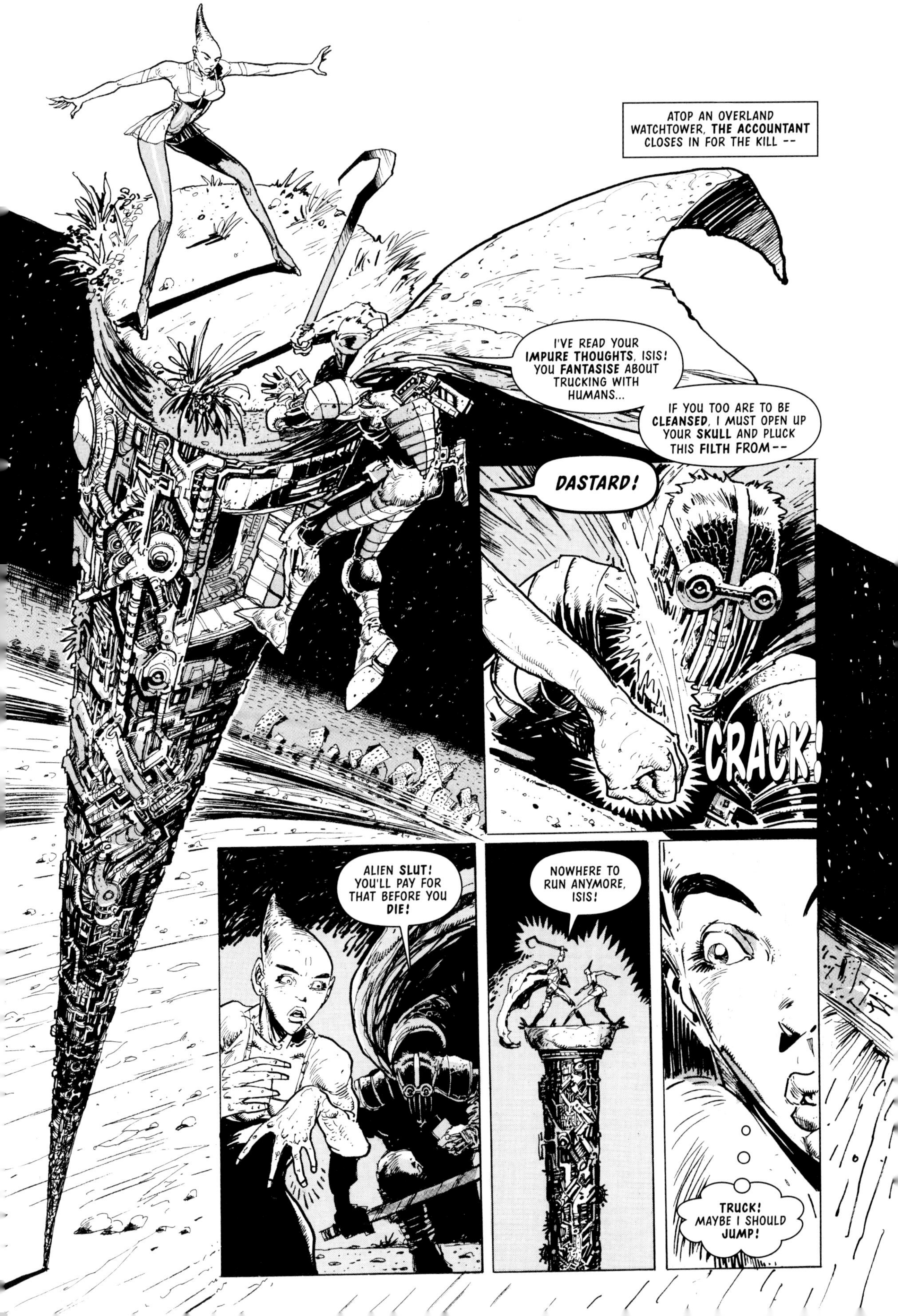
ATOP AN OVERLAND WATCHTOWER, THE ACCOUNTANT CLOSES IN FOR THE KILL --
I'VE READ YOUR IMPURE THOUGHTS, ISIS! YOU FANTASISE ABOUT TRUCKING WITH HUMANS...
IF YOU TOO ARE TO BE CLEANSED, I MUST OPEN UP YOUR SKULL AND PLUCK THIS FILTH FROM--
DASTARD!
CRACK!
ALIEN SLUT! YOU'LL PAY FOR THAT BEFORE YOU DIE!
NOWHERE TO RUN ANYMORE, ISIS!
TRUCK! MAYBE I SHOULD JUMP!

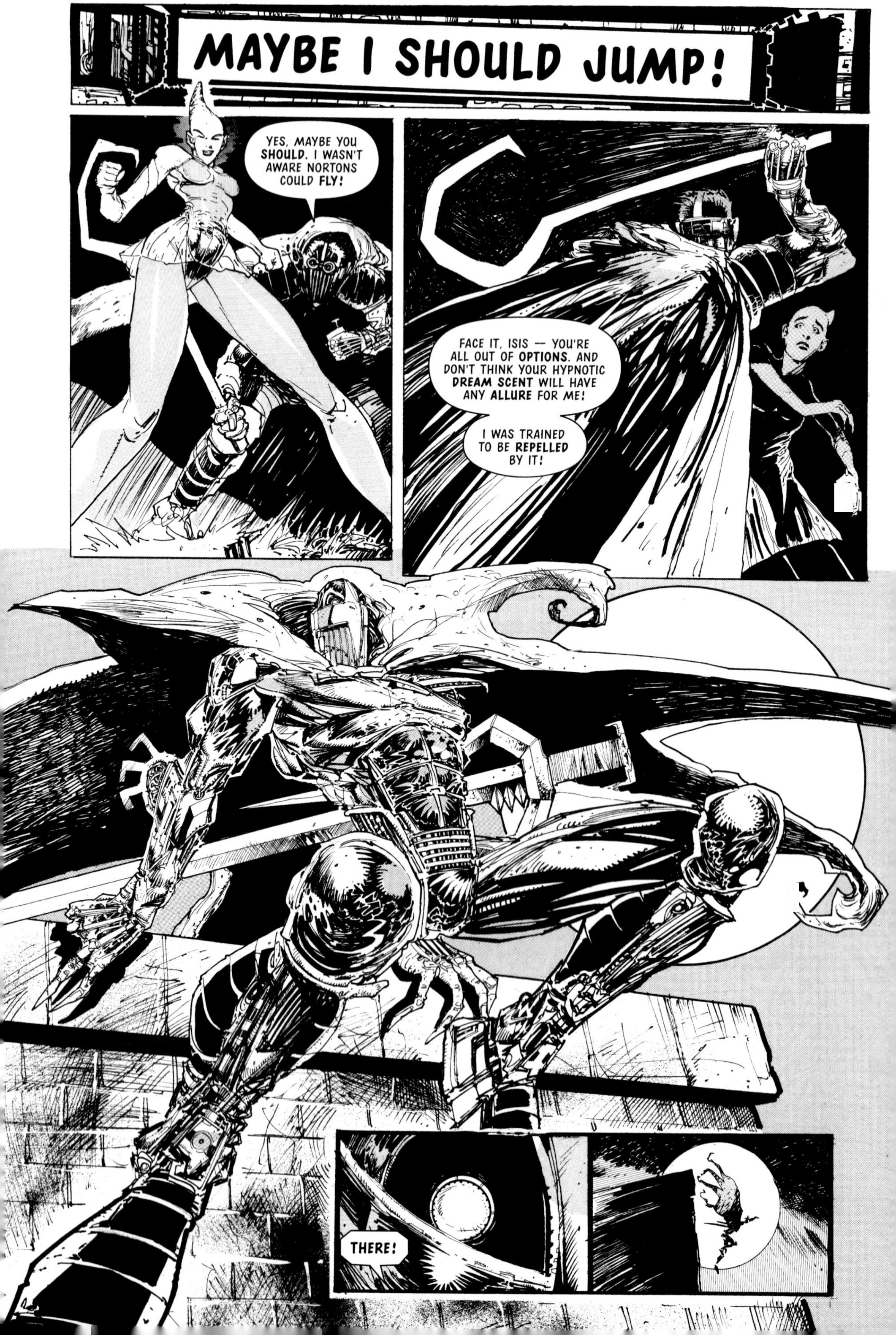

MAYBE I SHOULD JUMP!
YES, MAYBE YOU SHOULD. I WASN'T AWARE NORTONS COULD FLY!
FACE IT, ISIS -- YOU'RE ALL OUT OF OPTIONS. AND DON'T THINK YOUR HYPNOTIC DREAM SCENT WILL HAVE ANY ALLURE FOR ME!
I WAS TRAINED TO BE REPELLED BY IT!
THERE!

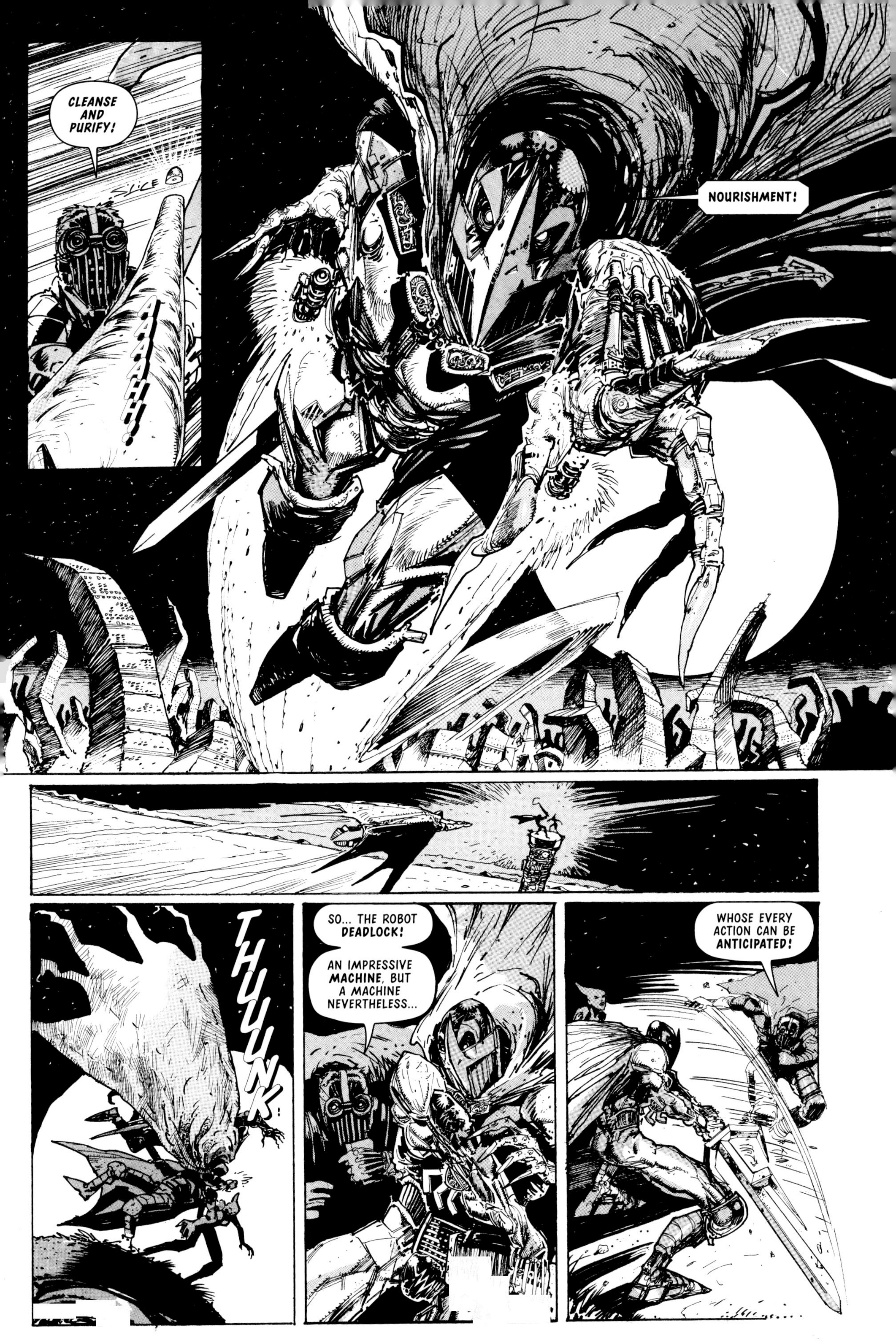
CLEANSE AND PURIFY!
SLICE
AAAAAHH!
NOURISHMENT!
THUUUNK!
SO... THE ROBOT DEADLOCK!
AN IMPRESSIVE MACHINE, BUT A MACHINE NEVERTHELESS...
WHOSE EVERY ACTION CAN BE ANTICIPATED!

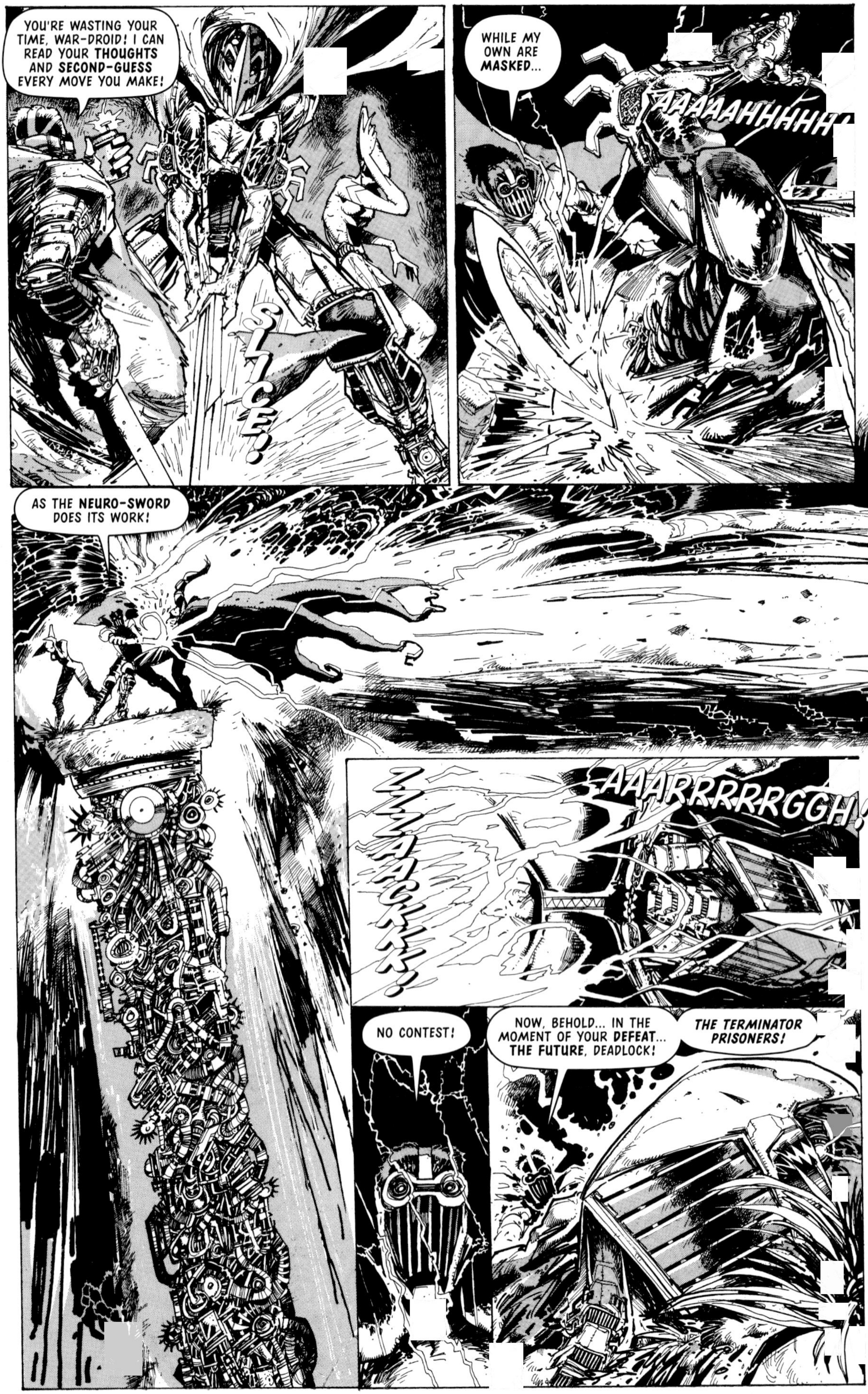
YOU'RE WASTING YOUR TIME, WAR-DROID! I CAN READ YOUR THOUGHTS AND SECOND-GUESS EVERY MOVE YOU MAKE!
SLICE!
WHILE MY OWN ARE MASKED...
AAAAAHHHHHH
AS THE NEURO-SWORD DOES ITS WORK!
ZZZZAACKKKK!
AAARRRRRRGGH!
NO CONTEST!
NOW, BEHOLD... IN THE MOMENT OF YOUR DEFEAT... THE FUTURE, DEADLOCK!
THE TERMINATOR PRISONERS!

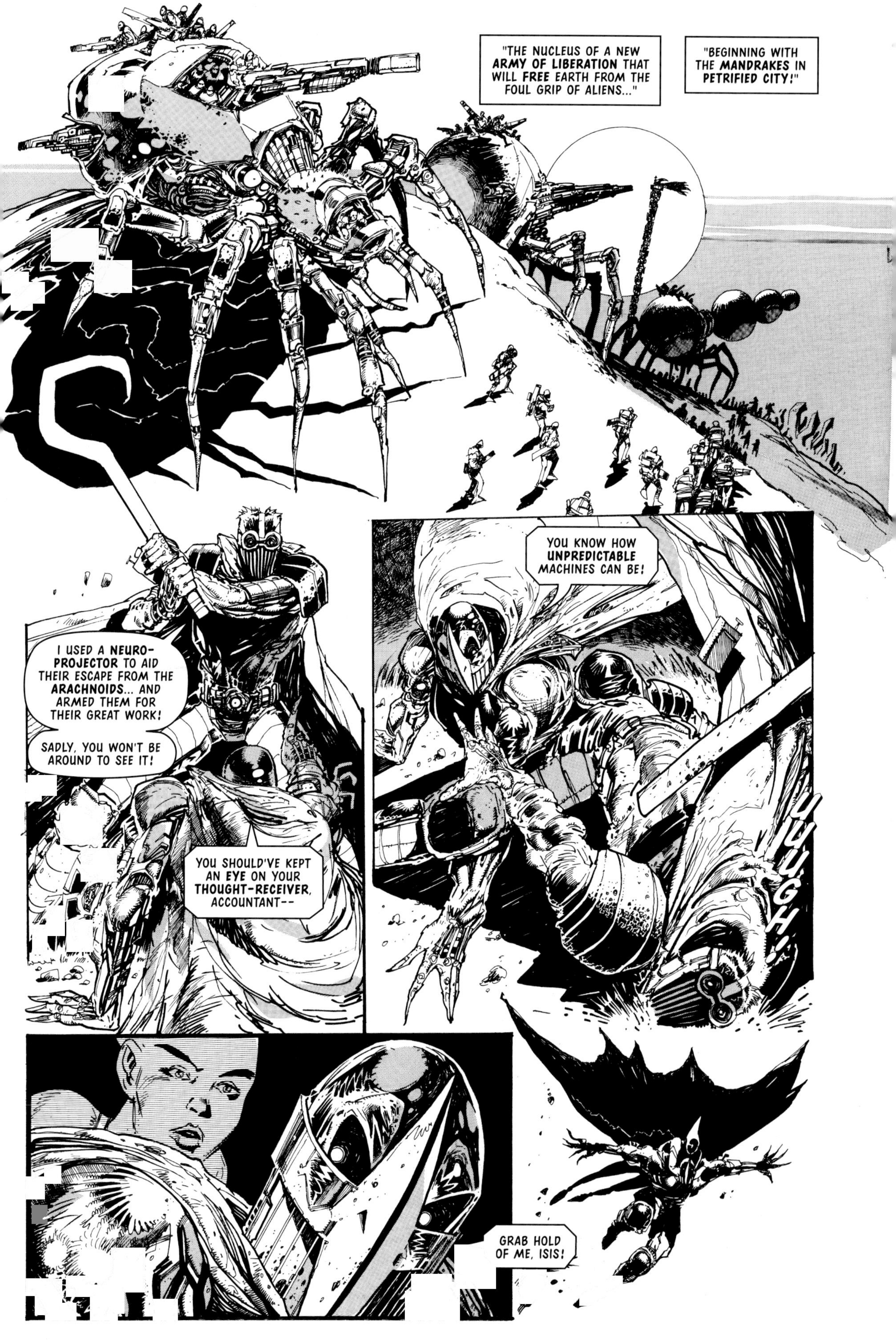
"THE NUCLEUS OF A NEW ARMY OF LIBERATION THAT WILL FREE EARTH FROM THE FOUL GRIP OF ALIENS..."
"BEGINNING WITH THE MANDRAKES IN PETRIFIED CITY!"
I USED A NEURO-PROJECTOR TO AID THEIR ESCAPE FROM THE ARACHNOIDS... AND ARMED THEM FOR THEIR GREAT WORK!
SADLY, YOU WON'T BE AROUND TO SEE IT!
YOU SHOULD'VE KEPT AN EYE ON YOUR THOUGHT-RECEIVER, ACCOUNTANT--
YOU KNOW HOW UNPREDICTABLE MACHINES CAN BE!
UUUGH!
GRAB HOLD OF ME, ISIS!

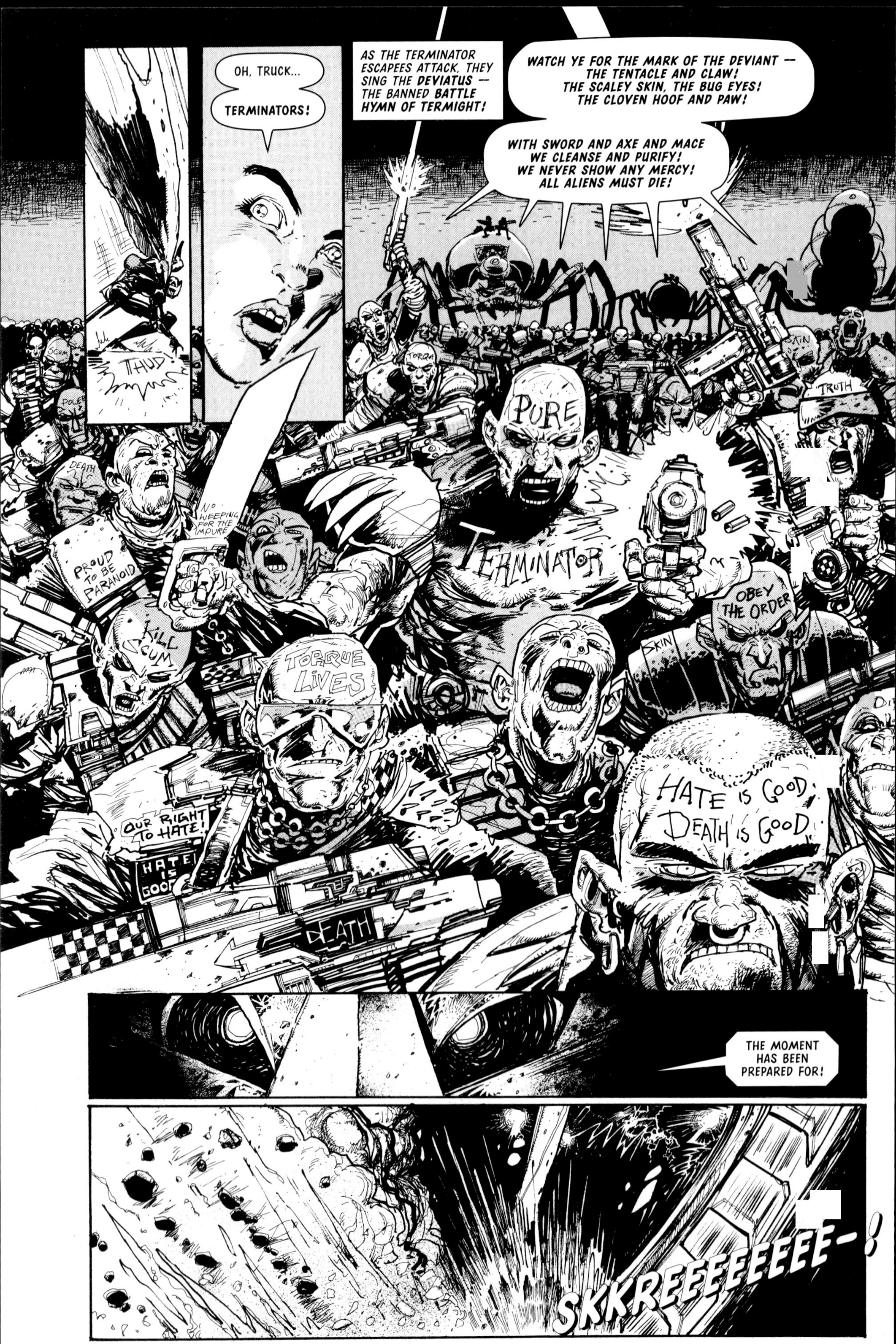

OH, TRUCK...
TERMINATORS!
THUD
AS THE TERMINATOR ESCAPEES ATTACK, THEY SING THE DEVIATUS -- THE BANNED BATTLE HYMN OF TERMIGHT!
WATCH YE FOR THE MARK OF THE DEVIANT -- THE TENTACLE AND CLAW! THE SCALEY SKIN, THE BUG EYES! THE CLOVEN HOOF AND PAW!
WITH SWORD AND AXE AND MACE WE CLEANSE AND PURIFY! WE NEVER SHOW ANY MERCY! ALL ALIENS MUST DIE!
PURE
TERMINATOR
TRUTH
NO WEEPING FOR THE IMPURE
PROUD TO BE PARANOID
OBEY THE ORDER
TORQUE LIVES
HATE IS GOOD DEATH IS GOOD
OUR RIGHT TO HATE!
HATE IS GOOD
DEATH
THE MOMENT HAS BEEN PREPARED FOR!
SKKREEEEEEEEE-!

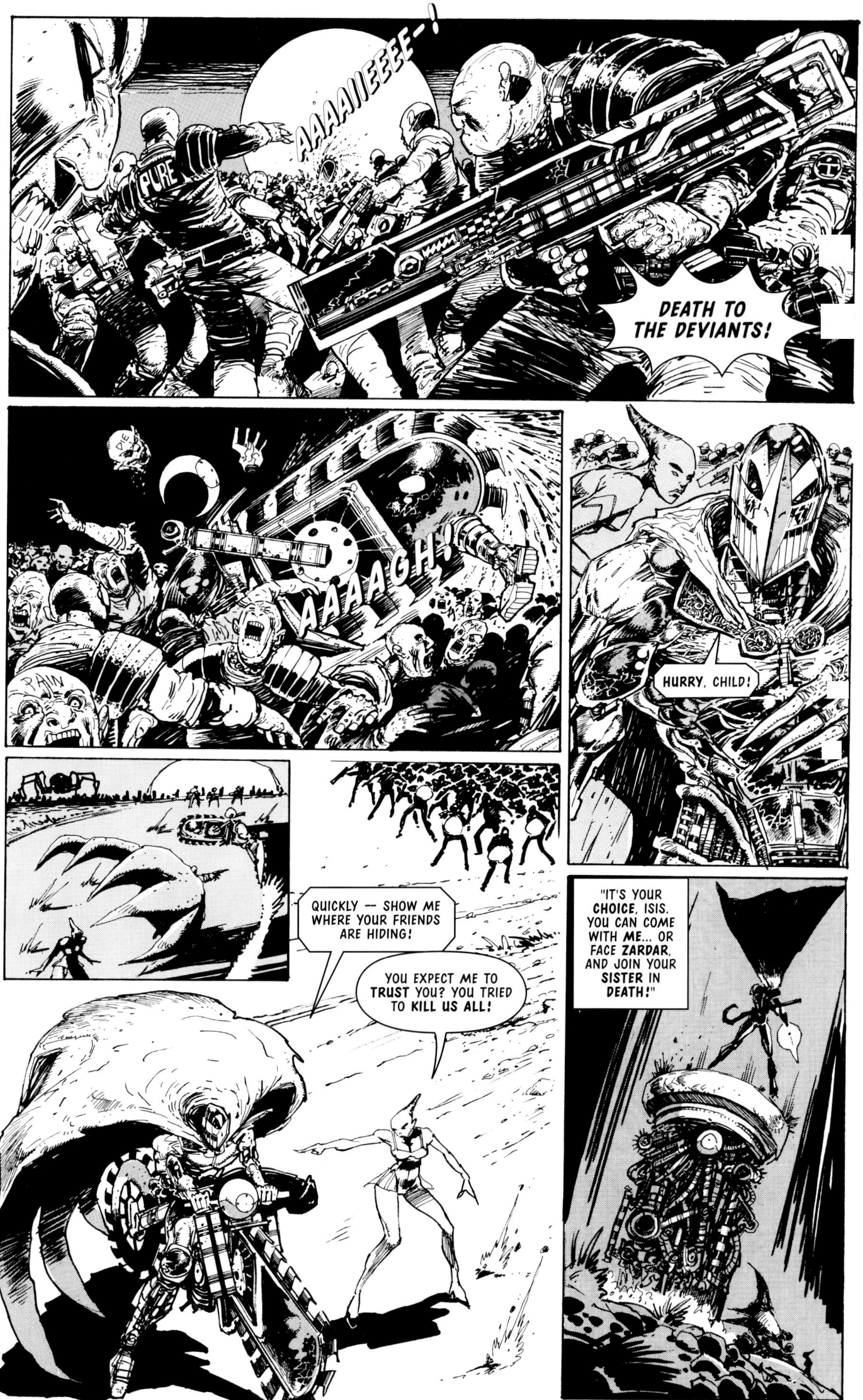
AAAAIIEEEE-!
DEATH TO THE DEVIANTS!
AAAAGH!
HURRY, CHILD!
QUICKLY -- SHOW ME WHERE YOUR FRIENDS ARE HIDING!
YOU EXPECT ME TO TRUST YOU? YOU TRIED TO KILL US ALL!
"IT'S YOUR CHOICE, ISIS. YOU CAN COME WITH ME... OR FACE ZARDAR, AND JOIN YOUR SISTER IN DEATH!"

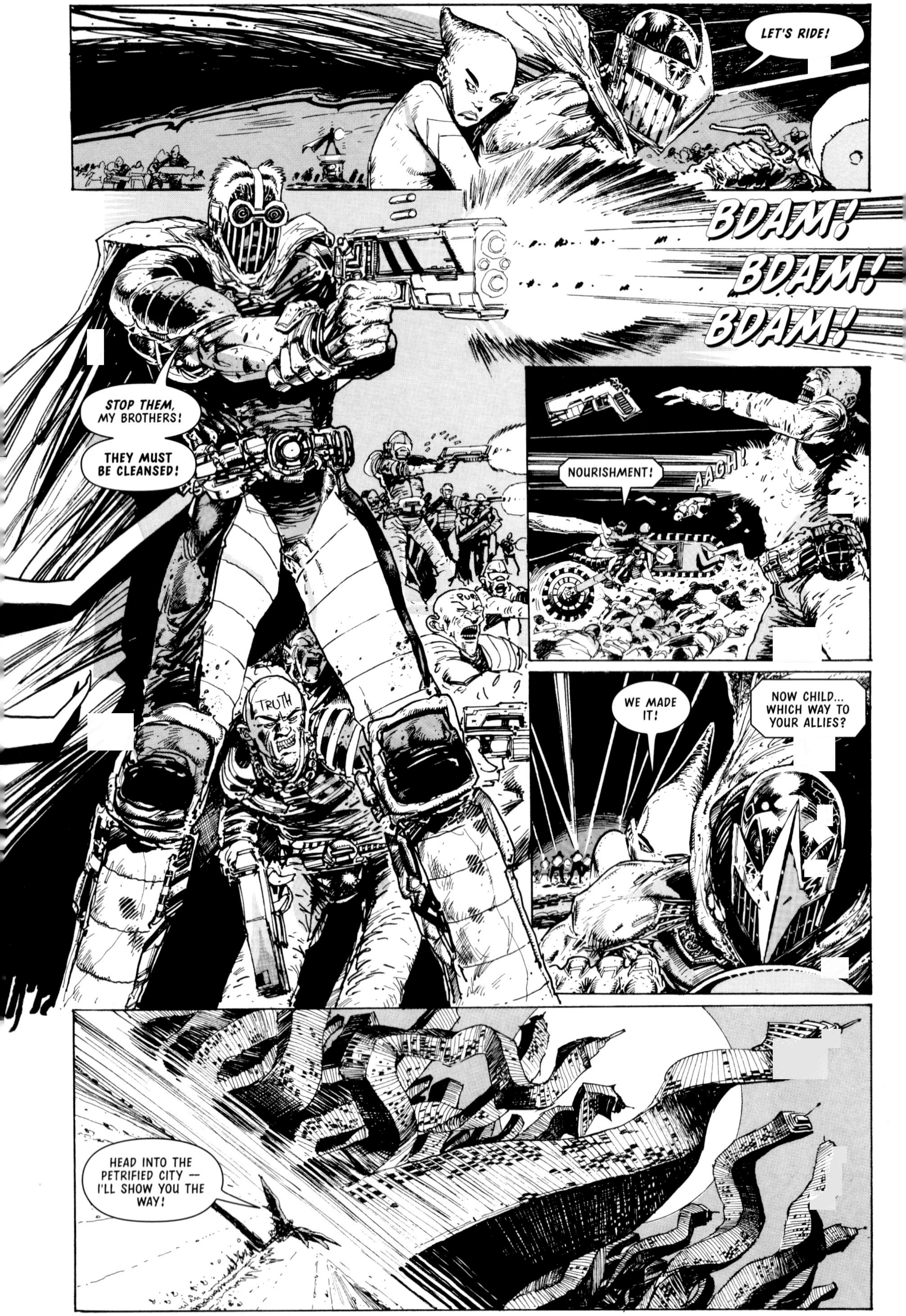
LET'S RIDE!
BDAM!
BDAM!
BDAM!
STOP THEM, MY BROTHERS!
THEY MUST BE CLEANSED!
TRUTH
NOURISHMENT!
AAGH!
WE MADE IT!
NOW CHILD... WHICH WAY TO YOUR ALLIES?
HEAD INTO THE PETRIFIED CITY — I'LL SHOW YOU THE WAY!

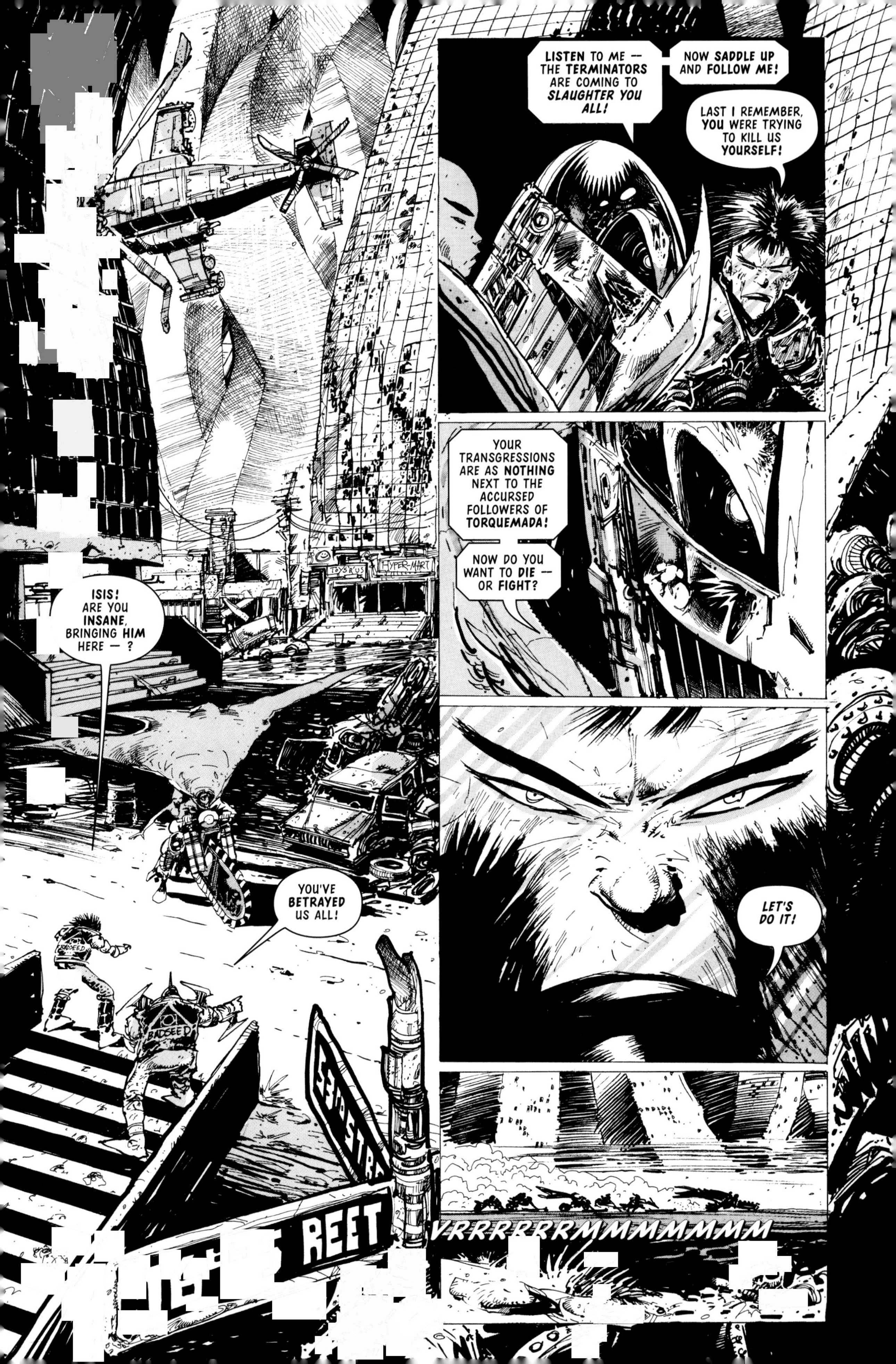

ISIS! ARE YOU INSANE, BRINGING HIM HERE — ?
YOU'VE BETRAYED US ALL!
REET
LISTEN TO ME — THE TERMINATORS ARE COMING TO SLAUGHTER YOU ALL!
NOW SADDLE UP AND FOLLOW ME!
LAST I REMEMBER, YOU WERE TRYING TO KILL US YOURSELF!
YOUR TRANSGRESSIONS ARE AS NOTHING NEXT TO THE ACCURSED FOLLOWERS OF TORQUEMADA!
NOW DO YOU WANT TO DIE — OR FIGHT?
LET'S DO IT!
VRRRRRRRMMMMMMMM

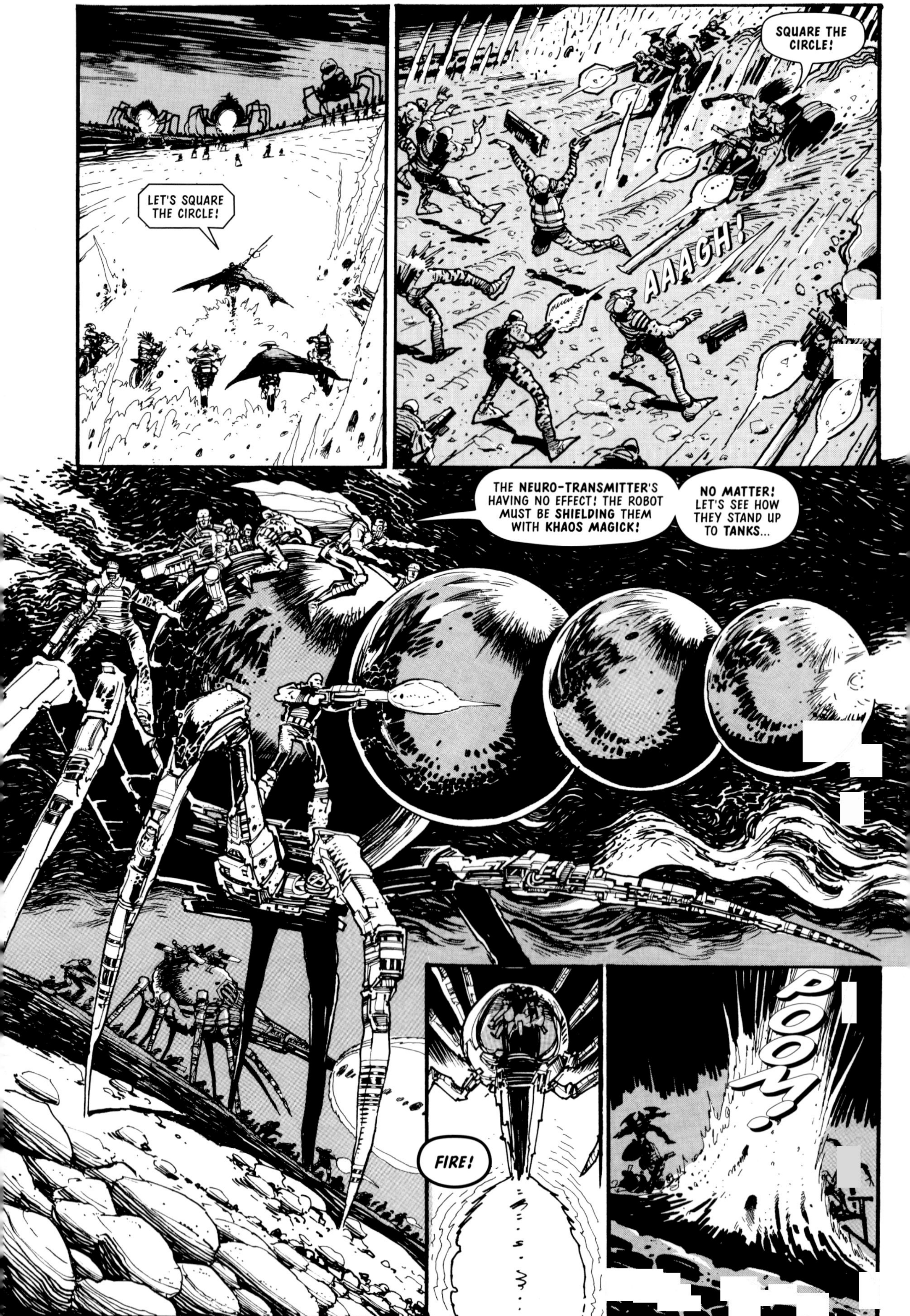
LET'S SQUARE THE CIRCLE!
SQUARE THE CIRCLE!
AAAGH!
THE NEURO-TRANSMITTER'S HAVING NO EFFECT! THE ROBOT MUST BE SHIELDING THEM WITH KHAOS MAGICK!
NO MATTER! LET'S SEE HOW THEY STAND UP TO TANKS...
FIRE!
POOM!

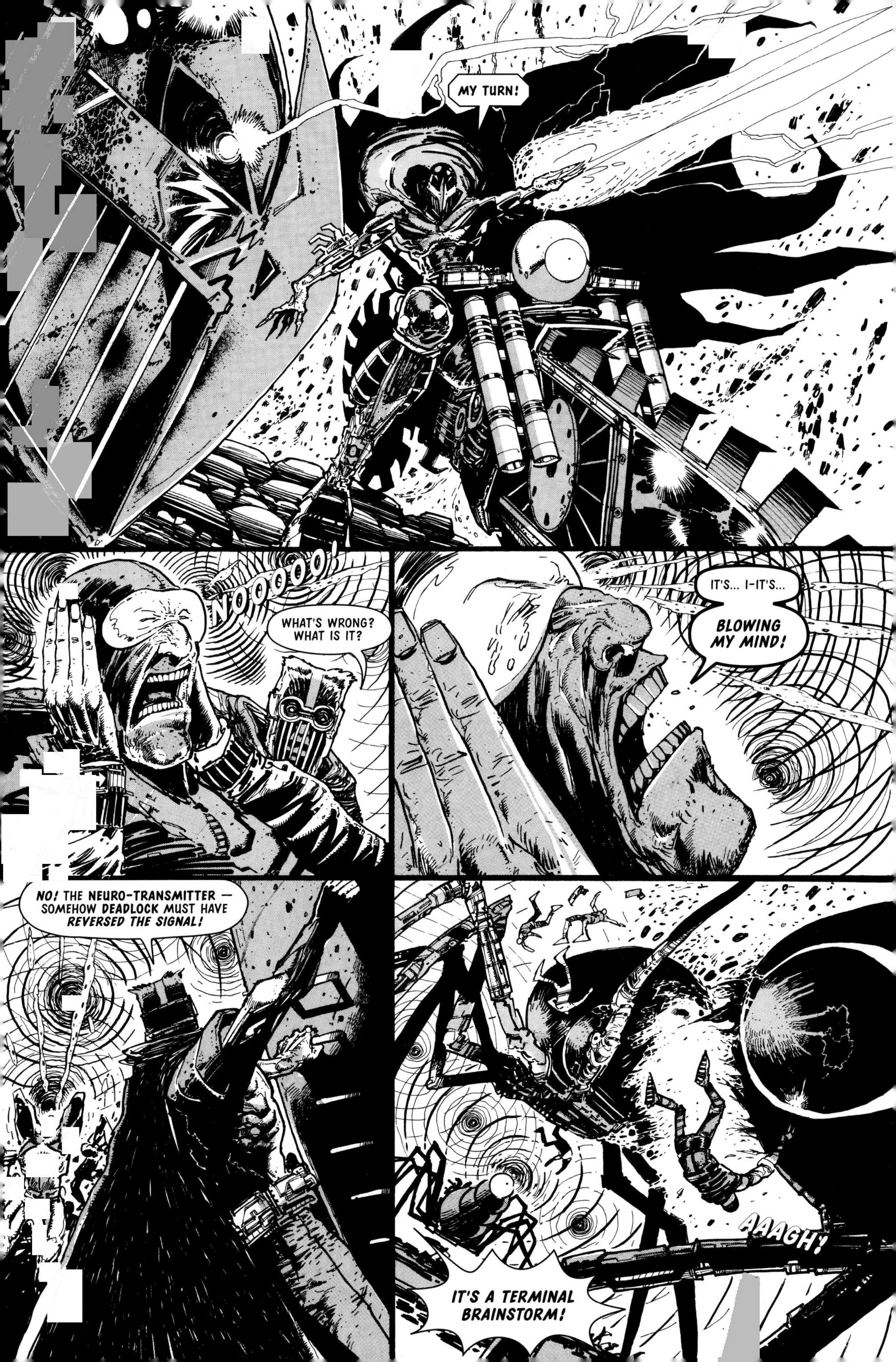
MY TURN!
NOOOOOO!
WHAT'S WRONG? WHAT IS IT?
IT'S... I-IT'S...
BLOWING MY MIND!
NO! THE NEURO-TRANSMITTER — SOMEHOW DEADLOCK MUST HAVE REVERSED THE SIGNAL!
AAAGH!
IT'S A TERMINAL BRAINSTORM!

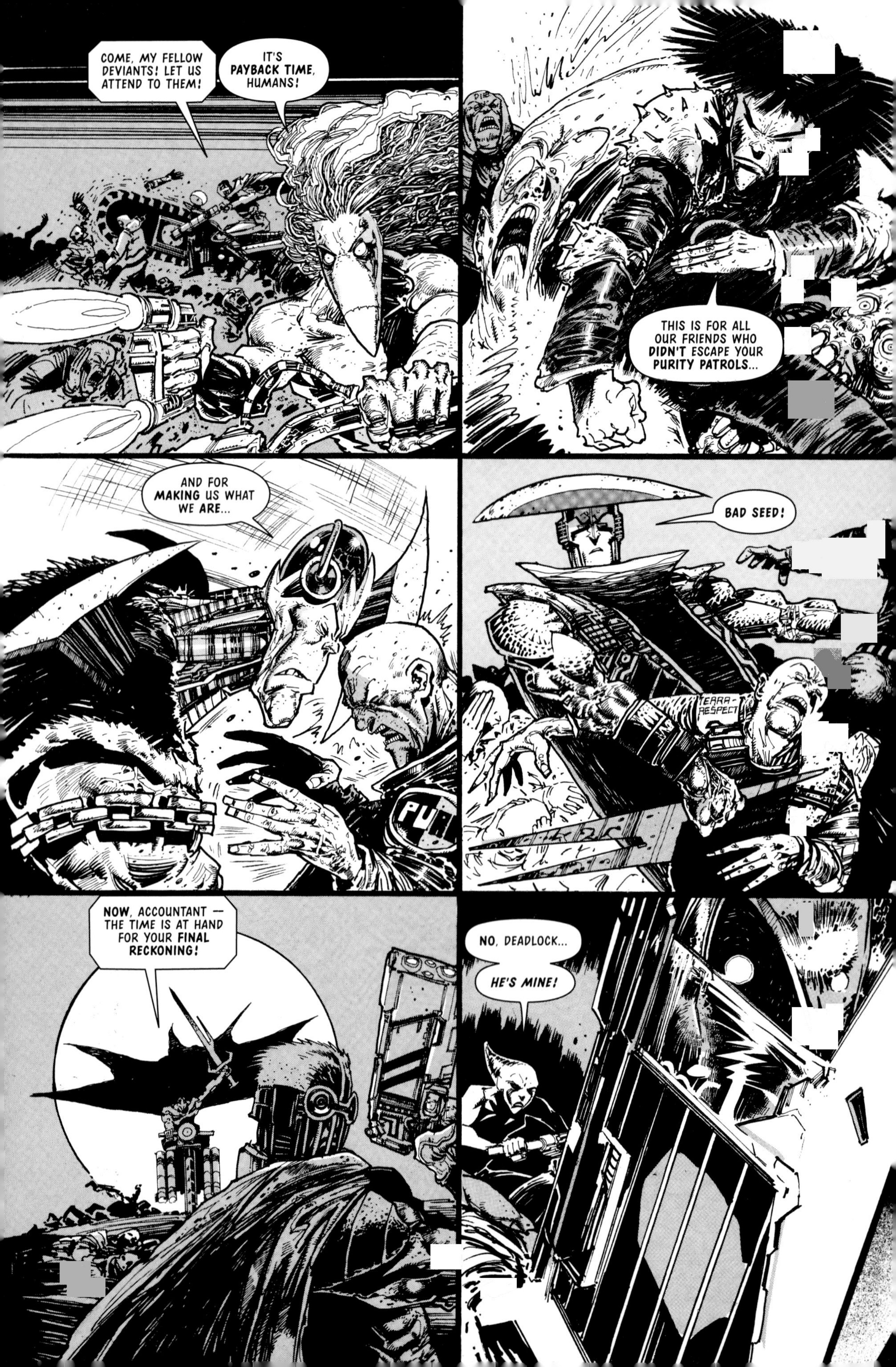
COME, MY FELLOW DEVIANTS! LET US ATTEND TO THEM!
IT'S PAYBACK TIME, HUMANS!
THIS IS FOR ALL OUR FRIENDS WHO DIDN'T ESCAPE YOUR PURITY PATROLS...
AND FOR MAKING US WHAT WE ARE...
BAD SEED!
TERRA-RESPECT
NOW, ACCOUNTANT — THE TIME IS AT HAND FOR YOUR FINAL RECKONING!
NO, DEADLOCK...
HE'S MINE!

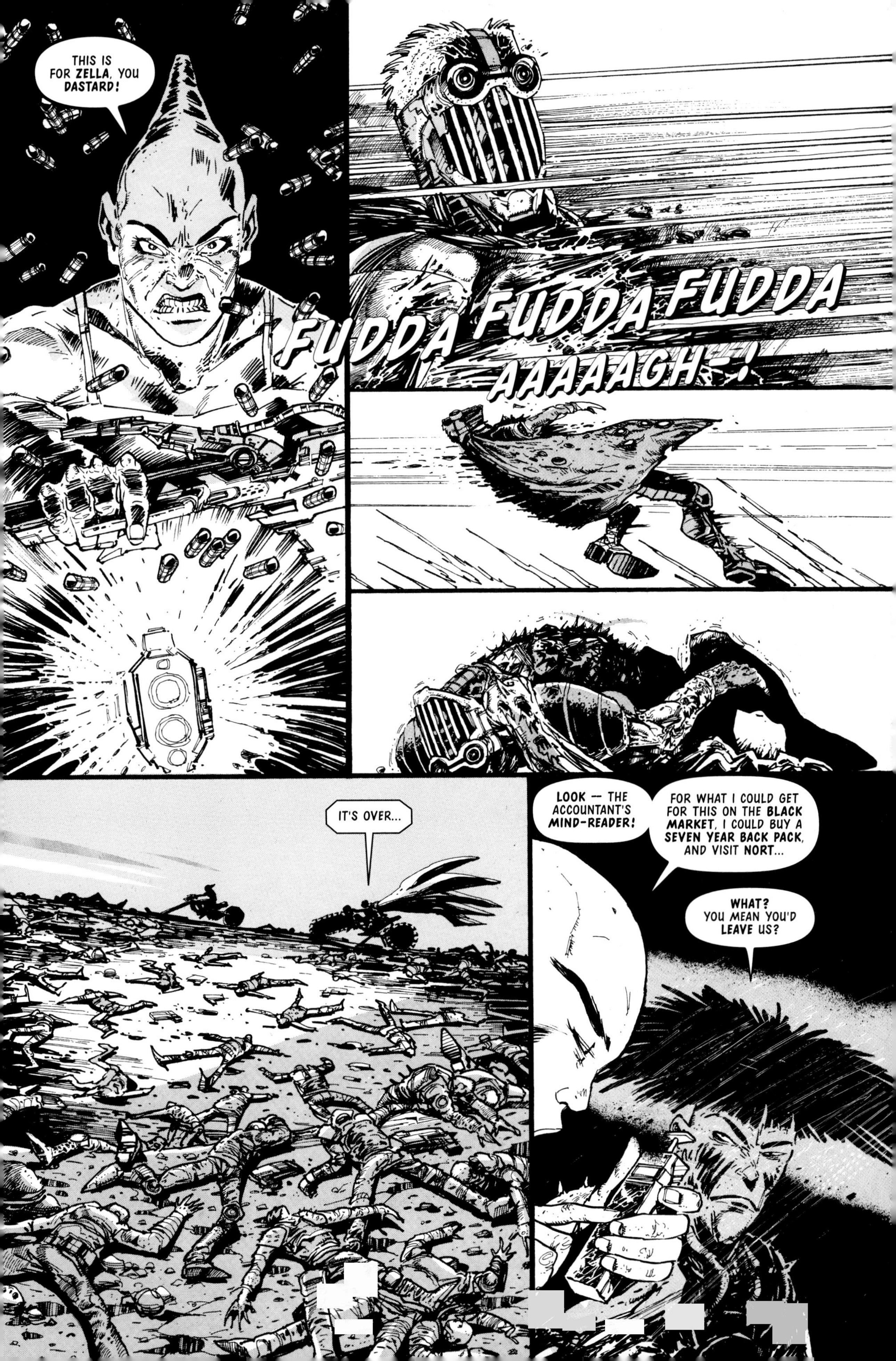
THIS IS FOR ZELLA, YOU DASTARD!
FUDDA FUDDA FUDDA
AAAAAGH--!
IT'S OVER...
LOOK -- THE ACCOUNTANT'S MIND-READER!
FOR WHAT I COULD GET FOR THIS ON THE BLACK MARKET, I COULD BUY A SEVEN YEAR BACK PACK, AND VISIT NORT...
WHAT? YOU MEAN YOU'D LEAVE US?

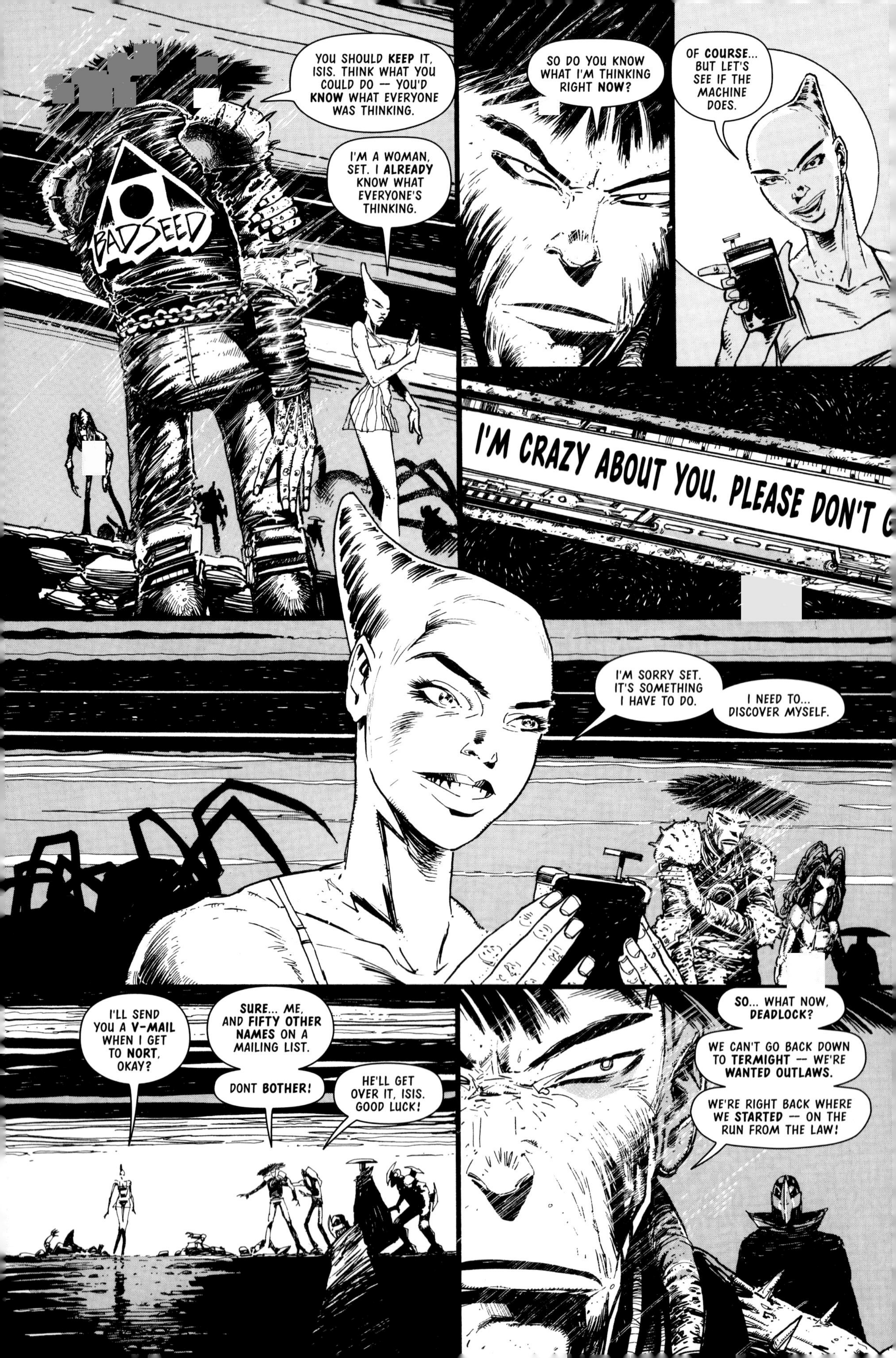
YOU SHOULD KEEP IT, ISIS. THINK WHAT YOU COULD DO — YOU'D KNOW WHAT EVERYONE WAS THINKING.
I'M A WOMAN, SET. I ALREADY KNOW WHAT EVERYONE'S THINKING.
BADSEED
SO DO YOU KNOW WHAT I'M THINKING RIGHT NOW?
OF COURSE... BUT LET'S SEE IF THE MACHINE DOES.
I'M CRAZY ABOUT YOU. PLEASE DON'T G
I'M SORRY SET. IT'S SOMETHING I HAVE TO DO.
I NEED TO... DISCOVER MYSELF.
I'LL SEND YOU A V-MAIL WHEN I GET TO NORT, OKAY?
SURE... ME, AND FIFTY OTHER NAMES ON A MAILING LIST.
DONT BOTHER!
HE'LL GET OVER IT, ISIS. GOOD LUCK!
SO... WHAT NOW, DEADLOCK?
WE CAN'T GO BACK DOWN TO TERMIGHT — WE'RE WANTED OUTLAWS.
WE'RE RIGHT BACK WHERE WE STARTED — ON THE RUN FROM THE LAW!

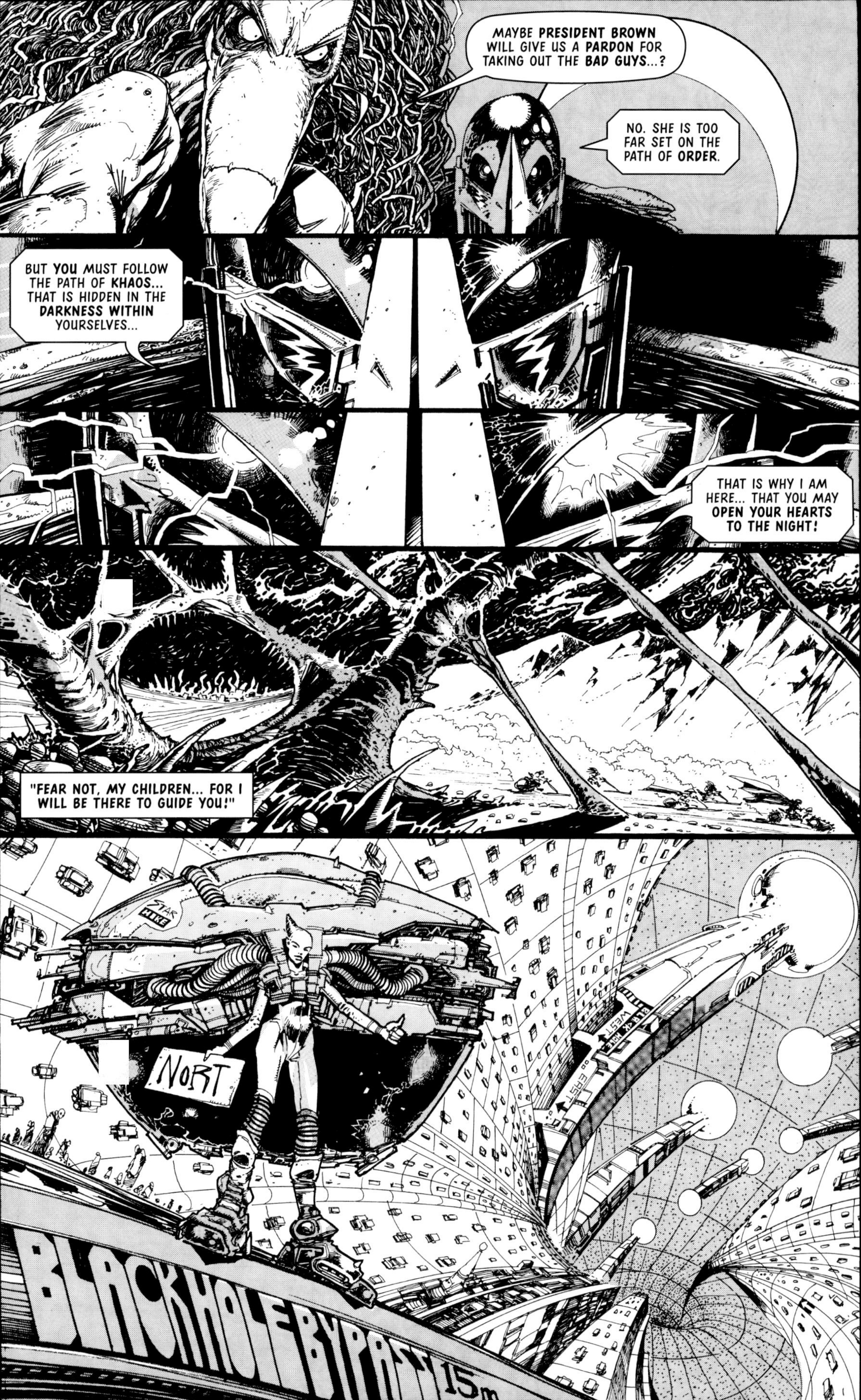
MAYBE PRESIDENT BROWN WILL GIVE US A PARDON FOR TAKING OUT THE BAD GUYS...?
NO. SHE IS TOO FAR SET ON THE PATH OF ORDER.
BUT YOU MUST FOLLOW THE PATH OF KHAOS... THAT IS HIDDEN IN THE DARKNESS WITHIN YOURSELVES...
THAT IS WHY I AM HERE... THAT YOU MAY OPEN YOUR HEARTS TO THE NIGHT!
"FEAR NOT, MY CHILDREN... FOR I WILL BE THERE TO GUIDE YOU!"
STAR HIKE
NORT
WEST
EAST
BLACK HOLE BYPASS 15m

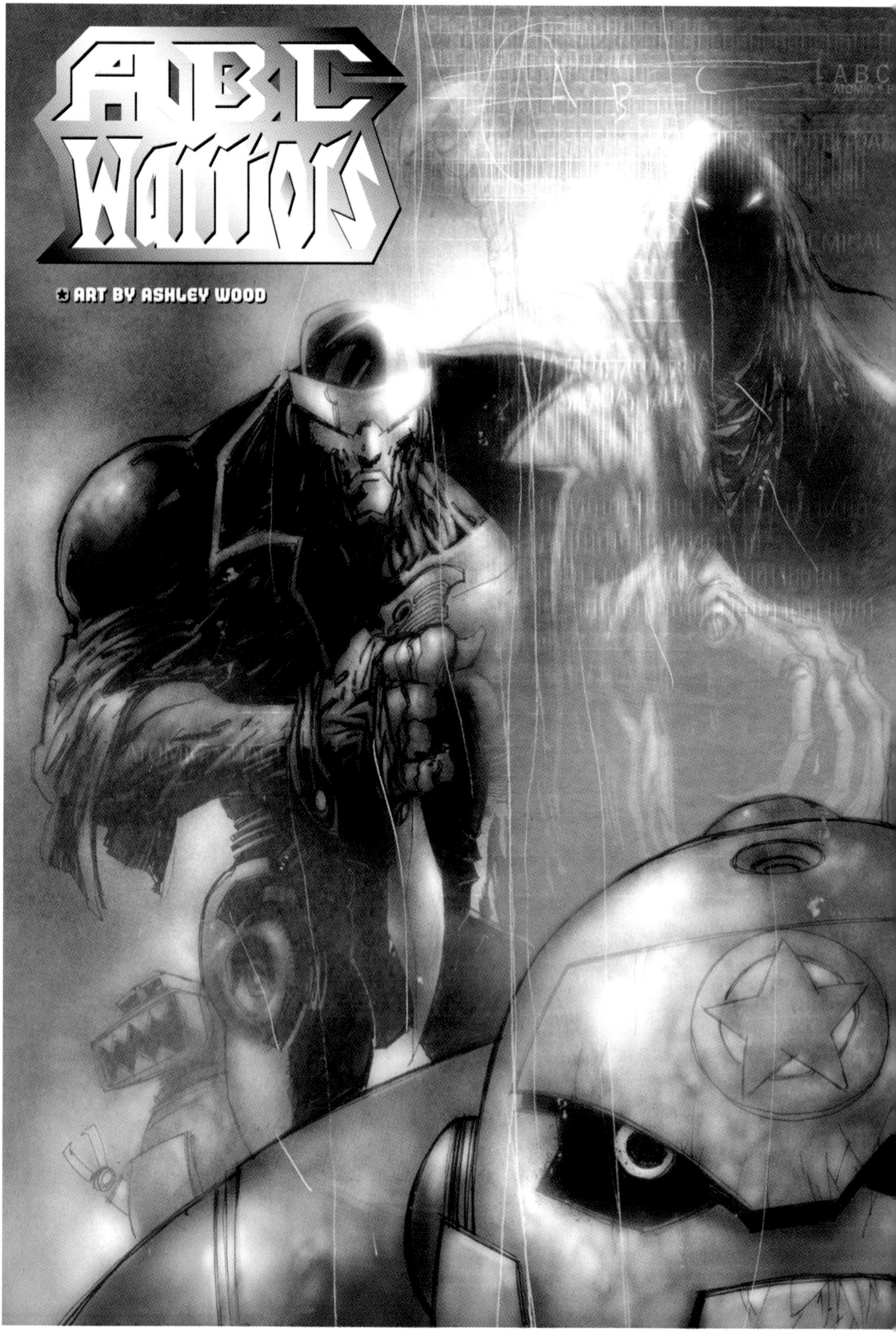
ABC Warriors
ART BY ASHLEY WOOD

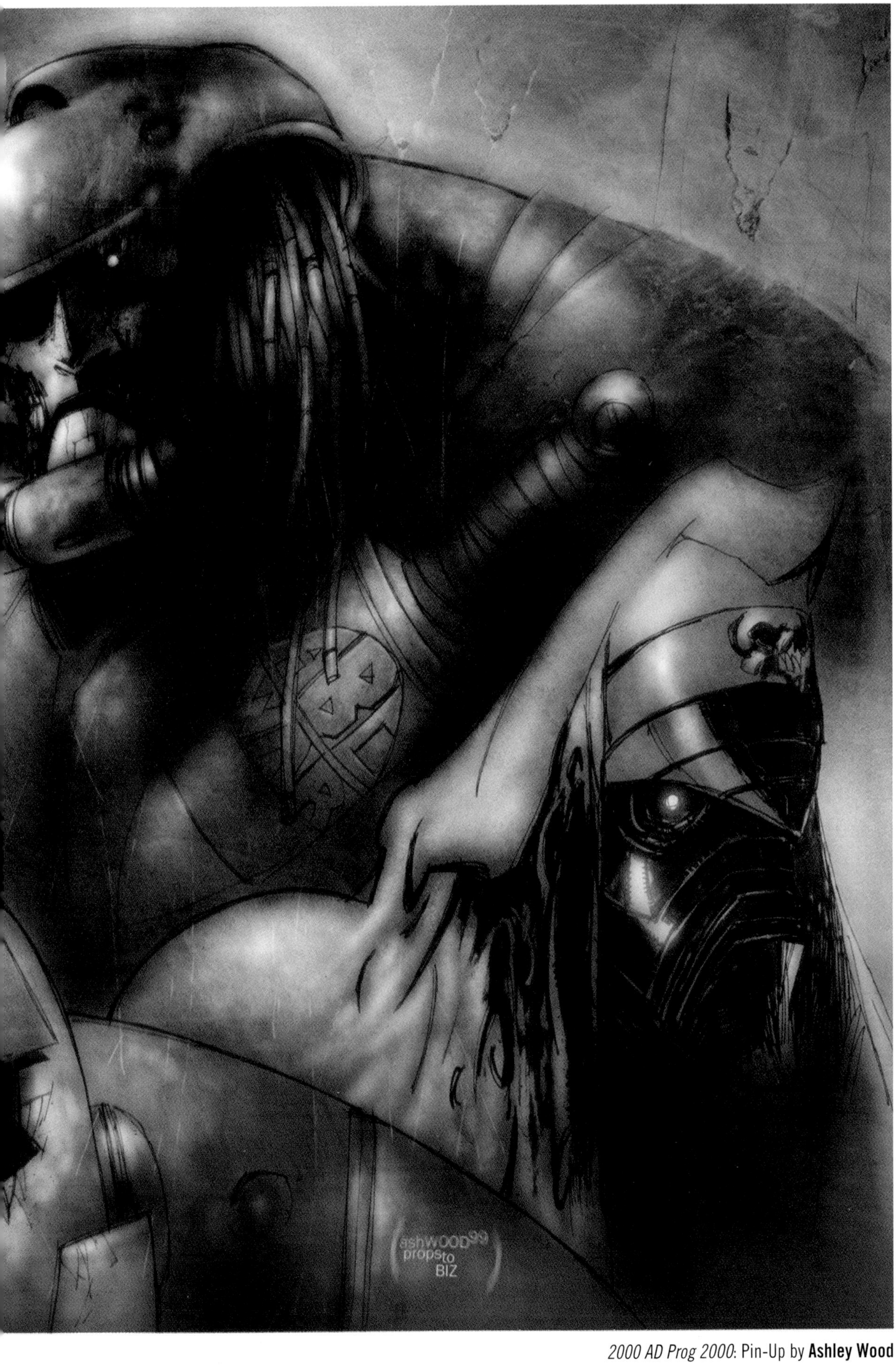
ashWOOD99
propsto
BIZ

2000 AD Prog 2000: Pin-Up by **Ashley Wood**

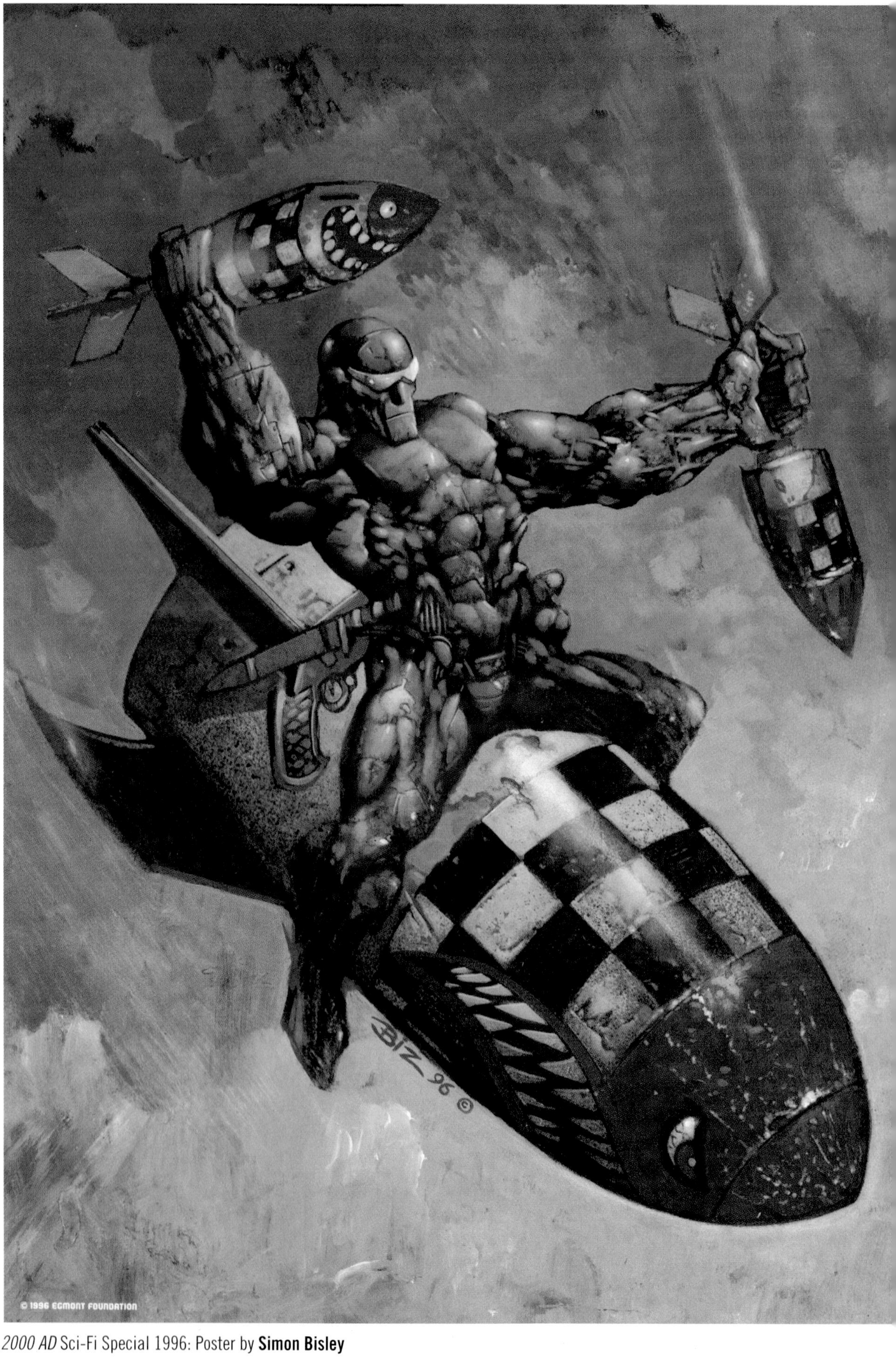
BIZ 96 ©
© 1996 EGMONT FOUNDATION

2000 AD Sci-Fi Special 1996: Poster by **Simon Bisley**